MW01043003

You Never Asked Me to Read

Useful Assessment of Reading and Writing Problems

Jay Simmons

Boston University

Allyn and Bacon

Boston ■ London ■ Toronto ■ Sydney ■ Tokyo ■ Singapore

To
Mary Camac Simmons (1910–1977)
and J. W. Simmons (1909–1985),
who started life poor but bought me a rich education

Senior Editor: *Virginia C. Lanigan*
Editorial Assistant: *Bridget Keane*
Director of Education Programs: *Ellen Mann Dolberg*
Marketing Manager: *Brad Parkins*
Editorial-Production Administrator: *Annette Joseph*
Editorial-Production Coordinator: *Susan Freese*
Editorial-Production Service: *TKM Productions*
Electronic Composition: *Publishers' Design & Production Services, Inc.*
Composition Buyer: *Linda Cox*
Manufacturing Buyer: *Suzanne Lareau*
Cover Administrator: *Jenny Hart*
Cover Designer: *Brian Gogolin*

Copyright © 2000 by Allyn & Bacon
A Pearson Education Company
160 Gould Street
Needham Heights, MA 02494

Internet: www.abacon.com

Library of Congress Cataloging-in-Publication Data

Simmons, Jay
   You never asked me to read : useful assessment of reading and
writing problems / Jay Simmons.
      p.   cm.
   Includes bibliographical references and index.
   ISBN 0-205-28854-5
   1. Reading—Ability testing—United States—Case studies.
  2. Language arts—Ability testing—United States—Case studies.
  3. Educational tests and measurements—United States—Case studies.
  4. Learning disabled children—United States—Case studies.
  I. Title.
  LB1050.46.S535 1999
  428.4'076—dc21
                                      98-46509
                                         CIP

Printed in the United States of America

10 9 8 7 6 5 4 3 2 1   04 03 02 01 00 99

CONTENTS

PREFACE

You Never Asked Me to Read was written in response to my dismay at working with seven children over the course of several years—children whose lives and educations had been disrupted due to their inability to learn to read and write as their peers had been able to do. Over that time, they had variously been tested for mental disorders, lack of academic ability, faulty perceptual processing, and lack of achievement. They had been diagnosed as learning disabled and had been placed on medication; one had even been sent to a residential school. As part of their diagnoses, however, none of these students had ever been asked to read a book or to write a piece that they cared about in order to discuss or share the piece with another human being who also cared about the meaning.

To play on a phrase from Paolo Freire (1985), reading and writing occur outside the book, inside the book, and inside the mind. To understand how children read and write, we must examine what they know about reading and writing in the world, what they bring to the page, and how they construct the page in their minds in order to read the words of others or to compose their own.

Writers and readers must know what print is for in their worlds: to keep track of information, from grocery lists to medical reference volumes; to get things done, from reminders to oneself to have the oil changed to proposals for new programs at work; to delight and instruct in the form of stories, poems, plays, biographies, or essays; and to reflect on experience, emotion, or understanding in the form of journals, daybooks, or discovery drafts.

Today, educators know that such reading and writing knowledge of children can be assessed by using the work they actually do in school. Anthony, Johnson, Mickelson, and Preece (1991) suggest four areas from which to collect data to evaluate literate activity: observation of process, observation of products, classroom measures, and decontextualized measures. Clearly, decontextualized measures dominate the folders of students who have had trouble learning to read and write. Classroom teachers can add to this impoverished record. In their pursuit of curriculum coverage, many teachers have relied on classroom measures such as the text-related activities and tests mentioned by Anthony and colleagues. In this book, I will show that as teachers and specialists, we can observe process—that is, see children engaged in literate activities and record their retellings or responses to texts. We can interview parents, children, and colleagues to learn what literacy means at home as well as at school and to learn how the students think while they read and write. I will also show how to collect and interpret products such as writing folders, learning logs, and self-assessments.

Organization of This Book

In this book, I demonstrate both where traditional testing approaches to assessment fail and how teachers can improve in this area. I will reveal the steps I take to learn how to help readers and writers by telling you the stories of students such as those teachers encounter every day. Each chapter ends with a formal written report sent to parents who hired me to work with their children or of a second-language learner whose teacher assessed him or her for my university course. Of course, I have renamed the people, institutions, and places, but otherwise, the reports remain unchanged.

In the chapters, I call on the stories of these children to illustrate points, but the reports stand alone. Information about the children will be cited repeatedly throughout the book, sometimes before the reports are presented and sometimes afterward. I use their examples to demonstrate how to read student files, how to make sense of test results, how to interview their parents or them about how they read, and how to observe what goes on in the classroom. Therefore, as you read Chapter 1 and learn about Sadie, whose formal report appears at the end of Chapter 2, feel free to stop and read Sadie's case report, if you need to.

Chapter Summaries

Chapter 1 discusses the useful assessment of reading problems based on actual texts, not standardized tests. You will meet Andrew, Sadie, Terry, Mike, Jason, Tara, Kristen, and Jeff and see how much testing and how little useful assessment they have undergone. By comparing tests to what people do outside of school, you will see how little tests tell teachers about the goals of instruction. When examining the nature of contemporary classrooms, you will see that tests even fail to do their traditional job of predicting school success. In Andrew's case study, you will find a young man for whom medication has made an enormous difference, allowing him to gain practice and change his attitude about himself as a reader and writer, once useful assessment showed him how much he could actually do.

Chapter 2 shows how factors typically ignored in testing can be addressed by authentic assessment. I discuss the advantages for examining the texts as well as the reader, the teaching history as well as the learning record, home behavior as well as school performance, and observations as well as numbers. In planning instruction, I will show how to be practical when considering how much change you can expect from any school, while emphasizing what you can do in your own classroom. Sadie's case report shows how home information can change the way a teacher interprets what a student does at school.

Chapter 3 explains how to read reports of testing and anecdotal evidence generally included in student records. You will see how to interpret what students are asked to do on tests and in class in terms of how language is processed. It is the teacher's job to decide what knowledge, practice, or change in conditions will help children develop automatic language functions and personal reasons for reading and writing. In Terry's case report, you will see reasons not to test, or assess, any further.

Chapter 4 shows that parents and school colleagues have valuable information about a student's reading and writing that is often ignored. Occasionally, the classroom teacher asks for such information, but usually by following a script or simply sending out a questionnaire. I will demonstrate how to prepare a few general questions and then ask follow-up questions based on language theory and your growing knowledge of the child. Throughout the chapter, I reiterate the need to respect parents for what they do know and to seek out direct observations of reading and writing behavior, such as from teacher aides who work with children. In Jason's case report, you will have to look diligently for signs of success, despite lengthy and sincere efforts by family and schools.

Observing classroom activity, a source of data generally ignored when children are assessed for services, is the focus of Chapter 5. Teachers need to stand at a variety of distances from the child and the text so that they are able to question the constraints that classrooms may place on children's reading or writing. Perhaps daily classroom routines create the habits that need correcting; perhaps what is working for others actually impedes the progress of this particular student. In Kristen's case report, you will find evidence that modifying class procedures may permit a child to take part in class activities, but deny the child the opportunity to improve as a reader and writer.

Chapter 6 explains how to design assessment for each child based on the principles of language functioning. Teachers must seek to describe how the child reads and writes, not to find evidence of problems they know how to fix. Most important, teachers must invite the student to participate in the assessment by permitting him or her to select the books to be read, the writing to be discussed, or the topics to be developed in writing. Once you sit with the learner to consider a text, you can follow the child, giving proper instruction and noting the reaction, changing the conditions for reading or composing, trying to find what works. When you finish, you will know not only what the student does but also what he or she thinks reading and writing are for, and under what conditions he or she does best. Mike's case report is somewhat unusual. His parents and his Montessori school had avoided testing, so his file is thin, but so is adult knowledge about what Mike can and cannot do.

Chapter 7 focuses on recommending or redesigning instruction. Often, teachers, specialists, and administrators try to fit a child into an existing program or package. I warn against solving problems with packages; rather, I explain how to plan realistic instruction, within existing school structures, based on the principles of language learning. Tara's case report shows that classroom rules and materials can sometimes deepen problems that the teacher is trying to solve.

Mileidis Gort, author of Chapter 8, describes the relationship between what a reader knows about his or her first language and how he or she needs to learn a second. Gort reviews the literature on assessment of culturally and linguistically diverse students, and uses the methods prescribed in this book to evaluate Jeff's reading and writing.

Chapter 9 is devoted to catching up with Andrew, Jason, Kristen, Mike, Tara, and Sadie. Unfortunately, I have lost touch with Terry and his family, but you will be able to see how useful assessment of reading and writing has helped families, schools, and the students themselves change. For Sadie, I present two years of follow-up examinations, and we will celebrate her success with her.

Acknowledgments

I would like to thank Grant Cioffi of the University of New Hampshire—my friend, doctoral advisor, and mentor—for teaching me how to assess the reading and writing of all children but especially those who have had trouble learning. I also thank Don Murray for changing my life by teaching me to think like a writer. Ralph Fletcher read an early draft of this work and insisted I tell the students' stories. I am grateful for his wise counsel. Alan Gaynor of Boston University also read an early draft and challenged me to organize my data more logically. I thank Rebecca Leo, a doctoral student at Boston University, for expeditiously obtaining permissions. Without Millie Gort's chapter on assessing culturally and linguistically diverse students (Chapter 8), this book would be much less useful. Jennifer Jacobson, sales representative, encouraged me to send this book to Allyn and Bacon. I also gratefully acknowledge the following reviewers for their comments and suggestions: Jill Burk, Tarleton State University; Connie B. Cadle, West Virginia University–Parkersburg; Donald D. Pottoroff, Grand Valley State University; and Deborah L. Tidwell, University of Northern Iowa. I further thank Lynda Griffiths of TKM Productions for her patient and meticulous editing.

Finally, I would like to thank my son Zack for letting me tell his stories and for insisting that I have a life away from the computer, sometimes.

ABOUT THE AUTHOR

Jay Simmons has always worked as a reader and a writer. Armed with a degree in English, he covered the superior court beat for the *Springfield (MA) Union* before moving to Maine to teach English in grades 6 and 8. Simmons was a junior high reading specialist in 1977, when Donald Murray of the University of New Hampshire recruited him to teach freshman composition and newswriting. He subsequently taught high school writing, literature, and remedial reading for 13 years.

In 1991, Simmons earned a Ph.D. under Donald Graves at the University of New Hampshire, researching the use of portfolios for large-scale writing assessment. For two years, Simmons learned how to teach third grade from the staff of Moharimet School in Madbury, New Hampshire. Since joining the Boston University School of Education, he has taught teachers how to teach reading and writing. He also helps school districts evaluate their literacy programs and is a reading coach for a middle school in the Roxbury section of Boston. In addition, Simmons writes for trade journals and professional books and co-directs a three-year grant from the Fund for the Improvement of Postsecondary Education to improve the teaching of composition in high school and college. Simmons feels he has always been better informed about student reading and writing abilities by observing students engaged in reading and writing than by administering isolated tests.

1 You Never Asked Me to Read

The Children and the Tests

During one recent year, I assessed the reading and writing abilities of many students, but seven in particular—Andrew, Sadie, Terry, Kristen, Jason, Tara, and Mike. A doctoral student and bilingual teacher, Milcidis Goıt, evaluated the reading and writing of a bilingual boy, Jeff. Either their schools, their parents, or both were concerned about these students' progress in reading. Sadie had taken 22 language tests in her first three years of school; by the end of second grade, Kristen had been tested 15 times; Terry, a fourth-grader, had been the subject of 16 standardized measures; and Andrew, although in high school, had been tested with 17 instruments in just three years (grades 3, 5, and 10).

The students had variously been examined by clinical psychologists, special education teachers, school psychologists, and speech and language therapists. These professionals had administered a total of 52 different tests, some of them three times with a given child. With each of these children, the specialists used one of the Wechsler intelligence scales to measure intellectual ability. Clinical psychologists tended to use word fluency or automatic naming tasks, whereas special education teachers almost always administered the Woodcock-Johnson Psycho-educational Battery–Revised.

Andrew had taken the Scholastic Assessment Test (SAT I), and Sadie had attended a private educational tutoring service that administered an informal reading inventory. Four of the students had taken a group reading achievement test such as the Stanford Achievement Tests, Metropolitan Achievement Tests, or Gates-MacGinitie Reading Tests. These were the only measures of the 52 used requiring more than three sentences of connected reading. (See Appendix A at the back of this book for descriptions of many of the tests listed.) Not once had Andrew, Sadie, Terry, Kristen, Jason, Tara, or Mike been asked to read from a book or periodical of his or her choice, to discuss his or her reasons for reading, or to write something he or she cared about as part of this extensive educational record.

Andrew

Andrew was preparing to enter his senior year of high school in the fall. One sultry August morning, Andrew, his mother, and his sister, a biology major in college, pulled into the parking space by my apple tree about 9:00 A.M. His father was at work as a police officer. Andrew shouldered his way out of the blue Chevy sedan, shook my hand with the sinewy grip of a middle linebacker, and ducked his brown eyes as we said hello. When I asked about his job delivering pizzas, Andrew said he was not working as much since football practice had started. He had done pretty well this summer, usually picking up a $3 tip or more with each delivery. I promised myself to be less cheap in the future.

The previous spring, Andrew had been diagnosed with an attention deficit and had been prescribed medication. He said he believed the medication had helped him concentrate. Andrew was initially referred for his reading problems and attention deficits after grade 3 in a parochial school. He was identified as learning disabled by the local public schools, repeated third grade, received counseling for anxiety and depression, and worked with tutors specializing in learning disabilities through middle school.

Upon entering high school, Andrew and his parents decided he would try learning on his own in classes in the lowest two tracks of a three-track system. His academic record and his testimony as well as that of his mother indicated that he had consistently refused voluntary reading and, whenever possible, avoided assigned reading.

Sadie

Sadie's reddish-blonde hair shined as brightly as her smile. I met Sadie and her mother at school to observe Sadie in her third-grade class and have her read for me. When we left to continue the assessment at her home, Sadie asked if she could ride with me so she could work the sunroof of my car.

Sadie lived in a brightly restored cottage within walking distance of the Atlantic Ocean. If her mother would have let her, Sadie would have worn her Rollerblades in the house. She also loved to play soccer and would head for food as soon as she got home. Her college-educated parents read and wrote daily, and her mother worked in the publishing industry. Sadie loved to learn and write about marine life and worked with her mom to prepare her class reports via desktop publishing.

Sadie was identified with a reading disorder in the second grade. She was placed in inclusionary second- and third-grade classrooms and given extra help using the grade-level assigned texts.

Terry

Terry, a fifth-grader, could read but did not. He read slowly and he watched the clock when doing a reading assignment. His father had concerns about Terry's comprehension. Both parents worried that they had let Terry's problems with print be swept under the rug for too long.

At his parents' request, Terry had been tested several times. He consistently scored in the high-average range for intelligence, but below expectations in reading and writing. School as well as independent psychologists found Terry to have difficulty with word retrieval. One private school refused to accept him into its regular program, but said he qualified for their learning disabled group. The group was full, however, and school officials refused to provide Terry's father with details of the testing that led to their conclusion. Terry was tired of testing.

Kristen

Kristen was an active girl who loved horses, and, like Sadie, loved to wear her Rollerblades in the living room when she could get away with it. She changed from a whole-language kindergarten to a literature-based basal program in first and second grades, when her family moved to a new home in the southern part of the state. In second grade, Kristen still read and wrote much as she did in kindergarten, substituting one graphically dissimilar sight word for another, guessing from context and first letter, and memorizing stories during repeated readings before reading aloud in class.

Kristen's room was dominated by a bunkbed and a tent, which she had set up in the middle of the shag rug. In one corner a bookshelf offered a variety of children's books, many about horses. A desk sat next to the bed, and when I asked her to write with me, Kristen chose to use her own pencil and paper, which she found immediately in their own, neat drawer.

Jason

When I met him, Jason was a fifth-grader who ran through the halls of his elementary school and jumped to touch the overhang leading to an added wing. His mother told him to stop. He was small, with dark hair and a tentative but genuine smile. When he got over his initial nervousness, Jason told me stories of building a soapbox-type car and racing it with his sister. He liked the part when she fell off.

Jason had been in special education classes for three years and taking medication for an attention deficit and hyperactivity during the same period. When I met him, he was taking Prozac. Through second grade, Jason continued to read and write in a consistent manner, dictating brief texts to be transcribed and being read to. In third grade, he began tutoring sessions in a single-letter phonics system, but continued to listen to books on tape and dictate his stories to an aide. Jason's mother felt the school had given up on Jason learning to read.

Tara

Tara said her problem was remembering what she wants to write. She could think of ideas, she stated assuredly; she just forgot them as she wrote the words. Tara was all business; she had brought books to read with me and a selection of her best writing to share, as well. She brushed her hair back from her freckled face as she read both a familiar basal story and a grade-appropriate children's book, impatient to get on to the writing part. She knew she could read.

Tara, a student at a parochial school, had been coached to write with accurate conventions. Her best pieces were neatly handwritten with perfect spelling and punctuation. She also played the piano and wrote about how easy it is to learn to play songs that people recognize.

Mike

The day I met Mike, he nervously scanned the notes and pictures on my refrigerator as I got my assessment materials ready on the kitchen island. We sat in high, green, ladder-back counter stools, and he noticed my son Zack's soccer pictures. Mike was in fifth grade and enjoyed soccer, too. He had brought *The Whipping Boy* to read to me, since it was the book he was reading in class.

Mike had attended a Montessori school for three years, after his parents had removed him from the local public school that wanted to evaluate him for special education. He was briefly tutored in tactile phonics methods, such as finger spelling, and had been hard to keep on task in both public and Montessori classes. He worked quietly and steadily with me for nearly two hours; we did take juice breaks, however, during which he joined his mother, who was reading in the living room.

Mike's parents and teachers were concerned that his handwriting, spelling, and punctuation continued to lag behind his peers, as did his oral reading accuracy and comprehension. He generally did well on isolated phonics tests, however.

Jeff

Jeff was a dedicated and hard-working student who strived for perfection in everything he did. As a second-language learner, he had learned to use his two languages very strategically. Although his current educational setting was monolingual, it was clear that he continued to scaffold his English development through the use of his native language. As he consolidated his second-language literacy and conversational skills, though, Jeff became increasingly aware of his native language loss. This realization caused him frustration and aroused mixed feelings about his status as a bilingual/bicultural individual.

Jeff had only recently begun to experience academic difficulties. It appeared that his second-language skills were not up to par with those of the other children in his fifth-grade classroom, and this affected his performance across the curriculum. Jeff continued to put forth his maximum effort, but was becoming increasingly frustrated with his current academic performance.

Missing Information: The Folders of Students with Reading Problems

I am amazed that I can read the cumulative records of students like these who have been tested for three to eight years and never see a reference to a book title or piece of writing finished. In fact, I have never seen a miscue analysis or a report of an informal reading inventory, except in terms of so-called levels of reading the child may have attained. (Appendix B, found at the end of this book, describes authentic natural measures mentioned in this text.) How useful can "grade level 3.0" be, if we do not know what the student knows about language, about how to read, about how to write, or about how to solve problems in these areas?

Denny Taylor wrote *Learning Denied* in 1991. *Windows into Literacy* by Rhodes and Shanklin appeared in 1993. Taylor discusses the dangers of ignoring naturally occurring evidence of student ability while accumulating norm-referenced evidence of disabilities. She tells of playing a tape recording of oral reading by Patrick, a boy being forcibly coded as learning disabled over the protests of his parents. The director of special education refused to accept this evidence of the boy's ability because test results had shown he could not read. Rhodes and Shanklin show classroom teachers how to assess the developing literacy of their students in more authentic ways (e.g., having students retell what they have read or share their finished writing in class while the teacher observes). Yet, students continue to be referred for special programs with no more than the testing records of Andrew, Sadie, and the rest.

Schools need to keep records of students' abilities (i.e., habits, preferences, judgments, information, and strategies) in doing things outside of school that literate adults do, such as:

- Reading books, newspapers, and magazines
- Writing letters, reports, requests, and memos
- Finding information

Assessment teams need to know what children think reading is and what readers do and what they believe reading can do for them. Decision makers need to know the same things about writing. They need to know what information these children have about language, how they use it in normal reading and writing situations, and what strategies they have for solving problems that arise during reading and writing.

Reading the Test, the School, and the World

In order to decide what is missing in reading folders, we would do well to start with reading and writing outside of school (see Table 1.1, p. 8). What do readers and writers do outside of school? They read magazines, newspapers, and books for enjoyment. And in some literature-based classrooms, or any classroom practicing Drop Everything and Read (DEAR) or Sustained Silent Reading (SSR), opportunities to do the same are given in school. Never have I read a testing record of a person reading from a book, magazine, or newspaper he or she chose for enjoyment.

People also read books, magazines, and newspapers for information, both in school and out. Certainly, test items ask readers to read for information and then test the readers on their acquisition and possibly synthesis of this information. Yet, typically the selections are just snippets chosen by the test maker or the examiner as being appropriate for a certain sort of reader or for showing a certain sort of weakness.

When not in school, readers find their own books, magazines, and newspapers by browsing, from friendly recommendations, or from long-standing lists of favorite writers. Students may be given the chance to choose their own books, but most reading instruction still takes place with assigned basal readers. I have yet to see test results stating, "Sam chose to read *Bridge to Terabithia* for our assessment session."

Independent readers connect their reading to their lives, finding stories about people like themselves or seeking information for work or hobby needs. Teachers practicing the Directed Reading and Thinking Activity (Stauffer, 1975) may ask students to predict what their reading will be about by referring to the prior knowledge of their lives, but even this application generally ignores the chance to allow students to choose reading that fits into their lives.

I remember helping Reggie Hannaford, one of my professors at Bowdoin College, put up a ceiling in a new family room. As we were working, his family came bursting in, all seven fresh from the library, each carrying six or seven new books. I was impressed! Even the youngest kids were planning to read a half dozen books. "Oh, no," Reggie explained. "They'll skim through them, try them out, and return the ones they don't like." Now I was shocked! Not finish a book I started? My required reading lists (and my mother) would not hear of it! Yet, as Reggie's kids taught me, readers regularly abandon books, magazines, or newspapers that are not working for them. Of course, I would learn later, as a newspaper reporter, to plan on being abandoned by the reader before the final paragraph and thus to write my good stuff early in the article.

Students have few chances to abandon reading assignments, unless they are in workshop-style classes such as those advocated by Atwell (1998). Such classes are proliferating, as can be seen in the recommendations for all learners by the writers in *Talking about Books* (Short & Pierce, 1990), or by those of Cunningham and Allington (1994) for "students to whom learning did not come easily" (p. xiii), or by the suggestions of Rhodes and Dudley-Marling (1996) for students classified as learning disabled and remedial. In these response-centered classes, students talk to each other and the teacher about the books and other materials they are reading and writing in order to share, to recommend, and to understand. Seldom do such authentic conversations that Atwell (1998) would call "across the dining room table" occur across the testing desk.

Writing to Ourselves and Others

Outside of school, people write for audiences that may be categorized as spectators, participants, or themselves (Britton et al., 1976). When writing to a *spectator audience*, one attempts to give them an experience without asking any opinion, change, or action on their part. In the case of people one knows, the writing might be a letter or an article sharing thoughts on a common experience, such as a recent holiday visit. In the case of people one does not know, the writing might be a story or a poem.

In some schools, students often write notes to each other or the teacher to discuss recent events or readings. From the "Author's Chair," they share their stories, plays, and poems, or their published pieces are kept in the classroom library. At best, in a test, a student might be asked to write a letter "as if" to a friend or relative. The limited time available for testing naturally precludes writing meaningful complete stories or poems, although students often attempt them when given a sufficiently open prompt (Simmons, 1990, 1992).

When we write to get something done—to change a company representative's mind about a refund, to apply for a job, to request information—we write to *participant audiences*. We ask our readers to think and take action, not simply to sit back and enjoy the show. Again, in response-oriented classes, students might be writing to each other, to the teacher, or to the principal. More commonly, however, writing consists of "authentic" extension activities to literature as letters from one character to another, or to the company in Dr. Seuss's *The Lorax*, or other such tasks as listed in Johnson and Louis (1987). Authentic participant writing takes place much less often in testing, especially individual, diagnostic testing. In some large-scale writing assessments (O'Brien, 1992; Valencia et al., 1994), of course, students either write to a standard prompt or collect pieces of formerly completed work into a portfolio. Never have I seen a portfolio in the cumulative record of a student with reading and writing problems.

Finally, we all write every day to *ourselves*—lists, notes, reminders, journals (for the more ambitious of us), even poems or stories that we may never publish but just enjoy writing. These constitute what Britton and colleagues (1976) classify as "expressive" writing that is done for ourselves, to aid our thinking or our action, or to help us decide what to say to others. Increasingly in classrooms where portfolios are kept, these notes, drafts, and false starts are becoming part of the assessment record (Porter & Cleland, 1995). It is time for diagnostic testing to catch up.

Scoring the Tests

Table 1.1 shows the ten things regularly done by readers and writers outside of school; only two are sure bets in classrooms—reading for information (what Rosenblatt [1978] calls "efferent reading") and spectator writing (stories). In secondary school, many will argue that students write fewer stories and more essays—surely writing for the purpose to get something done. Actually, no. School essays actually perform the same function as elementary teachers' display questions—they show that students have been paying attention and mastering the material. These essays are not written to an unknown audience (since the teacher reads them), but students are usually told (or expected without explanation to understand) that they should write as if the teacher does not know the subject at hand. In other words, if high schoolers do not have the chance to write spectator pieces, they do not write to authentic participant audiences either.

TABLE 1.1   Ten Things Readers and Writers Do

Action	Outside School	In School	In Testing
Read books, magazines, and newspapers for enjoyment	Yes	Maybe	Not likely
Read books, magazines, and newspapers for information	Yes	Yes	Sort of
Find something to read	Yes	Maybe	Not likely
Connect our reading to our lives	Yes	Maybe	Maybe
Stop reading if it is not working	Yes	Not likely	Maybe
Talk to someone (share) about our reading	Yes	Maybe	Not likely
Write to someone we know about new ideas or a common experience	Yes: letters	Maybe	Not likely
Write to someone we do not know to get something done	Yes: article, business letter	Maybe	Not likely
Write to someone we do not know to share or create an experience or realization	Yes: story, poem, play, article	Yes	Not likely
Write to ourselves to recall or reinvent our knowledge	Yes: journals, poetry, stories, lists	Maybe	Not likely

On the bright side, seven of the activities in Table 1.1 rate a "maybe" in school. That is, in literature-based or response-centered classrooms, as opposed to so-called recitation classes dominated by teachers (Brown, 1993), students may indeed be reading for enjoyment from books of their own choice, connecting their reading to their lives, sharing their reading and writing with others, and writing to themselves and others for authentic reasons. With so much change occurring in the classroom, then, we can at least expect tests to begin to reflect what goes on in school, if not outside the brick walls.

Unfortunately, in seven of the cases shown in Table 1.1, tests are "not likely" to ask students to read or write as if they were outside the examiner's office. "Maybe" the student will be asked to connect the reading with what he or she knows of the world, and "maybe" the examiner will stop the reading when the frustration level is reached. Any reading for enjoyment in testing is largely a lucky accident, since students have no choice in what they read or write. And although the students certainly must carry information away from the reading act, it is unlikely they will be reading any whole piece of work for a useful purpose outside generation of scores and results.

Clay (1993) asserts that a test's likeness to what the child will do in the real world establishes the test's validity. Since large-scale assessment and classroom practice have begun to incorporate more authentic literacy, individual, diagnostic testing of students with a history of problems in learning to read and write must follow. Certainly, we would like to think that our tests tell us how well our students read and write in general, but failing such authenticity, we should at least know how well they read and write in school. As tests continue to lag behind schools in authenticity of reading and writing required, even this minimal result is doubtful.

Purposes of Testing

Grade-level performance on standardized achievement tests means the average score of students of the specified grade using material on the test. The reading selections on standardized measures are drawn from books intended for the grade levels to whom the test is administered, or are written to readability formula guidelines for those grade levels. Therefore, it is assumed that if a student can succeed as well as other third-graders on materials intended for third-graders, he or she can be placed in a third-grade reading book. Now that students in classrooms are reading trade books rather than instructional texts, such placement data are less useful. Conversely, students need to be assessed with a variety of trade materials to see how they read in these. In Sadie's case, testing did not show if Sadie could read classroom books under natural reading conditions in a way that would allow her to develop fluent reading habits.

What Can Sadie Read?

Sadie was tested at a private academy during her second-grade year with the primer level of the Metropolitan Achievement Test and scored as follows:

Subtest	Grade Equivalent	Percentile
Reading Comprehension	1.9	63rd
Vocabulary	2.0	78th

On an unspecified informal reading inventory, Sadie performed as follows:

Grade Level	Comprehension Percentage
Pre-primer	100%
Primer	87%
First	75%
Second	Too difficult

Sadie was unable to use the testing materials intended for her grade level, and she scored only marginally as a second-grader on primer-level testing materials. That means that she was unable to read very brief passages and answer specific questions as well as the average second-grader reading primer materials. Sadie was also unable to read even a brief, first-grade passage with more than instructional comprehension on the informal reading inventory. (For a listing of independent, instructional, and frustration levels and percentages, see Appendix B.)

Despite these results, Sadie was tutored in a second-grade basal reader. Perhaps of more concern, Sadie's performance appeared more at grade level on the formal test than on the informal inventory in which more connected reading was required. In other words, the standardized tests inflated her performance relative to more natural reading. In the future, however, only standardized scores were obtained for Sadie, and decisions were therefore based on these inflated estimates. In September of her third-grade year, Sadie took the Metropolitan Achievement Test Primary 1 and scored as follows:

Subtest	Grade Equivalent	Percentile
Vocabulary	1.9	21st
Reading Comprehension	1.9	21st

She was placed in a third-grade classroom using the Houghton-Mifflin literature-based basal series, and in the spring had just been assigned a Beverly Cleary book typically used with third-graders. Testing in March produced these scores:

Wechsler Individual Achievement Test

Subtest	Score	Percentile
Reading Composite	85	16th
Basic Reading (word recognition)	84	
Reading Comprehension	94	
Predicted Score (based on WISC-III)	101	

Sadie's performance was termed unusually low:

Woodcock-Johnson Psychoeducational Battery–Revised

Subtest	Grade Equivalent	Score	Percentile
Broad Reading	2.4	88	21st
Letter Word Identification	2.5	89	23rd
Passage Comprehension	2.2	88	22nd

In May, Sadie's private academy reported her reading "at the middle to the end of third grade," although no testing or reading performances were provided to defend this claim. The evidence, so far, supported placing Sadie in grade-level materials. She was less than a grade level behind in grade 2 and about one grade level behind in grade 3. Even though the International Reading Association and the National Council of Teachers of English have for years urged professionals not to use or report grade-level scores, even her percentile ranks put Sadie in the low-average range.

However, it is important to remember that none of these tests required more than a few sentences of reading. Nowhere was a check run on the number of words Sadie had to stop and decode, nor on how she read as she proceeded past a few minutes. The school personnel had noted, however, her high levels of activity and distractibility during testing (see Chapter 2).

Reading Real Books

In May, I asked Sadie (see the case report at the end of Chapter 2) to read from books that she chose as easy, just right, and challenging. She read from the easy one (*Reading Milestones,* level 3, book 3) with 99 percent accuracy and one miscue, which she self-corrected. She had chosen the passage for its brevity and subject (animals). She predicted the events based on her knowledge of animals and story sense, and after reading, she noted that her prediction had not come true. However, Sadie read the passage in a word-by-word manner, indicating a lack of automatic word recognition even in her easiest choice.

Sadie read two passages from her "just right" book, *Focus: Up and Over* from Scott Foresman. Early in the session, she read with 97 percent accuracy, usually self-correcting, but at the end of the session, I asked her to read a page of the same book, which she did with only 83 percent accuracy, clearly at her frustration level.

Finally, between the two passages from *Focus: Up and Over,* Sadie read less than a paragraph from *Mystery of the Lost Village* from the Boxcar Children series of Gertrude Chandler Warner, a book commonly read by third-graders. She selected the book as challenging, and she chose the paragraph because the page contained an illustration of a horse. Sadie read with 77 percent accuracy and few self-corrections.

I was worried that the school setting, possible nervousness with me, or the rather insipid nature of the programmed texts or the difficulty of the Boxcar Children book had unfairly affected Sadie's performance. I asked Sadie to read aloud some of her own books from home, at home, with her mother.

Even reading at home with her mother, Sadie tired quickly and her strategies failed as she tired. Sadie read from an easy second-grade book, *Small Wolf,* with 90 percent accuracy and frequent self-corrections. In a slightly harder book commonly used with second- or third-graders, *Junie B. Jones and Her Big Fat Mouth,* she read with 70 percent accuracy, still maintaining self-correction and preserving meaning, while working hard on 3 out of 10 words. Again, when she read another passage from the same book later, Sadie read with marginal accuracy, but much less self-correction, preserving meaning only 57 percent of the time.

Bad Placement, Mixed Results

Sadie could obviously "read" test materials better than books. Perhaps that is why her private academy found her to have "come a long way." When working with brief passages and workbooks, she seemed not to tire as she did when reading whole, unconstrained children's books that required her to use all of her very good contextual fix-up strategies to accommodate limited word recognition skills. When she read trade books at school or at home, she tired quickly, and instructional or independent material quickly became frustration-level material. Moreover, because all of Sadie's reading in the Houghton-Mifflin series was at her frustration level, she never had the chance to practice easy, fluent reading, nor to develop a store of sight words through repeated practice. Assessment with books and analysis of her integrated reading behaviors revealed what testing on subskills did not.

Skills and Knowledge

In addition to testing students in order to form reading groups or assign books, schools also test to decide which skills or awarenesses children need to learn. I might administer the Shanker and Ekwall Phonics Assessment (Shanker & Ekwall, 1998), for instance, to decide which letter sounds a student can recognize and blend into nonsense words. Or I might use the Woodcock Reading Mastery Test of passage comprehension to see if a student can read a few sentences and supply a missing word. If the reader does well with the word recognition task but poorly with comprehension, then I can teach that child what he or she needs to know.

Classroom teachers no longer present phonics only with worksheets of nonsense words. Teachers now more frequently show young readers how to decode words while they read whole children's stories (Trachtenburg, 1990). Many teachers have abandoned sentence completion worksheets to develop reading comprehension in favor of reading response journals (Atwell, 1998) or extension activities (Johnson & Louis, 1987). Is it really important for a student to know how to blend nonwords (Rhodes & Shanklin, 1993)? We might prefer data from miscue analyses that show students' strategies for recognizing words during the act of reading whole, connected texts. We will know more about a reader's understanding by listening to the reader summarize a passage or by watching the reader find information or references we have questioned (Paratore & Indrisano, 1987).

Can Jason Write?

Jason, diagnosed as learning disabled and taught by an inclusionary model for the last three years, was able to participate in class activities by having books read to him, or taped for him, and by having his dictated stories transcribed by an adult. He then copied the adult transcription. In other words, Jason's school decided that Jason could not write. Testing would seem to encourage this view. On a recent administration of the Woodcock-Johnson, Jason scored as follows:

Woodcock-Johnson

Subtest	Percentile
Writing	
Dictation	0.2
Writing Samples	0.1
Broad Writing	0.1

He also had trouble with spelling dictation and recognition of sight words:

Test of Written Spelling	*1.4 grade*
Dolch Sight Word List	*Preprimer (38 words recognized)*

When I worked with Jason, I asked him to write a sentence about a book he had just read to me, an activity modeled on a Reading Recovery lesson (Pinnell et al., 1991). He chose to copy the title of the book instead. When I asked him to write all the words he knew how to write, he tried the same copying strategy. Perhaps he could not write, as his test scores indicated. It occurred to me that Jason had learned that writing is copying, since that was the way it had been presented to him in class. I decided to see what he knew about writing when he did not have to compose the message (which is what copying is, in a sense) but still had to encode the words to print (which copying is not).

I dictated the passage, "My friend and I like to go and see the big sail boat. It has a blue flag" (Johnston, 1997), and asked Jason to write down the words as best he could. He wrote, " Me FND the I LIK to eo is c the BOe Cal Bot it hac u Bo hlae" (see the case report in Chapter 4).

Jason used several strategies to write this message. First, he succeeded most frequently with first and last consonant sounds: *Me* for *My, fnd* for *friend, lik* for *like, to, boe* for *big, cal* for *sail, bot* for *boat, it, hac* for *has,* and *bo* for *blue*. Actually, he probably wrote what looks like an *e* for *g*, since they are spatial transpositions of each other. Therefore, he got *go* and the final *g* in *big* and *flag*, as well. He used *h* to represent *f* in *flag* since they are articulated in similar ways, and he used *c* for *s* and the letter name *C* for the word *see*. He placed vowels, though not always the right ones, where vowels belong, and he used one sight word for another, as he did in his reading, probably because they were presented to him as isolated drill lists and were not associated in his memory with meaningful contexts.

Therefore, Jason used sound, graphics, articulation, letter names, and sight words, but not reliably. He knew and remembered the sounds, shapes, and names of letters and words, but he could not retrieve the knowledge each time he needed it. He also had not yet developed cueing systems to tell him when there was a problem and which fix-up strategy to use. For instance, if Jason was not sure that *t-h-e* spelled *and,* then he could listen for the sounds at the end and think, "Does *the* end like *friend?*" He didn't know that he didn't know (Johnston, 1997) nor did he know to switch to sound patterns when visual memory did not work.

Clay (1993) questions relying on standardized test scores for young children "in the tail end of the distributions" (p. 7), because problems of significance do not appear in the test scores until well after they have begun appearing in literate activity. In Jason's case, this writing of a whole text provides many data for deciding which knowledge and "skills" Jason knew and what he still needed to be taught. The percentiles derived from the normed tests reveal little, and may have led his teachers to conclude that Jason did not have the ability to write. Further, the results of isolated subskill testing led to isolated skill instruction (composing orally without ever encoding, learning sight words from lists not from meaningful context), which led to Jason learning ineffective strategies for writing and reading.

Dynamic Assessment

Through dynamic assessment (Cioffi & Carney, 1983; Paratore & Indrisano, 1987; Dixon-Krauss, 1996), an evaluator can try various strategies with the reader to find out what sort of help or instruction improves reading performance, thereby helping teachers plan methods as well as content and materials. For instance, if a student has difficulty sounding out longer words in context, I might try covering, then gradually revealing, syllables. If the student can sound out each syllable and blend them into a known word, then rules for syllabicating may help him or her.

In Jason's case, he stopped at the word *pal* in his oral reading of a linguistic reader and said he did not know the word. He also said he had no ideas for figuring it out. I suggested the rerunning strategy, in which a person rereads the sentence from the beginning to see if the context helps him or her guess. Jason reread and got the word. Therefore, switching strategies may help Jason.

Later in the same text, he read, "The van is out gas" instead of the printed sentence, "The van has no gas." Then he stopped himself and said, "That should be 'out of gas'." Here again, Jason substituted basic sight words for each other. In addition, he kept the length of the sentence the same (five words). He knew what the more sensible phrase was, but the book was focusing on the short *a* sound and used the verb *has* instead of *is*.

I asked Jason what the phrase looked like, and he said, "Out of gases," clearly focusing on the least familiar word, *gas,* as the likely culprit and not recognizing the syllable difference between *gas* and *gases*. I covered words on either side of *no* to see if he recognized the word in isolation, and he did. Then I asked him to rerun the sentence and he got it correct. This dynamic assessment session, then, showed that Jason could benefit from the rerunning strategy, that he could use his sense of natural language, and that he could focus on sight words individually, but that he needed help (as in Reading Recovery lessons) integrating these separate kinds of information as he read.

Useful Assessment of Reading and Writing Problems

Norm-referenced subskills testing dominates the folders of children who have reading and writing problems. Teachers and specialists identify learning disabilities on the basis of these tests and then plan instruction in the content and the form of the tests. Yet, as you have seen, these tests do not reflect how literate adults read and write outside of school, nor do they assess students doing the things teachers increasingly ask students to do with reading and writing in school. These scripted measures fail to serve the traditional purposes of diagnostic language testing—to determine appropriate instructional materials, to identify needed information and skills, and to suggest successful teaching strategies.

At the same time, educators have begun to see that when children and adults read from trade books and periodicals, a great deal can be learned about their reading and writing abilities. In the next chapter, I will show that when we ask students to read and write whole texts for meaningful purposes, as much as possible of their own devising, we gather information that clarifies and extends the data obtained from tests as often as it contradicts or discredits testing.

Finally, this chapter ends with a case report of Andrew, the high school junior who thought he could not do anything at all as a reader and had been avoiding reading and writing consistently since third grade. From this report, Andrew and his parents learned that he knows a great deal about how to read and write and that with this change in attitude, he can begin to gain what books and periodicals have to offer.

CASE REPORT: What Is the Problem?

Background

I was asked by Mrs. Mary Billington to evaluate the reading and writing abilities of her son, Andrew, who was entering his senior year of high school in the fall. Andrew had been diagnosed with an attention deficit the previous spring and had been prescribed medication that he felt helped him concentrate. We decided he would take his dosage prior to the session in order to focus on his reading behavior devoid of any inattention unrelated to the reading act.

Andrew was initially referred for his reading problems and attention deficits after grade 3 in a parochial school. His initial WISC–R scores were generally superior, except for coding and information, and the school reported his decoding to be at the 1.8 grade level. He was identified as learning disabled by the Ripley Public Schools, repeated third grade, received counseling for anxiety and depression, and worked with a tutor specializing in learning disabilities in reading. Records from grades 4 and 5 indicated tutoring on word recognition and spelling patterns, comprehension of brief passages built from controlled vocabulary, and writing from a given prompt with emphasis on spelling and punctuation rules covered.

Andrew's intelligence testing results are summarized here:

Verbal				*Performance*			
	11/85	*4/89*	*5/94*		*11/85*	*4/89*	*5/94*
Information	7	8	7	Picture completion	15	14	10
Similarities	18*	15	9	Picture arrangement	16	15	13
Arithmetic	11	9	9	Block design	13	14	13
Vocabulary	14*	8	6	Object assembly	14	14	14
Comprehend	13*	9	8	Coding	8	9	9
Digit span	10	10	9				

Notice that the abilities (marked with asterisks) to do word analogies (similarities), to understand vocabulary, and to solve practical problems (comprehend) dropped significantly from grade 3 (11/85) to grade 10 (5/94). Analogies were also the lowest part of Andrew's SAT in grade 11. After third grade, the ability to comprehend language and to work analogies generally depends on vocabulary development from wide reading. Andrew's academic record as well as testimony by his mother and himself indicated that he consistently refused voluntary reading and, whenever possible, avoided assigned reading. Moreover, tutoring materials were focused on controlled vocabulary designed to reinforce decoding and spelling patterns. Therefore, lack of practice and experience with natural printed language may account for much of Andrew's reading difficulty.

There is good evidence that Andrew had learned what he had been taught, however. Grade-level scores reported on various reading measures showed growth:

	Grade 4	Grade 5	Grade 10
Stanford Diagnostic Reading	4.3	4.6	8.8
Morrison McCall Spelling	4.5	5.2	7.5
Woodcock Word Identification	6.0	6.1	12.9
Woodcock Word Attack	NA	NA	12.9
Gray Oral Reading	4.0	2.8	8.6

These tests showed significant gains in reading ability, spelling ability, word recognition, and word attack, although Andrew was not up to grade level in overall reading or spelling of dictated lists.

On the SAT I in May, before beginning the attention medication, Andrew scored 400 on the verbal test and 490 in math, putting him above 42 percent nationally in math and 17 percent nationally in verbal reasoning. Within the reading test, he scored above 25 percent nationally in critical reading of short passages and completion of sentences with missing words. He scored above only 14 percent nationally in verbal analogies.

These scores indicated that Andrew used context to understand passages and complete sentences, but that he lacked the academic vocabulary to complete verbal analogies, a trend consistent with earlier WISC–R and WAIS–R intelligence testing. Since the SAT I is a timed test, attention and reading speed as well as a limited vocabulary may account for Andrew's performance on the test.

Current Assessment

Spelling and Phonics.   Andrew pronounced the 35 names on the Names Test (Duffelmeyer et al., 1994) with 98 percent accuracy for phonic knowledge. When asked to write a brainstorming list, titles, and the beginning of a piece on a topic of his own choosing, Andrew made only three spelling errors in 77 words (96 percent accuracy), even though spelling was not emphasized in the directions (see Figure 1.1). Therefore, Andrew has learned to sound out both nonsense words (Woodcock Word Attack test) and naturally occurring names (Names Test) and to

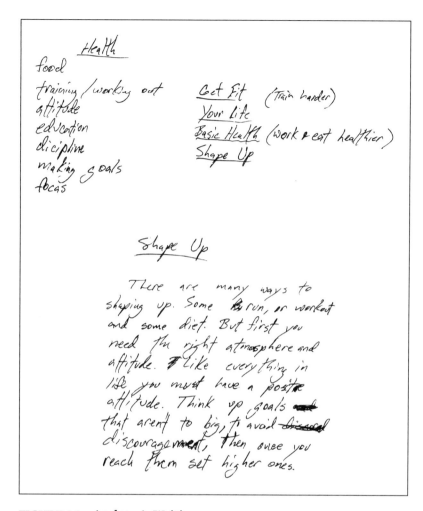

FIGURE 1.1 Andrew's Writing

spell accurately in his own writing, when he has the choice of subject (and therefore vocabulary). Tests of his ability to recognize errors in printed lists, or of his ability to spell dictated words not of his choosing, would probably be lower, but less related to actual writing.

Reading for Meaning

Andrew chose to read aloud a 207-word passage from the *Eagle-Tribune* because he felt the Red Sox were doing well and sports are an interest of his. He initially predicted the article would be about their most recently played game, because of the picture accompanying it, but when directed to the headline, he changed his prediction to reading about the team's upcoming road trip to the West Coast, where the Sox hoped to win, despite the better recent performance of the western teams. Andrew read with 98 percent word accuracy and a full and accurate retelling after the reading. He made five misreadings of words:

Passage 1 (Oral).   *Eagle-Tribune,* "Sox Look for More West Success," August 17, 1995, p. 21: 207 words, 98 percent accuracy, 60 percent self-correction rate

Andrew	*Text*	*Matches Preceding Context*	*Matches Following Context*	*Self-Corrects*	*Preserves Meaning*	*Corrected or Preserves Meaning*
game	days	no	no	yes	no	yes
a	the	yes	no	no	yes	yes
monumentum	momentum	no	no	yes	no	yes
of	—	yes	no	yes	no	yes
the	a	yes	yes	no	yes	yes
		60%	20%	60%	40%	100%

These miscues indicated that most of the time (60 percent, column 3), Andrew predicted the upcoming word from the preceding context, which is a positive habit. Few of the miscues fit with the words that followed, however (20 percent, column 4), so Andrew corrected most of the miscues (60 percent, column 5). Again, this is a positive fix-up strategy for word recognition errors. When asked, Andrew described this use of context to check on his own reading. As shown in column 7, 100 percent of his word errors were either corrected or did not change the meaning enough to need correction.

Passage 2 (Oral).   *Let's Live,* "Medicinal Mushrooms. Part I: How Mushrooms Fit the Mold for Health and Healing," August 1995, p. 78: 246 words, 61 words per minute oral reading speed, 94 percent accuracy, 58 percent self-correction rate

Andrew also selected a passage to read that he predicted would be hard because it contained technical vocabulary. He used the cover of the magazine to find the subject of the article he planned to read, used the table of contents to find a related title, and turned to the appropriate page. From the title and headings, Andrew predicted the article would be about mushrooms and how they are nutritious. He said he expected to learn about different types of mushrooms, but admitted that he never eats mushrooms and does not know much about them.

Andrew read the first 246 words with 94 percent accuracy, and was able to give a retelling of the major ideas and some of the most striking details. He was able to use the technical word *herbology* after reading in order to complete his retelling and he used his knowledge of suffixes to figure out the meaning. He made 14 word errors:

Andrew	Text	Matches Preceding Context	Matches Following Context	Self-Corrects	Preserves Meaning	Corrected or Preserves Meaning
—	should	yes	no	yes	no	yes
formulas	formulations	yes	yes	no	yes	yes
elements	ailments	yes	no	yes	no	yes
diver-	devastating	yes	no	yes	no	yes
boosts	boasts	yes	no	yes	no	yes
engineered	engendered	yes	yes	no	yes	yes
dissolving	discovering	yes	no	yes	no	yes
the	and	yes	no	yes	no	yes
leggitimit	legitimate	no	no	yes	no	yes
starting	startling	yes	no	no	no	no
tradition	traditional	no	no	no	no	no
herbal	herbology	yes	no	yes	no	yes
expensive	expressive	yes	no	no	no	no
for example	i.e.	yes	yes	no	yes	yes
		86%	21%	58%	21%	79%

Again, Andrew predicted most words from preceding context (86 percent, column 3) and self-corrected most (58 percent, column 5) of his errors after noticing that they did not fit with following context (21 percent, column 4). Most of the errors were corrected or meaning was preserved (79 percent, column 7). In fact, the writer of the passage misused the expression *i.e.* to mean *for example* (it should be *e.g.*), but Andrew read the intended meaning instead of the literal meaning, *that is*. Therefore, he continued to show excellent use of context to gain meaning from his reading.

Andrew did not correct *starting* for *startling*, *tradition* for *traditional* or *expensive* for *expressive*, even though meaning was changed. Here, he may have been overloaded with the number of new words to recognize, or perhaps unfamiliar with the uses of these expressions.

Andrew explained that he reads better silently, because he makes errors reading aloud, trying to keep up with the pace of his eyes. Earlier testing noted that Andrew would "perseverate" on an error he had made, losing concentration on upcoming text. Andrew indeed confirmed that he often worries about an error he has made so much that he cannot concentrate on his reading. Therefore, I asked Andrew to read the next 250-word section silently. He logically predicted the next part would be about where the nutritional mushrooms are grown, how they are grown, and what tests are run on them.

Passage 3 (Silent).   *Let's Live,* "Medicinal Mushrooms. Part I: How Mushrooms Fit the Mold for Health and Healing," August 1995, p. 78: 258 words, 115 words per minute silent reading speed

Andrew read silently nearly twice as fast as he read aloud, so he was indeed faster when processing silently. However, his reading speed was about half the average of high school reading rates, so we can expect him to have difficulty completing assigned homework on time or doing well on timed reading tests, such as the SAT I.

Andrew retold the passage with less detail than he did with the earlier piece on the Red Sox, probably because of the presence of technical vocabulary explaining the medical reasons for the benefits of the mushrooms. He did, however, recall details about mushrooms' growing habits, their size and composition, and their therapeutic effects with cancer and the immune system.

Overall, Andrew demonstrated the ability to set a purpose for reading, to check on word recognition problems at the sentence level of meaning, to decode words based on their structure, to recognize main ideas and to recall details, and to be aware of his own reading processes and the structure of sophisticated text. He reads slowly and lacks a wide vocabulary, probably due to lack of sustained reading in challenging material.

Writing

Andrew was able to discuss his writing process as used on his research paper on Hugh Hefner. He chose the topic, he said, because it was one of two names left on the list allowed by the instructor, although he did not know who Hefner was prior to the assignment. He went to the library and used the computer cataloguing system to find a book on *Playboy* magazine, and he later saw a television special on Hefner's life.

After he took notes, Andrew wrote the paper right before the deadline, sitting on the couch while his mother typed the pages he had already written. She confirmed this to be Andrew's standard method of report writing. I asked him how he decided what information to use, and he said he tried to decide what the teacher wanted.

In English class, Andrew said, the students wrote drafts (usually on books they had read), had the drafts checked by the teacher for completeness and mechanical correctness, then typed the drafts at the computer lab. That process generally took a week or two, he said.

Such assignments do not really allow discussion of Andrew's ability to write. Writers must decide on a topic they know something about, decide what they can offer a reader about that topic, get information they may need to achieve that purpose, and obtain feedback from readers before publishing a final draft. Andrew normally was not given the opportunity to do what writers do.

However, I asked Andrew to brainstorm with me a list of things he knew about, to come up with some titles for a piece on this information, and to begin such a draft (Murray, 1985). He was able to list seven items quickly on the subject of *health:* food, training/working out, attitude, education, discipline, making goals, and focus. He was able to focus on a purpose for a piece, in the form of writing four titles: Get Fit (Train Harder), Your Life, Basic Health (Work and Eat Healthier), and

Shape Up. He chose Shape Up as his title and topic, because Get Fit sounded too much just like working out and Basic Health sounded too much like a textbook. He wrote five sentences in about five minutes and was able to point out that the ideas might be sections or chapters in a longer work.

From this information, it was clear that Andrew could generate ideas for writing, focus on a subject, and begin a draft in short order when given the chance and given a helpful model of someone working with him to do so.

Study Habits

As noted earlier, Andrew knew generally how to do library research, and he understood book and text structure well enough to read for reports and home-work. I asked him how he studied for tests. He said that he usually did not study at all. His mother confirmed that Andrew did almost no homework. If he felt the test or the studying was impossible, he would not undertake it. When he did study, say for Spanish, he reviewed the textbook for sections he remembered covering. In social studies, he would go over vocabulary with a friend he believed was smart. Andrew said that in class, the social studies teacher would at times splatter words on the board, and Andrew would then attempt to write down what the teacher said when he discussed those words, or anything else that sounded important.

Regarding his plans for the coming year, Andrew said he felt his new med-ication helped him in focusing, so he was planning to take typing this year, because typing would help him in his reading and writing abilities. He could always pick out the correct spelling on a spell-checker list using a word processor, he said. He also felt the medication would help him with anatomy and physiology, a subject needed for his career interest in physical therapy, and he hoped to be able to concentrate enough to do well in the class.

Conclusions and Recommendations

Andrew read slowly but accurately and with comprehension in material intended for adults on technical and general topics. He showed solid knowledge of phonics, word structure, and text organization. He was able to set a purpose for reading, preview a piece to see if it fits that purpose, and check up on his reading to see if he achieved his purpose. Andrew was aware of his own reading processes and could generally fix errors when he made them. In addition, the medication seemed to help him concentrate, as he showed no signs of distractibility until the end of our 90-minute session. He did not, however, view himself as a good reader and he avoided reading for pleasure or classwork whenever possible.

Since Andrew was a linebacker on the football team, I explained to him that trying to read while maintaining this attitude about himself was like trying to play linebacker while imagining himself to be Elmer Fudd. In other words, Andrew's fear of failure prevented him from getting into the game. Even when he did play, he had less playing experience and training to produce good results; he stumbled rather than glided quickly; he avoided challenging opponents rather than attacking them. My assessment showed that Andrew had learned the tools necessary to become an all-pro linebacker in reading.

His current training schedule should include lots of "playing time": wide reading in easy or only slightly challenging material in order to build speed and fluency with his newly acquired concentration. He should also pursue new words he comes across in reading. He had the abilities to use context and structure to figure out most of them, and could ask for help or use a dictionary with the others.

Andrew's tutoring records from middle school showed that he had been taught organizational and study skills; however, his resistance to using them over the years had left the skills fuzzy or absent in his mind. I would suggest that future tutoring concentrate on how to take notes in class, emphasizing how to select the important ideas in reading. If he applied these principles to lectures, he could do well there, too. Skills should include the following: Set a purpose for listening, guess (by thinking of questions you want answered) the speaker's probable topics, check up and refine your predictions if the speaker does something else, and write down the answers to your prelistening questions.

Andrew also needed to learn and practice time management, from getting to school on time (this is another example of fleeing the game rather than playing it) to computing how long it will take him to read a page of social studies, English, or science homework, then setting aside time (in manageable chunks for him, perhaps 30 to 60 minutes at a time) to complete the pages required. In addition, Andrew needed to practice studying his notes for tests. He seemed to have a good idea of how this worked, but fear of failure discouraged him from practicing the method.

I would suspect that an untimed or extended timed SAT I would produce higher results in reading and sentence completion. In order to improve in the analogies section, Andrew needed to practice analogies specifically and to use words generally included on SAT lists. Such practice materials are readily available on computer disks or in book form.

Despite what they had thought all these years, Andrew and his family should be impressed with how much Andrew has learned about how to read and write under difficult conditions. With the benefit of better concentration, and a mental image of himself as a successful reader, Andrew can give himself the practice time to acquire more speed and stronger vocabulary needed for enjoyable reading.

CHAPTER

2 What Reading Teachers Can Add to the Record

Reviewing the list of tests used on Andrew, Sadie, Terry, Kristen, Jason, Tara, and Mike, we can see that the medical-model practitioners had all been looking for the problem inside the child. The lack of reading proficiency was tested for the following:

- Low intelligence (Wechsler scales)
- Inadequate word fluency (Rapid Automatized Naming, Rapid Alternating Stimulus Naming, Boston Naming Test, Word Fluency Task)
- Limited receptive or expressive vocabulary (Peabody Picture Vocabulary Test–Revised, Gardner Expressive One-Word Picture Vocabulary Test)
- Below-average language development (Clinical Evaluation of Language Fundamentals–Revised, Language Processing Test)
- Limited store of sight words (Dolch Sight Word List)
- Psychological problems (Children's Apperception Test, Rorschach)
- Abnormal visual-perceptual functioning (Bender Visual Motor Gestalt Test)
- Auditory perception deficits (Test of Auditory Perception Skills)
- Mental processing problems (Kaufman Assessment Battery for Children)
- Abnormal perception and motor coordination (Beery Developmental Test of Visual Motor Integration, Purdue Perceptual-Motor Survey)

Johnston (1997) might look for the problem in the school, and in some cases, there is a good deal of evidence to indict the school. Andrew left parochial school feeling ashamed of his inability to read like the other kids. Sadie's school district recently changed to a literature-based basal reading system, according to Sadie's mother, in order to provide multiple levels of reading materials in each classroom. However, Sadie has only third-grade books available in her selection of extension reading books, so if she cannot read these, she cannot read. Mike attends a competitive private school and feels his books must look like those of the other students.

Jason defines reading as "getting the words right." He has no favorite writer, no idea of what reading and writing can do for him, and no favorite story he can ask for by name or description. All his instruction, in the past and planned for the future, has been aimed at the word level—how to recognize basic sight words and sound out unknown, phonetically regular words. When Jason needs to read or write in class, he is read to or dictates his ideas to an adult who then writes for him. He has no responsibility for or contact with literacy above the word level.

Factors Beyond the Student and the School

Taylor (1991) says that when we look for problems inside the child, we will find them, even if the child can read and write. If I follow Johnston's (1997) advice and look to the school, I will find problems there, as well. Rhodes and Shanklin (1993), however, suggest looking at the process of reading, not just the reader. When we consider the *process,* the reader becomes only one factor, as does the school. We must also consider the *text,* the *immediate context* in which the reading or writing takes place, *history* (including family and educational history), and the *larger setting* in which the assessment has been conceived and will be used.

The Text Read

Mike read very differently in different texts. When he attempted to read *The Whipping Boy* (Fleishman, 1986), a novel appropriate for most fifth-graders, he could only follow the story very generally, mostly from reading the illustrations. He was unable to use his prior knowledge to sound out words or interpret phrases. However, when Mike switched to easier material, such as *Nate the Great and the Boring Beach Bag* (Sharmat, 1987), he was able to react to the story in great detail and solve his own confusions about the text.

Immediate Context

Andrew said he had no idea how to plan a piece of writing; instead, he generally put off writing until the last minute, avoidance being his primary strategy for literacy frustrations. His mother confirmed that the night before a paper was due, Andrew would write as she typed. The total number of pages completed was Andrew's sole criterion to decide whether to continue writing; he stopped when he got to the required number.

Andrew said his paper topics were assigned from a teacher-generated list, first come, first served, and due dates were given. Only the teacher read the finished piece. Clearly, Andrew was not writing for a purpose recognized outside the school's walls nor on a topic within his realm of knowledge. The processes of research, question finding, drafting, and revising had never been modeled for him.

I asked Andrew to brainstorm topics, information, and titles on subjects of his own choice. I did the same for topics of mine and shared my results with him. We discussed our alternatives and evaluated our tentative beginnings. Andrew wrote with clarity and purpose for half an hour. He misspelled only a few words and he could clearly see where he needed to change focus and search out more information in order to continue the piece. In other words, given the immediate context of an open-entry task and supportive modeling of what writers do, Andrew employs different writing procedures and produces a more meaningful product than when his context for writing is an intellectual vacuum that assumes he already has the procedural knowledge he is supposed to be learning.

History

Andrew also furnishes a good example of the role played by family and educational history in interpreting a child's literacy performances. For instance, Andrew brought a newspaper article about the Boston Red Sox and a fitness magazine to the assessment session. Neither he nor his mother described him as a reader. In fact, Andrew said he loses track of his reading because he keeps thinking about his mistakes as he tries to read on. He also says that he will not attempt a task that seems impossible and that his homework record is "horrendous." Meanwhile, his mother describes Andrew's father as a smart man who is not a reader but enjoys crossword puzzles and the newspaper. She herself is a slow reader, but Andrew's older sister (who is studying biology in college) is an avid reader. In fact, it was her magazine Andrew brought to the session.

In the context of his family, not the school, Andrew is a normal reader: He does not especially enjoy reading but, like his father, he reads the newspaper sports section well and by choice. He has academic plans similar to that of his sister, thinking about studying sports medicine or physical training, and is willing to read more difficult material on that subject. Andrew reads slowly (like his mother), probably accounting for his lack of performance on the SAT I and his inability to keep up with homework assignments, thus leading to his long-standing habit of avoidance.

Both Andrew and his mother said that Andrew can attend to academic tasks now that he is taking medication for his attention deficit. The rest of his reading behavior is consistent with an underdeveloped, slow reader who lacks vocabulary and fluency from inadequate reading experience and easy reading practice.

The Larger Setting

Referring to special education staff meetings intended to diagnose, identify, and plan for a child, Rhodes and Shanklin (1993) suggest that regular classroom teachers can add to the proceedings by doing the following:

- *Balancing the evidence* from standardized measures with data collected from the student's classroom engagement with whole texts, highlighting conflicting data and data demonstrating strengths as well as weaknesses
- Making sure that parents feel that *school information matches their home observations*
- *Keeping open the option of not identifying the student as learning disabled*
- Forcing the team to consider *which set of data should take precedence* by emphasizing the theoretical stance assumed by any educational plan created, preventing the domination of a behavioristic stance, and making sure people realize that

the identification and the plan are only first steps in getting to know the child as a learner

■ *Making sure the plan is practical* by insisting that the teachers and the parents receive the support necessary to implement it (pp. 396–397)

Each of these suggestions is considered next in terms of the readers you are getting to know.

Balancing the Evidence

Despite the fact that Sadie had taken 22 language tests in three years, I could find nowhere in her cumulative special education or regular education files samples of writing she had completed in school. In the spring of her third-grade year, Sadie was reevaluated with the Wechsler Individual Achievement Test (WIAT). As part of the WIAT, she was asked to write a complete letter, which was then rated better on its expression (standard score = 89; 23rd percentile) than was the accompanying spelling test (standard score = 71; 3rd percentile). Sadie also did poorly on the reading comprehension measure (16th percentile). In contrast, she scored in the 90th and 84th percentiles, respectively, in oral language and listening comprehension.

As Johnston (1992) notes, embedding percentile ranks and standard scores in paragraph form hardly constitutes a full narrative report. The letter Sadie wrote is nowhere to be found nor is the scoring system explained. These test results show that Sadie does well with listening and speaking but does poorly with written language—things her classroom teacher could have told us in the first week of school.

I asked Sadie's mother to have Sadie review any writing she had brought home from school or that she had done on her own. I then asked Sadie to choose three pieces that she felt showed how good she is at writing and to be prepared to talk with me about her work. Figure 2.1 shows a sample letter of such requests. Sadie chose a computer-printed report on killer whales as her best piece, an unedited fictional narrative about herself and her friend Caroline as her second best, and a classroom response to a film about the *Titanic* as her third best (see Figures 2.2, 2.3, and 2.4).

Sadie told me that she wrote the whale piece (Figure 2.2) on the computer, with the help of her mother, after she found information on killer whales in reference material. She chose this selection as her best because she found the topic interesting. She recalled that her major problems came with typing, spelling, and sizing the pictures she included. When I asked her how she solved spelling problems, she told me she sounds words out, asks the teacher, or uses another word.

Responses made by Sadie are typical of third-graders, who often choose their best work not on the quality of the product but the topic. Her three strategies for spelling—sounding out when she is isolated from other help, asking for expert help, or switching to a known word—are techniques used by many children and adults. She knows how to write a report around information and organize it into related paragraphs. She also uses a rather wide variety of sentence types for a third-grader.

FIGURE 2.1 Reading and Writing Assessment Preparations

Before you and your child come for your reading and writing assessment appointment, please collect and forward to me the following materials:

1. **Three passages to be read aloud** that your child has not read before. They should be 200 to 500 words long, depending on your child's age, and may be entire picture books, sections of books currently being read, or magazine or newspaper articles. **Please have your child think about why the passages were chosen and what they are likely to be about. Include:**

   a. one **easy** passage that your child expects to read comfortably without help

   b. one **just-right** passage that your child will be able to read but might need a little help or have some difficulty with

   c. one **challenging** or hard passage of the type that your child might try from time to time but would need help to understand or to get the words right

Please photocopy the passages and send them to me prior to the appointment so that I may be familiar with them.

2. **Three pieces of writing** your child has done in school or at home that he or she feels show how good a writer he or she is. Have your child be prepared to say:

   a. why each is good

   b. how each was written

   c. any problems encountered while writing each

   d. any help he or she got during writing

3. **All the records of your child's testing and instruction that you can get**. For example, try to get copies of school special education evaluations, individualized education plans, school standardized test results, and your child's cumulative regular education folder, especially including teacher comments and notes about work done, material used, or teaching strategies employed.

I know that this is a lot to ask. Thank you in advance for your time and effort. I would like to have as much information as possible about achievement and past instruction before I see your child. Then I may try to fill in areas not explored or try strategies not used, in order to make suggestions for the future.

I look forward to working with you.

Sincerely,

Jay Simmons

Killer Whale (Orca)

I am doing the Killer Whale. The Orcas is exciting. I want to learn more about it.

When it is a baby the killer Whale is only seven feet long. The male Killer Whale grows up to be thirty feet long but the female is only half that size. The Killer Whale is black on top, white on the bottom and has a white patch above his eye. They have ten to fourteen teeth on each side of the jaw. Killer Whales have a large dorsal fin which is visible most of the time. They have a blow hole. It is behind the fin, but also close to it. They live in the Antarctic and the Arctic Oceans. The water is very cold. They like to live there because there are small whales, small walruses, seals and penguins. They eat those animals.

The Killer Whale works as a team. They hunt in packs. They go next to whaling boats. When the fishermen shoot the whales the Killer Whales eat the dead whales. When the killer whale is chasing the humpback whale, the humpback turns on his back, opens his mouth and let the killer whale go in his mouth and take out a piece of his tongue.

The Killer Whale travels in a pack with about 40 other killer whales. When the killer whale is far away from an iceberg and he sees a seal, walrus or penguin on the iceberg, he takes a deep breath, goes under water and swims up to the iceberg. And with a great surprise he crashes into it and splits the iceberg in half. Then the animal slips into the water and the Killer Whale chases the animal and swallows it whole.

All Killer Whales and dolphins use echolocation to catch their victim. Echolocation comes from their organ named a melon on the front of their heads.

Lots of Killer Whales get killed for their teeth and blubber. Some get caught in nets. I think that Killer Whales were fun and exciting to learn about. They do exciting things.

FIGURE 2.2   Sadie's Best Piece

Sadie also chose the other two pieces because she liked the topics *and* they were done with a friend, often a third-grader's next best reason for determining the quality of a piece. She said she wrote the piece about her friend Caroline by piecing together exciting stories she knew. (Similarities to *The Secret Garden, Black Beauty*, and any number of cartoons [alligators in the sewer] and fairy tales [goblins and trolls] can be seen.) Sadie also used the normal third-grade techniques of starting her writing with "One day" and ending with the end of the day, sleeping over at her friend's house—a "bed-to-bed" story.

Sadie's second choice (Figure 2.3) took only one day to write, so it is unedited and full of misspellings. Notice, however, that most of the spellings are phoneti-

Own bay my frand Caroline and me 1/5/95
were walking aloing one are horsis Aplasu
and Blackbuotey, We wer one the sidwock
and Caroline foned a cey one the sidwock
She picd up the cey and we saw a forist.
one the uter sid of the rod. So we loct both
wase and crost in to the forist. And we
woct 20 mils and finley we stopt.
taer wus a dore taer. Sow we got of are
horsis and I sad to Caroline "I see a cey
hole madey it is the cey hole fore the
cey mabe it is the cey we hav lats tritt
out." "OK" sad Caroline "lats go" we both sad
So Caroline hadid me the cey and I tern
the cey and the dore opingd. And in
sid was a buotfel garting. So we want in.
and Caroline saw a dimind on a rock
so we got a litel closer to the rock
but wan we got clos anufe we saw
chrols and godlins donsing arongd the
rock and I saw a stacheow of a uoncorn
I gumpt on the uoncorns back and we
tock of and the uoncorn cild all of the
chrols. We cweclley got of of the uoncorn
and got the dimidd. And want out. And
loct the dor and want to tel the
peppl and I fale in to a souer weth
algaters but Caroline savd me rit wan
algater gust was gowing to bite me.
So we want over to my hous and
slept over Carols hous. The End.

FIGURE 2.3 Sadie's Second-Best Piece

cally recognizable, indicating that Sadie does have and use (as she said she did) a sense of English phonetics, but her sight vocabulary is so limited that she must invent most spellings. Notice that she punctuates most complete sentences correctly and is beginning to use quotation marks around the words actually said. The paragraphing structure in the whale piece must have been added in editing, because this story is one long paragraph.

A combination of Sadie's fiction and nonfiction writing techniques is seen in the *Titanic* piece (Figure 2.4). She included as much information as she could from the lesson (e.g., the levels of passengers) as well as other information she knew about ships (e.g., they pass dolphins, whales, sea turtles, and sharks), even if it was anachronistic (e.g., the TV and air conditioners on the *Titanic*). She began her writing with a favorite third-grade opener, "Hi. I am . . ." and ended with her and her mom and dad being saved.

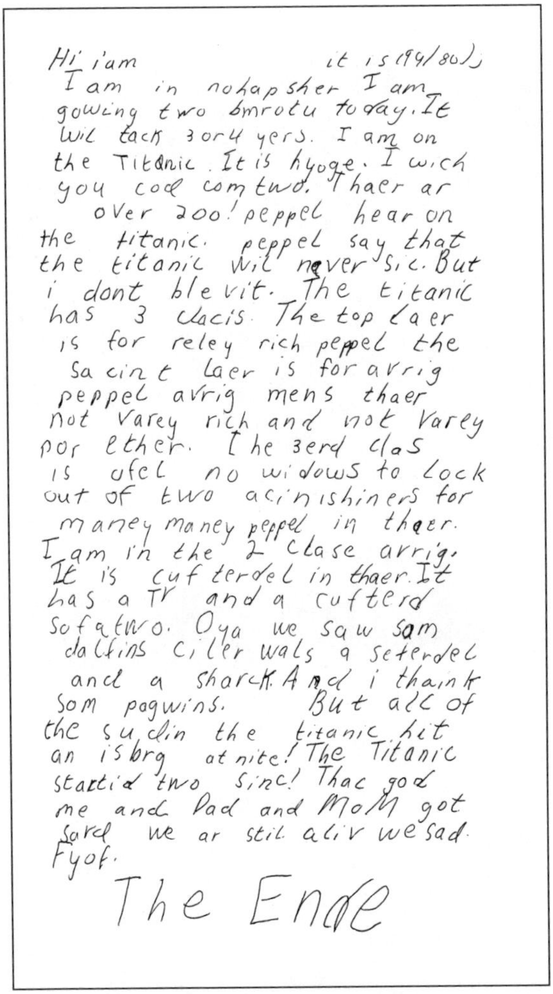

Hi' i'am   it is (9/4/80);
I am in nohapsher I am
gowing two bmrotu today. It
wil tack 3 or 4 yers. I am on
the Titanic. It is hyoge. I wich
you coed com twd. Thaer ar
    over 200! peppel hear on
the titanic. peppel say that
the titanic wil naver sic. But
i dont ble vit. The titanic
has 3 clacis. The top laer
is for reley rich peppel the
sa cin t laer is for a vrig
peppel avrig mens thaer
not varey rich and not varey
por ether. The 3erd clas
is ufel no widows to lock
out of two acin ishiners for
maney maney peppel in thaer.
I am in the 2 clase arrig.
It is cufterdel in thaer. It
has a TV and a cufterd
sofa two. Oya we saw sam
dolfins ciler wals a seterdel
and a sharck. And i thaink
som pagwins.   But all of
the suclin the titanic hit
an isbrg at nite! The Titanic
startid two sinc! Thac god
me and Dad and Mom got
sared we ar stil aliv we sad.
Fyof.

The Ende

FIGURE 2.4   Sadie's Third-Best Piece

Not Balancing but Extending

Rhodes and Shanklin's (1993) suggestion that we balance test data with classroom data derived from encounters with whole texts implies that the two sets of information must oppose each other. Sadie's case, however, demonstrates that tests, work sample analysis, and interview responses lead to similar conclusions. The analysis of classwork simply tells us much more about Sadie's writing abilities and is less mysterious.

Clearly, Sadie expresses herself better than she spells. She writes with spirit, information, and voice. I doubt that anyone reading her report on whales could miss the fact that she enjoyed learning about them and was fascinated by the details of their hunting and eating. Her mythical trip on the *Titanic* was told with an enthusiastic child's voice, as well, giving us all the details of the voyage that a child interested in marine animals and housing arrangements would remember! Sadie's strategies and preferences seem so typical of third-graders I have taught that I wonder what criteria led the test scorers to conclude that her expression was "low average."

Scoring in the 3rd percentile in spelling as well as her two unedited stories tell me that Sadie has trouble with conventional spelling, but after reading her work, I know much more. Most important of all, I know she can write. Some students who might score in the 3rd percentile are so overburdened with the need to "get the words right," despite limited visual memory and undependable knowledge of sound-letter relationships, that they cannot write at all. Juggling the tasks of composing, printing, retrieving word forms, transcribing from the retrieved memory, and checking the written product proves to be too much for them—either they will not even make an attempt, will copy what is available in print around them, or will tire quickly (see Jason's case report in Chapter 4).

Sadie plunges right in. When she has time (a week for the whale report) and help (her mother and spell-checker), she can spell correctly and punctuate well. When she writes one day in class (the magic key story), she can still punctuate well—so long as she can invent the spelling and write about familiar subject matter (e.g., her friend and favorite stories). When she must write on a given topic (the *Titanic* film), she punctuates considerably less well but continues to invent spellings (*nohapsher* for *New Hampshire*) and substitute homonyms (*hear* for *here*). She also reverses letters at times (*bay* for *day*) but indicates that she hears the sounds of letters and knows the difference (*rod* for *road*). Obviously, the varying demands on Sadie's attention during composing prevent her from compensating on a regular basis for her poor visual memory. Sadie does show consistent difficulty with consonant digraphs, however, indicating that she may not hear all those letter sounds (*sic* for *sink* and *paguins* for *penguins*). This lack of awareness also appears in her reading of the Names Test (see the case report at the end of this chapter).

In Sadie's classroom work we can see how she strategically handles spelling while composing. The varied performances of her three pieces of writing, done under very different conditions, allow us to interpret the state of her language knowledge and her ability to access the knowledge, as suggested by Lahey and Bloom (1994) in their model of a limited capacity processor.

The Limited Capacity Processor

Lahey and Bloom (1994) note that variability of performance often characterizes the records of children with language-learning difficulties. These variations often frustrate teachers and students alike and derail attempted instruction that seems not to be working. The authors argue that working memory is a limited capacity system and that different tasks or contexts require differing amounts of capacity. Therefore, variations in performance offer teachers chances to interpret how an individual's language processor works and what demands it places on working

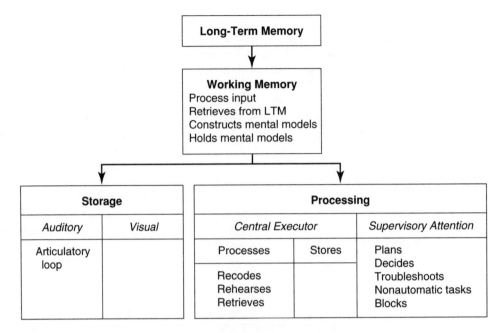

FIGURE 2.5   Lahey and Bloom's Limited Capacity Processor
Source: Adapted from Lahey & Bloom, 1994, with permission of the publisher.

memory. The authors describe a working memory system that processes input, retrieves information from long-term memory (LTM), constructs mental models of ideas under consideration, and holds the mental models in memory long enough for a person to think, write, or speak about them (see Figure 2.5).

Working memory, then, must both process and store information. It stores auditory information (the phonological processor of the interactive model), including articulatory information that can be self-reinforcing (as when one mouths an unfamiliar word to keep it fresh in mind while analyzing it). The human brain also stores visual data, such as when one looks away from a page and tries to remember what an unfamiliar word looks like.

Processing occurs on two fronts. The central executor processes language in the form of recoding, rehearsing, or retrieving. I may need to recode heard words to graphic forms in my mind to understand them, to sound out printed words that seem strange to me, or to think of what the sounds or spellings mean. I rehearse a word as I prepare to transcribe it to the page, after I have retrieved it from long-term memory or another section of working memory. I may have to sound it out, syllable by syllable or letter by letter, requiring me to hold each graphic model in memory while the next is generated. Unfortunately, the capacity I use to store the pieces is subtracted from the capacity I have left to process the thoughts.

Working memory also requires supervisory attention, according to Lahey and Bloom (1994). This system plans the steps needed to understand the sentence or to write the word, decides when each piece has been done, and troubleshoots for errors in the model or the data retrieved. More to the point for students such as those in this book, the supervisory attention system performs nonautomatic tasks and blocks inappropriate responses to given situations. For instance, a fifth-grade girl cannot hold information in her mind to write about while performing nonautomatic spelling. A high school boy cannot focus on the meaning of a history chapter while feeling inadequate each time he encounters a strange word. When the supervisory attention system steps in to make up for a lack of knowledge or distracting emotion, it consumes processing capacity required in the other parts of the system.

Framework for Assessing Reading and Problems

From my work in classrooms for more than 25 years, I have derived a framework for assessing reading and writing performances. I combine the language systems described by Harste, Woodward, and Burke (1984) with the limited capacity processor of Lahey and Bloom (1994) and Vygotsky's (1986) *zone of proximal development (ZPD)*. Vygotsky demonstrated that learners progress best when they learn to do things they can do today with help, not things they already know how to do alone or things they have yet to show any ability to comprehend. Therefore, reading educators need to find that zone of growth between what students can do with help and what they have not learned to do at all.

Language systems include pragmatics (knowing what language is for and how to use it), semantics (knowing the meanings of words), syntactics (knowing the rules of language construction), and, at least for alphabetic languages such as English, graphophonics (knowing the sounds associated with certain letters and letter combinations). In Table 2.1, the systems are listed down the left side of the chart. Under the heading of *Pragmatics,* I include knowing the purposes of reading and writing and knowing their sources, such as where to go for books or ideas for writing. Literate people also have routine times, places, and habits associated with reading and writing. They know who they are as writers and readers—what they like to read or what sorts of pieces they can write best. Readers plan what they will read next. I have a stack of professional books on my night table that I plan to read as soon as I finish *Further Tales of the City* (Maupin, 1982), recommended by my colleague Ruth Shane. Writers make plans, too. One day, Zack and I watched a snake eat a toad next to our basketball court. "Cool!" he said. "This'll be great to write about tomorrow!" In addition, readers and writers know what structures to expect from print. Characters have needs to satisfy or problems to solve. Stories have beginnings, middles, and ends. In essays, the third point mentioned in the introduction comes third in the discussion.

As Vacca and Vacca (1996) explain, word knowledge (semantics) is built on experience and the concepts one derives from it. As I explore a child's vocabulary knowledge, I must be aware of his or her depth and range of experience relative to, say, cities or diverse cultures. Since affixes and roots carry meaning as well as sound, good readers and writers use morphemes to unlock or create new words. Even young children have a sense of what language should sound like, although they may not all come to school knowing what Standard American English sounds

TABLE 2.1   Framework for Assessing Reading and Writing

	Knowledge	Retrieval	Mental Models	Storage	Self-Monitors	Emotions	Automatic
Pragmatics							
*Purposes	Alone__	Alone__	Alone__	Alone__	Alone__	Alone__	Alone__
*Sources	Help__	Help__	Help__	Help__	Help__	Help__	Help__
*Routines	No__	No__	No__	No__	No__	No__	No__
*Identity							
*Plans							
*Structure							
Semantics							
*Experience	Alone__	Alone__	Alone__	Alone__	Alone__	Alone__	Alone__
*Concepts	Help__	Help__	Help__	Help__	Help__	Help__	Help__
*Words	No__	No__	No__	No__	No__	No__	No__
*Morphemes							
Syntactics							
*Sounds like	Alone__	Alone__	Alone__	Alone__	Alone__	Alone__	Alone__
*Book	Help__	Help__	Help__	Help__	Help__	Help__	Help__
language	No__	No__	No__	No__	No__	No__	No__
*Sentence sense							
*Grammar							
Graphophonics							
*Letters	Alone__	Alone__	Alone__	Alone__	Alone__	Alone__	Alone__
*Recoding	Help__	Help__	Help__	Help__	Help__	Help__	Help__
*Phonemic awareness	No__	No__	No__	No__	No__	No__	No__
*Spelling							

like. Those who have been read to will know intuitively that books have a language different from that used by people speaking informally. Most teachers of young children insist on correct usage of the period, but children often need more time to develop sentence sense and more sophisticated grammatical knowledge beyond what "sounds right."

Finally, users of alphabetic languages know what individual letters look like, can name them, and learn to associate certain sounds with them. Of course, to take this last step, a reader needs to be aware of the presence of individual phonemes in a string called a *word*. When these readers write, they transcribe their knowledge of sound-letter relationships into print on the page as invented or conventional spellings.

When Processing Fails

The left column of Table 2.1, then, lists what all readers and writers must know to be literate. When I work with students who have difficulty, however, I need some structure that allows me to look inside their *use* of this knowledge. When students have been taught the knowledge of language systems, and when they have been given opportunities to use this knowledge in practice exercises or actual reading and writing, and yet they do not learn, educators often assume there must be perceptual or motor problems, and specialists are dispatched to find them. Salvia and Ysseldyke (1995) say:

> The assessment of perceptual-motor skills is incredibly problematic. . . . We are of the opinion that if assessments cannot be done properly, they should not be done at all. We believe this is one domain in which formal assessment using standardized tests is of little value. Rather, we encourage those who are concerned about development of perceptual-motor skills to engage in direct systematic observation in the natural environment in which these skills actually occur. (p. 564)

I use Lahey and Bloom's (1994) analysis of the limited capacity processor to guide my observations. Following the top of Table 2.1, I ask: Does the student *know* enough pragmatics, semantics, syntactics, and graphophonics to read this text successfully? Unfortunately, the answer may be "Sometimes yes, sometimes no." In that case, I suspect *retrieval* may be a problem; the student may know the word but not be able to recall its pronunciation, anymore than I can recall the name of the familiar face of a co-worker when we next meet! If I try some inductive questions and the student recalls the word, I know he or she had the meaning all along.

Lahey and Bloom (1994) also postulate that literate people construct *mental models* of language as they use it. That is, as I write a sentence, I have in mind the necessary parts I must include and in what order, just as I would when I set out to make spaghetti sauce. Once created, the model must be *stored* so that I may refer to it to *monitor* my progress, checking to see if I put in the vegetable stock next or with what verb I was planning to connect that noun. When I discover I am out of vegetable stock or have forgotten that perfect verb that I had composed, I must control my *emotions* and find an appropriate solution that does not include spaghetti sauce on the floor or shredded manuscript in the trash.

I must finally check the *automaticity* with which the child conducts all this activity. Although I can drive into Boston through heavy traffic while pouring coffee and tuning the radio, I cannot use a cellular phone at the same time. My colleague Jeanne Paratore can accomplish all of these things, plus do her nails. Clearly, she must give less attention to traffic, coffee, or the radio, since she has some left over for the phone and her manicure. For anything one can do automatically, one needs to allocate no conscious attention. My observations of children may reveal, therefore, that they do not have memory or retrieval problems; rather, their processing of print simply is not automatic and eats up attention that could be devoted to retrieving words or following text structure.

Vygotsky's theory (1986) of the ZPD helps out here. Notice in Table 2.1 that "Alone/Help/No" appears in every cell of the table. This means that I ask, for instance, if the reader self-monitors (column 6) whether the sentence he or she is decoding sounds like book language (row 4) on his or her own ("Alone"), when I remind him or her ("Help"), or not even when I give assistance ("No"). Clearly, any process not done or requiring help is not automatic and consumes attention. Those functions performed alone may be automatic, but reading or writing fluency—or lip movement or finger pointing—can indicate lack of automaticity.

Comparing School and Home Observations

Lahey and Bloom (1994) might say Sadie's variations in writing under different conditions should alert us to a difference in processing ability across different parts of her language system. Obviously, she has more trouble with print than speech; more specifically, however, she can orchestrate print into readable (but incorrect) writing because she understands the alphabetic nature of English and has mastered some of its generalizations, even if she cannot reliably retrieve the exact visual representation when needed. Sadie cannot produce correct spelling for the lists in the WIAT nor in running prose. Moreover, she cannot self-correct and edit her own writing without help.

All of this information can be obtained from Sadie's school performance. Her mother's observations extend our conclusions: She explained to me that the spell-checker does not help Sadie much. "She probably can't pick the correct spelling from the list of choices," I predicted. The mother's eyes lit up. "Exactly!" she exclaimed. "No one has understood that!" she told me, as if relieved that someone had finally *seen* Sadie under all the tests and diagnosis.

Lahey and Bloom's (1994) limited capacity processor model helps explain Sadie's behavior when we look at her "engagement with whole texts," as Rhodes and Shanklin (1993) would say. She knows a good deal about sound-letter relationships, sentence punctuation, story grammar, popular culture, children's literature, and marine life. She also knows how to write historical information into a fictional setting. Sadie simply cannot do all of these things at once. Given more time, more help, or a more familiar topic, her mastery of the visual surface features of text improves and her mastery of the pragmatics of writing consistently remains strong.

Home and school observations do not always agree, however. Sadie's mother, Virginia, could not accept the suspicion of school personnel that Sadie had an attention-deficit or hyperactivity disorder. The speech and language specialist, in a single examination session, asked Sadie to complete the Clinical Evaluation of Language Fundamentals–Revised (CELF–R), with eight subtests: the Language Processing Test, the Peabody Picture Vocabulary Test–Revised (PPVT–R), the Expressive One Word Picture Vocabulary Test, the Mayo Tests for Apraxia of Speech and Oral Apraxia, the Test of Auditory Perceptual Skills, and two others.

In three one-hour sessions on two separate days, the educational psychologist administered the Woodcock-Johnson Psychoeducational Battery–Revised, with its 14 cognitive tests. During the same month, the occupational therapist, in a single examination session, administered the Test of Visual-Perceptual Skills (TVPS) and the Periodic Examination of Educational Readiness at Middle Childhood (PEERMID). The TVPS has four subtests; the PEERMID rates 14 skills.

The speech and language therapist reported that Sadie got up and walked around the room and frequently asked for repetitions on those tests involving lists of related and unrelated words and temporal and spatial relationships. During three one-hour sessions with Sadie, the educational psychologist noted the 9-year-old was frequently in motion, rocking in her chair, asking unrelated questions, chatting, and otherwise showing breaks in attention and extraneous thinking. By the end of the month, the occupational therapist found Sadie initially enthusiastic but finally fatigued and irritable. The third-grader was rocking around, twirling her hair, and squirming.

According to her mother, Sadie acted similarly at home only during homework time, not during nonschool-related tasks. Moreover, Sadie was examined by a neurologist who found insufficient evidence of hyperactivity or attention deficits. He did note that although the parent observation form did not show elevated levels of activity or inattention, the teacher form did.

During my work with Sadie several months later, I, too, saw that she tired quickly, so we took breaks and did some of our work at school and some at her home. She and her mother also completed some of her reading on tape and sent it to me. In all settings, Sadie initially read a passage from a book with approximately instructional-level accuracy and fluency (see the case report at the end of this chapter), but after a brief session of more *engagement with print,* she was unable to read the same book without frustration.

My colleague, Grant Cioffi, describes memory capacity in terms of a car wash on the main street of a town. The cars line up to enter the washing bay, trailing out into the parking lot, but when the line reaches the street, no more cars can fit into the line, and the prospective customers must pass by and continue down the street. So it is with Sadie and her capacity to process print. The recognition, retrieval, and integration of print- and word-level information consumes so much of her attention that soon all space is gone and new information cannot get in line. Hence, Sadie shows signs of limited attention when doing print-related activities, not because she lacks attention but because her mental capacity used for visual processing is not available for attention. She literally tires out as her capacity is used up.

Again, the observation of a child engaged with whole texts, not isolated subtests, and at home in both schoollike and unrelated tasks *extends* our knowledge of the child, and, in this case, contradicts some of the conclusions of the testing sessions. In Rhodes and Shanklin's (1993) terms, perhaps, the *holistic data* took precedence over the *behavioristic data.* I would argue, however, that the observations that Sadie tired equally quickly in the isolated testing and the reading of whole texts *complemented* each other, demonstrating that it is the processing of print that drains her capacity to attend to further processing. In whole texts, for example, she can succeed for a while (in reading) and in readable (albeit incorrect) form (in writing) by bringing to bear other information about language than merely print and sound.

Keeping the Options Open

Terry (see the case report in Chapter 3) and Mike (see the case report in Chapter 5) present opposite dilemmas. Mike "needed" testing; Terry did not. Neither boy, at least in my opinion, needed to be identified as learning disabled.

I agree with Johnston (1997) that the sole valid use of assessment is to improve instruction. In the case of large-scale assessment, schools, states, and the nation should be attempting to ascertain how well what we are doing is working and what might help. If there is no disposition to support change, there is no moral justification for testing. In the case of classroom assessment, teachers often believe grades legitimize testing; regardless, poor grades by an individual or class should be followed by changes in instruction, including how that instruction is put to use by the student (e.g., more after-school help or improved homework completion).

Individual diagnostic testing should be no exception. Educators should be attempting to find out what the reader knows and knows how to do, what the reader needs to know, and how best to develop that knowledge. In Mike's case, he had been considered for retention in first grade, but his parents resisted the decision and transferred him to a local Montessori school before any mandated testing was begun. At the Montessori school, Mike was given only Stanford Achievement Tests, and those had been read to him.

However, Mike's teachers in grades 2, 3, and 4 continued to report reading difficulty for Mike, especially when many words appeared on the page. His parents were concerned that he did not seem able to read successfully at home and that his spelling continued to be poor. He particularly resisted the switch to cursive writing.

In the absence of norm-referenced testing, it is fair to ask how well Mike read compared to most children his age. The Stanford scores indicated his vocabulary, comprehension, and word study skills were fine, when the test was read to him, but his spelling was extremely weak. I decided to have him attempt the Woodcock Reading Mastery Tests and found he scored in the average range for word attack (blending nonsense words) but in the low-average range in word identification (reading of lists of words), word comprehension (analogies), and passage comprehension (supplying the missing word in passages of one to three sentences read silently).

Here, we can see that Mike's word attack remains about average in isolated practice but that his vocabulary score drops well below average when he must recognize the words himself. Clearly, more analysis of how Mike uses what he knows in actual reading is needed, but we can see a pattern that is explainable without any recourse to arcane neurological testing.

Mike is a friendly, agreeable student who has not suffered through any extended, individual diagnostic testing by reading teachers, language specialists, or psychologists. He has continued to try reading differently based on the results of the assessment. In Chapter 3, we will see that Terry underwent extensive testing, mostly at the request of his parents, and became resistant to any more. The scores he obtained, except on one test with questionable norms, were not strikingly abnormal. Since his school program was about to change to a different school and teacher both he and his parents seemed to like, I suggested they leave well enough alone for the time being. If Terry began to have trouble reading and writing in his new school, and if *he* felt additional assessment would be meaningful to him, then they could call me later.

Determining Which Data Should Take Precedence

Too often in the lives of students with severe reading and writing problems, behavioristic data predominate (Rhodes & Shanklin, 1993). Jason provides such an example.

At 10 years old, Jason was being reassessed between his fourth- and fifth-grade years because his mother refused to sign his new educational plan (see the case report in Chapter 4). She believed that the emphasis on taped books and dictation instead of writing meant the school had given up on Jason learning to read and write.

Jason was first diagnosed with a learning disability at the beginning of his second-grade year and has been educated in both the regular classroom and the resource room during each of the last three years. He has taken stimulant medication for attention-deficit/hyperactivity disorder and recently switched to a new prescription. Both Jason and his mother believed Jason's behavior and attention improved with the new medication. Jason particularly liked the fact that he needed to take his medicine only once a day at home and not at school, where at times he chose to work under the aide's desk rather than be seen doing work different from that of his classmates.

In his most recent round of testing, Jason scored in the average range on both the verbal and performance scales of the WISC-III but below the 1st percentile on the comprehension and word recognition sections of the Woodcock-Johnson. In contrast, his knowledge of social studies and science facts in the general knowledge section of the Woodcock-Johnson fell into the 65th and 50th percentiles, respectively. Jason had average ability, except when he had to cope with print. The plan developed by the special education team attempted to capitalize on his ability to acquire information orally by eliminating his need to process print.

Jason's regular and special education files indicated that the school attempted to teach him to recognize words both at sight and through decoding. In second grade, he practiced recognizing letters, initial consonant sounds, and short vowels. He was still unable to write in class unless he dictated his story to an adult and copied the adult transcription.

In third and fourth grades, Jason was taught by a single-letter phonics system in which letter cards are blended into words and word cards are segmented into letter sounds. Each day, Jason also read sight word cards taped to the chalkboard. In third grade, his teachers reported that he recognized most letter names, short vowel sounds, and consonant sounds, and had begun to sound out and spell consonant-vowel-consonant pattern words. However, Jason was often unable to read what he had written himself, even after copying adult transcriptions of his dictated stories.

In fourth grade, Jason read linguistic readers focusing on short vowel patterns, first with his special education teacher and then by himself in order to be able to read aloud to his aide within two days and aloud to his regular classroom teacher within four days. He completed Accelerated Reader program books by listening to the books on tape but he was unable to recall any of them by name or content at the end of the year.

Clearly, the behavioristic model dominated the instruction Jason experienced. He continued to be taught isolated phonics patterns and spelling practice, to read isolated sight words, and to practice reading linguistic readers in order, as he said, "to get the words right." However, at the end of three years, his ability to recall sight words reliably in practice or to read for meaning or write independently had not improved. His mother told me that she and Jason's father read aloud to him at home most nights but that he never asked for a book by name and had no favorites. His aide said that although copying his dictated stories allowed Jason to participate in writing workshop groups, he never took suggestions for rewrites.

When I dictated two brief sentences to Jason, he was able to invent spellings, using sight word strategies, sound-letter relationships, articulatory codes, and the letter-name strategy. These behaviors are typical of emergent writers. Jason had the knowledge of the alphabetic system; he just needed to put it to daily, meaningful use. The taped books and copying may have allowed him to blend in with his peers, but they did not provide for continued hypothesis testing (Harste, Woodward, & Burke, 1984) regarding how English represents sounds in print. Since no single language system was likely to provide enough information for Jason to read and write effectively, I suggested that he be given Reading Recovery–based training, despite the fact that his age and grade placement would seem to preclude his inclusion in a normal Reading Recovery program. He had already experienced word-level drill without meaningful contextual practice in both decoding and encoding. More instruction from the same behavioristic frame seemed pointless.

Making Sure the Plan Is Practical

Unfortunately, Jason's district did not have a Reading Recovery teacher in his school. Reading Recovery specialists worked at other schools administered by Jason's superintendent, so some training of his special education teacher was a possibility. I noticed that one teacher on Jason's upcoming fifth-grade team had experience with the Language Experience Approach (Van Allen & Allen, 1966); however, Jason was not assigned to her language arts classes. Meanwhile, his special education teacher had given up Language Experience after Jason had not been able to read the stories immediately.

Neither Reading Recovery nor Language Experience work by themselves. Each program derives from a mindset quite different from the isolated skills training Jason had so far encountered. Use of either set of techniques would require someone with sufficient training and experience to integrate Jason's performance into a rich set of concepts about how language functions and to respond with more flexibility than simply abandoning instruction.

Jason's mother wrote me that his district had, indeed, hired a trained Reading Recovery teacher to work with him three afternoons a week for 30 minutes. In addition, this teacher helped the special education teacher learn the approach. Progress was predictably slow, but the teacher prepared Jason and his parents for the need to persevere. Unfortunately, his regular classroom placement was less successful (according to his teacher, Jason seemed to be "attending with no participation"). His parents began investigating an all-day one-on-one program or a transfer to a specialized private school.

Jason's story illustrates two points about practical solutions to severe reading and writing problems. Jason appears to be what Manzo and Manzo (1993) would call a *surface dyslexic,* meaning that he has trouble responding to words as wholes, makes many visual confusions, has trouble attaching meaning to printed words, and reads better orally than silently. The first point is that highly specialized knowledge is required to understand and design instruction for students with such problems. Therefore, tutoring techniques that may have helped others in Jason's school over the years produced only three years of the same behaviors from Jason, because instruction was not redesigned based on his inability to profit from the teaching thus far. Jason was taught as dyslexics generally are: with drill in isolated, single-word phonics combined with taped readings and dictated stories that avoid the need to read and write in class (Fink, 1995–1996).

Second, traditional classrooms and pull-out programs are both inefficient and ill designed to include all students in meaningful reading and writing (Cunningham & Allington, 1994). If emergent readers as well as proficient readers cannot read and write in the same classroom, then tutoring in the resource room—however well designed—will not transfer to the classroom setting. In Jason's case, for instance, if he read a natural-language children's book with his Reading Recovery tutor and wrote his own message about his reading, he would be learning to read meaningful text and to use his knowledge of words and sound-letter relationships to write his own ideas about what he had read. By working with the Reading Recovery teacher, he would be helped to become aware of his own knowledge, how to access it and how to put it together as he tried to makes sense of print. Such instruction matches what Fink (1995–1996) suggests based on her study of successful dyslexics. If Jason then returned to a classroom where everyone else was reading much more difficult material and where it would be socially inappropriate for him to read easy books or Language Experience stories, or to struggle with difficult books of passionate interest to him, then he would have no option but to listen to books on tape or to dictate his writing to an adult aide. Thus, Jason would fail to practice what he had learned in his pull-out tutoring.

One third-grade class I know of had 24 students, 5 of whom had been identified as having learning disabilities: 2 had taken or were taking Ritalin for hyperactivity, 1 received occupational therapy, 2 left the room for speech and language work, and all were visited in the classroom by the resource room teacher or aides. Another student worked with the English-as-a-second-language teacher both in the classroom and in private sessions. A total of 8 students had scored poorly enough on the Stanford Achievement Tests to receive Title I reading help, most of which occurred in the classroom. That left 10 students of 24 who demonstrated no problems that required remediation.

During the year, one student took over read-aloud time and read Katherine Paterson's *Bridge to Terabithia* to his classmates for two weeks. Several other students worked their way through the Boxcar Children series and most of Roald Dahl's and Judy Blume's work. Meanwhile, others read the Henry and Mudge and Horrible Harry series of beginning chapter books, and still others read pictures books such as *Shrek* by William Steig. Some children wrote stories that spanned 40 or 50 pages; others labeled drawings or wrote cartoon stories. All students conducted library research on topics such as animals, U.S. states, and planets, writing reports and making class presentations. All students read or summarized news articles in class each week.

By the end of the year, all students were able to read at least brief passages of grade-level material silently with good comprehension. All but two of the Title I children tested well enough to be discontinued from the tutoring. Also, the class's least able reader was able to read *Bunnicula* aloud with 92 percent accuracy and 50 percent self-correction, and this from a student who had demonstrated no significant decoding ability the year before. He volunteered to read aloud in this class because his classmates spontaneously applauded his success; and when he read one of his cartoon stories aloud from the Author's Chair, his classmates responded with questions because they expected him to make sense. He later rewrote to answer their questions.

Practical educational plans for children in this school, then, meant inclusion in classes in which meaningful practice of what they learned in brief pull-out sessions was expected when they returned to class, not having missed reading and writing time for the day. Since all reading and writing was honored, all reading and writing flourished.

Sadie's case report, which follows, also demonstrates the need for plans to include a practical assessment of what options are available at the child's school. The education plan should ask: How much meaningful instruction is available with the least disruption of the child's life in the classroom and at home? Sadie, happily, seems to have had better choices open to her parents and teachers than did Jason.

CASE REPORT: Matching the Person to the Data

Background

Sadie was a 9-year-old third-grader attending Cottleston Elementary School. Her inclusion classroom used the Houghton Mifflin literature-based reading system, and Sadie had recently been assigned a Beverly Cleary book appropriate for third-graders. She received help with these materials in the classroom from the special education teacher.

In March of her third-grade year, Sadie was reevaluated with the Woodcock-Johnson Psychoeducational Battery–Revised. She was found to be age appropriate in broad math and broad knowledge categories but to have moderate weaknesses in broad reading and broad written language, due to weaknesses in spelling, punctuation, and inefficient decoding. These results echoed findings of other testing conducted over the past two years. WISC-III scores placed her in the average intelligence range.

The previous June, a physician found evidence of language-based difficulties, especially in Sadie's automatized naming and word retrieval. He found insufficient evidence of attention-deficit/hyperactivity disorder.

In addition, Sadie has been tutored in reading and math at the Holmes Learning Center in Cottleston. At the beginning of third grade, the center found her vocabulary and reading on the Metropolitan Primary 1 test to be in the 21st percentile. The previous April, using an informal reading inventory, Sadie was able to read a preprimer passage with 100 percent comprehension, a primer passage with 87 percent recall, and a first-grade passage with 75 percent comprehension. The second-grade passage was deemed too difficult. The Holmes Learning Center used grade-level 2–2.5 materials from the Economy Press, as well as Phonics Is Fun, Sullivan Programmed Readers, New Practice Readers, Fry Words, following directions, and main idea and word activities.

Current Assessment

I met with Sadie in the room of the special education teacher, Jean Billings, at Cottleston Elementary School on an afternoon in May. Ms. Billings said Sadie had been quite nervous all day about the impending reading assessment. Sadie was initially observed in her regular classroom, traditionally arranged with desks in rows facing the front board. Sadie was seated in the front row and was talking with the teacher, Mrs. Taylor, about a math lesson.

Sadie had chosen three passages to read to me at school: an easy one, a just-right one, and a challenging one. She read 107 words from the easy selection (pp. 2–9 in *Reading Milestones,* level 3, book 3) with 99 percent accuracy and one miscue (*worried* for *wanted*), which she self-corrected. She had chosen this passage, as she did all her passages, because it was short and dealt with animals—in this case, a cat and a mouse that go fishing. She predicted that the mouse would be better at fishing because books are sometimes like that, having the smaller one be better by surprise. After reading, she noted that her prediction had not come true, for both the cat and the mouse had made mistakes and fallen into the water. Despite her accurate word recognition and clear comprehension, Sadie read the passage in a word-by-word manner, indicating a lack of automatic word recognition at any level of difficulty.

Sadie read two passages from her just-right book, *Focus: Up and Over* from Scott Foresman. Early in the session, she read with 97 percent accuracy and 100 percent self-correction of 8 miscues. At the end of the session, I asked her to read from another page of the same book (83 words), which she did with 83 percent accuracy and 43 percent self-correction of 14 miscues. The miscues for the two readings are summarized here:

Passage 1 (Oral).   *Focus: Up and Over,* Scott, Foresman, pp. 16–19: 222 words, 97 percent accuracy, 100 percent self-correction rate

Sadie	Text	Matches Preceding Context	Matches Following Context	Self-Corrects	Preserves Meaning	Corrected or Preserves Meaning
my	maybe	yes	no	yes	no	yes
my	maybe	yes	no	yes	no	yes
my	maybe	yes	no	yes	no	yes
desturb	desert	no	no	yes	no	yes
—	put . . . (2 lines)	no	no	yes	no	yes
my	maybe	yes	no	yes	no	yes
—	slide	no	no	yes	no	yes
take	talk	yes	no	yes	no	yes
		63%	0%	100%	0%	100%

Passage 2 (Oral).   *Focus: Up and Over,* Scott, Foresman, p. 20: 83 words, 83 percent accuracy, 43 percent self-correction rate

Sadie	Text	Matches Preceding Context	Matches Following Context	Self-Corrects	Preserves Meaning	Corrected or Preserves Meaning
little	ladder	yes	no	yes	no	yes
lander	ladder	yes	no	yes	no	yes
camels	climbing	yes	no	no	no	no
—	a	yes	no	no	no	yes
soft	lot	yes	no	yes	no	yes
lots	lot	yes	yes	no	yes	yes
the	there	yes	no	yes	no	yes
world	would	yes	no	yes	no	yes
quickly	loudly	no	yes	no	no	no
quietly	loudly	no	yes	no	no	no
in	on	yes	yes	no	yes	yes
—	a	yes	no	no	yes	yes
lots	lot	yes	yes	no	yes	yes
it	him	yes	yes	yes	no	yes
		86%	43%	43%	36%	79%

Finally, between these two passages, Sadie read less than a paragraph from *Mystery of the Lost Village* from the Boxcar Children series. She selected the book as a challenge and chose the page because it had a horse on it. It is a book commonly read by third-graders. She read the first 31 words with 77 percent accuracy and 14 percent self-correction. Miscues are summarized here:

Passage 3 (Oral). *Mystery of the Lost Village,* Gertrude Chandler Warren, p. 32: 31 words, 77 percent accuracy, 14 percent self-correction rate

Sadie	*Text*	*Matches Preceding Context*	*Matches Following Context*	*Self-Corrects*	*Preserves Meaning*	*Corrected or Preserves Meaning*
make	making	no	no	no	yes	yes
Betty	Benny	yes	yes	no	no	no
curtained	surprised	no	no	no	no	no
supare	surprised	no	no	no	no	no
—	laughed	no	no	yes	no	yes
—	each	no	no	no	no	no
—	handmade	no	no	no	no	no
—	designs	no	no	no	no	no
		14%	14%	14%	14%	28%

These patterns of miscue demonstrated Sadie's strengths and weaknesses as a reader. First, in passages at or below her instructional level (95 percent accuracy rate), Sadie predicted from preceding context (63 to 100 percent) and self-corrected (100 percent) based on a mismatch with following context (0 to 43 percent). Thus, her miscues were either meaning preserved or self-corrected (79 to 100 percent), and she had correspondingly high comprehension.

Moreover, Sadie demonstrated understanding, awareness, and use of fix-up strategies. When she miscued, she either reread the passage or substituted the word *something* while she continued to the end of the sentence, looking for following context to aid her decoding. She explained to me that these were her strategies she used to figure out hard words. She also said she looked for small words inside big words and broke words down into parts.

The discrepancy between the first and second reading of her just-right book indicated that her strategies ceased to help her when she became tired. For instance, in familiar material of the same level of difficulty as her earlier reading, Sadie read with 83 percent versus 97 percent accuracy (below 90 percent is considered frustrating). She self-corrected only 43 percent of the time, versus 100 percent in the first reading.

Finally, in the third-grade material from the Boxcar Children series, Sadie was unable to use her strategies at all, predicting from context only 14 percent of the time, self-correcting only 14 percent of the time, and losing meaning 72 percent of the time. In this passage, she even substituted her first nonword (*supare* for *surprise*). Always in the earlier reading, Sadie had expected to make a word with her decoding skills.

Current Levels of Functioning

Based on these results, I concluded that Sadie had no level of comfortable, independent reading, but could profit from instruction in materials intended for first-graders and could read brief pieces normally used with second-graders without frustration. She was clearly frustrated by material intended for third-graders.

Sadie's wide store of general information, knowledge of story sense, and well-documented oral and receptive language ability supported her comprehension in otherwise frustratingly difficult material. Her word-by-word reading, finger pointing, and poor spelling indicated such a lack of sight vocabulary as to make decoding necessary for almost every word. Hence, Sadie tired quickly, fidgeted, and appeared inattentive during tasks that require the processing of print.

Even reading at home with her mother, Sadie tired quickly and her strategies failed as she tired. Sadie read an easy second-grade book, *Small Wolf* (pp. 5–8, 75 words) with 90 percent accuracy and a 80 percent self-correction rate. Again, she predicted heavily from context (80 percent) and corrected from following context (miscue matches 0 percent). In a slightly harder book commonly used with second- or third-graders, *Junie B. Jones and Her Big Fat Mouth,* she read 44 words on page 20 with 70 percent accuracy and 73 percent self-correction, preserving meaning 86 percent of the time. Again, when she read another passage from the same book (p. 1, 62 words) she read with 89 percent accuracy, but only 29 percent self-correction, preserving meaning only 57 percent of the time. Clearly, the processing of print intended for second- or third-graders, not the setting or the teacher/examiner, reduced Sadie's capacity to employ her strategies and knowledge.

Knowledge of Sound-Letter Relationships

At her home, Sadie read for me the 35 names on the Names Test (Duffelmeyer et al., 1994; see Figure 2.6). She demonstrated a strength in recognition of initial consonant sounds (92 percent) and consonant digraphs (73 percent) but relative weakness with the vowels: short (50 percent), long (43 percent), digraphs (60 percent), *r*-controlled (56 percent), and initial consonant blends (63 percent). She performed worst on the most variably represented vowel sound, the schwa or short *u* (20 percent). These results were typical of a first-grader late in the school year.

Writing

Sadie selected three of her pieces of writing produced this year to discuss with me. She rated as best her research paper on killer whales (Figure 2.2) because she found the topic interesting. She said it took her about one week to finish and that most of her problems resulted from typing, spelling, and sizing the pictures she included. She got help from the computer and her mom. Sadie told me that in school she solves spelling problems by sounding them out, asking the teacher for help, or thinking of another word to write.

As her second-best piece, Sadie chose the story of Caroline and the magic key (Figure 2.3) because it had her friend in it. She said she wrote it in one day by mixing in parts of exciting stories she knew. Sadie's third piece, about the *Titanic* (Figure 2.4), was also done with a friend as part of a school assignment in response to a film they watched. It, too, took her one day to complete and she found the topic interesting.

Name _____ Grade _____ Teacher _____ Date _____

Concay ✓ *Curvay* Jay Conway	✓ Tim Cornell	✓ ✓ Chuck Hoke	*Yorland Chelank* Yolanda Clark
✓ *Barlek* Kimberly Blake	*Sland* Rober**t** Slade	✓ Homer Preston	✓ *Queeny* Gus Quincy
Sandy✓*Spoonan* Cindy Sampson	*Cheddar Wight* Chester Wright	*grale* Ginger Yale	*Park* ✓ Patrick Tweed
✓ *Shawl* Stanley Shaw	*Wenly Swan* Wendy Swain	*gled slippern* Glen Spencer	*Find/Fern* ✓ Fred Sherwood
Fol Thronard Flo Thornton	✓ ✓ Dee Skidmore	*gracie/gray/greg Whaster* Grace Brewster	✓ *Whystermore* Ned Westmoreland
Rown ✓ Ron Smitherman	✓ *Withlock* Troy Whitlock	*Vice Merribeth* Vance Middleton	*Zan Andon* Zane Anderson
Be Pereshala Bernard Pendergraph	*Shawn Feelerth* Shane Fletcher	*Flor Shanna* Floyd Sheldon	*Dan* *Den Beth* Dean Bateman
Asther Spencerd Austin Shepherd	*Beth Doll* Bertha Dale	*Newl* ✓ Neal Wade	*Jack Marry* Jake Murphy
✓ ✓ Joan Brooks	*gen Lons* Gene Loomis	*Tith Raybart* Thelma Rinehart	

Phonics Category	*Errors*	
Initial consonants	3/37	92%
Initial consonant blends	7/19	63%
Consonant digraphs	3/15	80%
Short vowels	18/36	50%
Long vowels/VC—final *e*	13/23	43%
Vowel digraphs	6/15	60%
Controlled vowels	8/25	68%
Schwa	10/15	33%

FIGURE 2.6 Sadie's Protocol Sheet for the Names Test

Source: Figure from Duffelmeyer, Frederick A., Kruse, Anne E., Merkley, Donna J., & Fyfe, Stephen A. (October, 1994). Further validation and enhancement of the Names Test. *The Reading Teacher, 38* (2), 118–129. Reprinted with permission of Frederick Duffelmeyer and the International Reading Association. All rights reserved.

These reasons for writing, durations of work, and writing strategies employed are typical of third-graders in teacher-directed classrooms. In her second and third stories, Sadie's spelling had not been edited, and although most of the words were misspelled, they were phonetically readable, demonstrating that she had developed a working sense of English phonics but not a sight vocabulary sufficient to overcome the attention drain of composing. Also, the variability of her letter reversals (*bay* for *day* but *rod* for *road*) indicated that she knew the difference between *b* and *d* and heard the different sounds but that under variable demands for attention during writing, her visual memory was weak.

Strengths

As a reader, Sadie demonstrated strong story sense and the ability to use text to gather information. She grasped main ideas, retained details, and made predictions about the content of upcoming reading. In addition, she self-monitored to assess the accuracy of both the information and the words she read.

When Sadie had difficulty with a word, she generally guessed it from the preceding context and the initial consonant sound. She used rerunning and blanking strategies to further incorporate context. She also demonstrated better knowledge of consonant sounds than vowels, and was aware of syllables and words within words, although she was less consistent using these strategies.

Weaknesses

Sadie had a very weak visual memory, as evidenced in earlier testing, a poor sight vocabulary, poor spelling, and word-by-word reading. In addition, her knowledge of sound-letter relationships broke down after initial consonant recognition and she tended to sample erratically from the rest of the word as the difficulty of the text increased and the demands on her attention became greater.

Instructional Needs

Sadie needed to develop a wider store of automatically recognized words, preferably through wide and sustained reading of *easy* text, not flash-card drill with isolated words. This meant that she should read books at her interest level but of easy readability.

In addition, Sadie had not learned the phonetic regularities of English by traditional basal reader and worksheet approaches. Because her sight recognition and decoding procedures were not automatized, she was unable to sustain the effort necessary to read connected text or to spell or utilize a spell-checker reliably.

I suggested a code-based approach several hours a week, such as Reading Recovery or an Orton-Gillingham system that is multisensory in the teaching of phonics. Lahey and Bloom (1994) propose a limited capacity processor model of language-based learning disabilities. Essentially, this model explains why some children have too little knowledge of language to retrieve it, to construct a mental model of it, or to hold the model in mind long enough to think about how to sound a word out, how to spell a word, or how to understand or construct a phrase. These more complicated procedures are disrupted by the lack of lower order information and automaticity. As can be seen in Sadie's excellent comprehension, use of reading strategies, and normal writing behaviors, she functioned well with the higher-order processes but lacked the automaticity and phonetic information to make the process less taxing.

Instructional Models Available at School

Sadie's special education teacher told me that Sadie would have four options available for her next year at Cottleston Elementary School:

1. *Inclusion in a Regular Fourth-Grade Classroom:* With support from the special needs teacher in class using Houghton Mifflin materials, this option would allow Sadie to remain part of the regular program, offering her a rich selection of grade-level literature and the chance to feel "normal." Unfortunately, the instructional materials in fourth grade would be well beyond her instructional range and the special help would focus on handling those rather than providing multisensory code instruction or wide reading in easy books. This was essentially the option that had not worked in the past three years.

2. *Special Readers' Program:* Sadie would continue to use grade-level Houghton Mifflin materials in class with special reading help two or three times per week with those books. Once a week, she would receive extra work outside class. This approach would share the same strengths and weaknesses listed earlier. The one special tutoring session free from the use of instructionally inappropriate materials would be an improvement but unlikely to be sufficient to produce the needed changes. In addition, the continuation of overly difficult reading would reinforce dysfluent reading habits.

3. *Morning Resource Room Program:* Sadie's special education teacher explained to me that this option would be a language-based program serving primary school severely delayed students with behavior problems. It is unclear whether the materials and methods would match Sadie's instructional needs; however, the social dynamics seemed completely inappropriate for an otherwise "regular" student.

4. *Retention:* There was no reason to believe that what did not work this year would work next year. No one had argued that Sadie had not worked hard enough on appropriate tasks nor failed to develop into a stage of language that will allow her to do so.

Suggested Instructional Plan

I suggest that Sadie be provided with three hours per week of special reading instruction on the Orton-Gillingham model. This multisensory approach to sound-letter relationships should provide Sadie with the knowledge she needs to automatize her decoding. I also believe Sadie should be placed in a regular third-grade classroom that allows her to read books at or below her instructional level—those appropriate for beginning readers or first-graders but as close to her interest as possible, such as beginning books on animals. She needs to increase her fluency, her stamina, and her store of automatically recognized sight words. Continued instruction in grade-level materials can only be expected to compound the problems already experienced.

Tutoring or extra help should be provided for Sadie along the lines of Reading Recovery (Lyons, 1991). These lessons should focus on helping Sadie integrate information from the visual, semantic, and syntactic systems as she reads in instructionally appropriate books, but they should not replace her wide independent reading.

CHAPTER

3

Reading the Files

Gathering Data

As a classroom teacher, I am usually reluctant to read a student's cumulative file before getting to the know the student myself. As a reading specialist, I have reviewed enough cumulative folders to have been bored and disgusted by useless and misleading records that are passed on from year to year, everything from dismissal notes to inappropriately reported grade-equivalent scores. Yet, as an inquirer seeking to know a student who is having difficulty reading and writing in my class, or one who has been referred to me by others, I need to gather as many data as possible, evaluating them in light of my theoretical foundations in reading, other observations I have already made, and ignoring the trivial or distorted.

In particular, I ask to see students' school files, special education files, and any files the parent has accumulated. Parent permission usually gains me access to any records I need to see. Complete sets of papers may not exist in every school, but many schools keep separate records for the regular classroom and school history versus the activity of the special education program. These are often kept in separate offices and controlled by different people.

Most parents of students who have a history of learning problems have collected large and complete files. Some parents, such as those of Terry (see the case report at the end of this chapter), have not made all private testing available to the school for fear of what the school authorities might do with the information. Meanwhile, Jason's regular education and special education paperwork reported completely separate lines of instruction (see Jason's case report in Chapter 4).

Purpose of the Collection

I am a researcher, not a test giver. I examine student records in the same way that a graduate student conducts a literature review. I look for the factors that have already been explored, the methods that have already been used, and the questions that have remained unanswered. In other words, I look for the reactions of the student (performance) to instruction (classroom methods and materials) or assessment (test tasks and contexts).

Thinking as a researcher, I filter the information through my theory and research knowledge—in this case, my framework for literacy that includes social contexts, language systems, and psychological processes. I am seeking to form hypotheses about how a particular student processes print to construct meaning in specific social situations, so that I may test out these hypotheses later with my own assessment techniques.

Finding the Instructional History

At age 10, Jason could not syllabicate his own name. I had examined his regular and special education files and learned that he had been taught letter-by-letter decoding but not syllabication of longer words during his first four years in school. I showed Jason how to hear and tap out the "beats" in the word *Jason* and he proceeded to do the same with my name and his sister's. He then divided *Jason* into *Ja-* and *son* when I wrote it on the chalkboard, and he could do the same for *Simmons*.

Although Jason's social context for learning (school) had demonstrated how to sound out words, it had given up on involving him with print. He listened to books on tape and copied stories others had written down for him. He had little reason to guess how the multiple beats of words might translate into print. In further assessment, I needed to see how he could put syllables to work in real attempts to read and write, not to copy or listen to tapes.

Sadie (see Chapter 2), on the other hand, was expected to write, despite her inability to spell most words correctly. She had been assigned to write a report on whales, to write a collaborative story with a friend, and to write a story as if she were a passenger on the *Titanic*. Because Sadie had to guess how to put her words into print, she had developed an alphabetic sense that had become closer to conventional spelling. In further assessment, I needed to find out how she could use more knowledge of the sound-letter relationships of English. Since she had not inferred conventional ones on her own, nor learned them from paper-and-pencil phonics practice she encountered at her learning academy, some multisensory instruction seemed to be in order.

Sadie and Jason, then, had very different immediate contexts for their interactions with text, in Weaver's terms (see Figure 3.1). In the larger social context of home, more similarities existed. Sadie's and Jason's parents read to them and had books and writing materials around for them. Jason's mother said that he never asked for a book or story by name, and Sadie's mother said that Sadie would rather do anything than read.

Does the Student Learn What Is Taught?

Jason was taught to decode with isolated lists of words and letters. Sadie's tutors used phonics worksheets. Neither child learned what he or she had been taught. We may argue all day about whether schools or teachers teach the right things, but

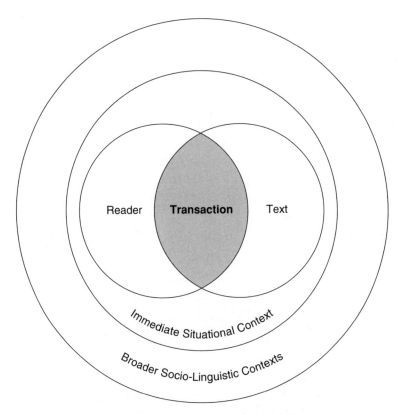

FIGURE 3.1   Weaver's Sociopsycholinguistic Model

Source: Reprinted by permission of Constance Weaver: *Reading Process and Practice: From Socio-Psycholinguistics to Whole Language, Second Edition* (Heinemann, A division of Greenwood Publishing Group, Portsmouth, NH, 1994, 1988).

when we finish assessing a student's learning and abilities, we need to know if that student is able to learn what is taught. If not, the student will likely not learn what we teach or we may not have discovered the requisite conditions for learning.

For example, Andrew (see Chapter 1) was taught word analysis, spelling, and comprehension through graded word lists and passages written around them. As well, he was tutored throughout the upper elementary and middle school years on keeping a notebook, completing homework, and studying for tests. In grade 10, Andrew was able to decode nonsense words at a twelfth-grade level and to spell standardized lists at a seventh-grade level. However, he did not do homework, did not keep records of his work, and seldom studied for tests. Andrew was a C student in classes from the lowest two levels of a three-track high school curriculum.

We may not like the unnaturally constrained language used to teach Andrew, but he did learn the decoding and spelling he was taught. He did not, however, benefit from the study skills tutoring. This prompts a further question: What is it about Andrew that makes it possible for him to learn the language functions but not the organizational functions he has been taught?

ORGANIZATIONAL PATTERNS

Students at this age seem to enjoy regularly scheduled events. Just like when they sing verses from a repetitious song, children like to know what comes next. As their teacher, you can take advantage of this by setting aside specific times throughout the week to study science. The National Center for Improving Science Education suggests between 120 minutes (for K–3 students) and 300 minutes (for 4–6 graders) per week. As discussed in Chapter 1, always try to be open to questions students bring up about science and the world around them. Strive to bring science into the other subject areas they study and also bring these other areas into the scheduled science time. Nothing in the world is completely isolated from everything else. Why should we try to keep them separate in school?

In addition to organizing your classroom and structuring your interactions with students, you must also consider how you will manage your records and materials. You might want to start a file of newspaper and magazine clippings. Videotapes of parts of interesting science shows (with a written summary of what's on the tape) can be used effectively. When you find or just happen upon science material that you can use (in a store, in your backyard, or in your class), save this material! You might want to keep everything for a particular topic in a shoebox or larger container. That way, everything you'll need will be in one place. Every good science teacher has a separate box (or drawer) set aside to hold "junk." Certainly keep a list of relevant books the children can find in the library. Better yet, start compiling your own science library in your classroom. You will probably also want to maintain your own reference materials so you can refresh your memory of certain areas and come up with new things to talk about or do. Keep files on each specific science topic.

The important question, "How do I set up my room?" also requires attention. Your own style of teaching may dictate that you want to keep the desks in a fairly traditional arrangement of rows. Perhaps you want to stress cooperative learning, so you put groups of four or five desks together. Our favorite arrangement is clusters of four flat-topped desks; two desks facing each other. You now have a team of four students or two teams of two for sharing science ideas and working on activities. Maybe you want to create "science centers" where students can go and easily find all the materials

Technology

they'll need to explore a particular topic. You also need to consider where to place your classroom computer(s) if you are that fortunate. If you will be displaying the screen to the whole class, put it where all can see it. If you will be assigning students to independent work on the computer, face the screen away from the class and think about whether headphones will be needed. Bulletin board space is always at a premium. Speaking of bulletin boards, can you devise a bulletin board that stimulates thinking, sparks curiosity, succinctly illustrates a complex concept, presents a problem to solve, provides an opportunity to apply learning, captures the essence of a delightful experience, or otherwise brings unforgettable ideas and images into the minds of children? In other words, bulletin boards can be a very important instructional tool! Plan early how you might have your students create a science-oriented display. Contact some publishers and vendors to see if they might have some colorful posters. Talk to your colleagues for their ideas. How about the classroom aquarium and small mammal (we prefer gerbils) set-up? Last, but not least, leave some window sill area free for growing plants.

PLANNING FOR GROUP INSTRUCTION

There is more to setting up a successful group experience than figuring out "how many to count by" when going around the room to assign groups. You may want to be a bit more sophisticated on how you decide who works with whom. Certainly there are times when simple counting off will provide a fast, easy start to a small project. There are other times, however, when you want to have more control over group membership. If you have students with disabilities, you need to form groups carefully—attending to academic skills, social skills, and other needs. On the one hand, you might want to consider keeping a quiet child with his or her best friend if that seems like a way to promote that child's active involvement. On the other hand, splitting up a pair of, shall we say, "enthusiastic" children, is often your only way of ensuring that either gets anything done!

Try to balance ability levels in each group. One approach to establishing groups of heterogeneous abilities is to rank order your students from highest to lowest in terms of academic achievement. Rankings are completed privately to avoid student embarrassment.

Students are assigned to teams on the basis of rankings: each team includes one high achiever, one low achiever, and two middle achievers. If handled carefully, having a faster, brighter student assist one who doesn't work at quite the same pace can be a positive experience for both. You certainly don't want one child to dominate the group. Nor should you allow any student to sit back and let the others do all the work. You can enforce this best by simply circulating around the room, listening to what's going on. Jump into conversations every now and then to keep the students on track or to suggest an important point they might not have considered yet. If you assign tasks for each individual in the group, rotate them regularly so that each member gets a chance to try each role. Having the best writer always taking notes does that student and the other group members a disservice. In order to make sure each student works to the best of his or her ability, make the group's success dependent on each member's equal participation. There's nothing like a little peer pressure to keep a student on task! Shared responsibility is an important lesson to learn—just as important as the science topic being studied.

Be careful of room arrangements when setting up for hands-on experiences. If the groups will be noisy, make sure they are well separated. If certain groups need access to specific resources, put them within easy reach. Map out a way for you to easily get around the room. You must be able to hop back and forth between groups without disrupting the work going on. It is often a good idea for each small group to report or demonstrate the results of its work to the whole class. Sharing findings is an important component of science. This strategy also is one way to transition from the small group setting back to the larger group.

When the class is working as a whole, you need to have clearly established guidelines for what is expected from each class member. Certainly, the noise level often associated with small groups won't work well when the class is gathered back together. There must be respect for what each person is saying or doing. Since you might want to stimulate debate (or at least discussion) of a particular topic, enforce rules that will help maintain order. You need to decide (before the first day of school) whether students can speak without being called on, how they get your attention, and where and when they can talk among themselves. Classroom rules should be the backbone of defining the behaviors you expect of your students. In fact, rules are a proactive strategy to decreasing problems in a classroom. Discuss rules with the students and why they are important. Elementary school children can be remarkably cooperative when they understand *why* they should do things a certain way. Or better yet, let older children develop the classroom rules. Rules should be worded simply and positively when possible, should describe observable behavior, should be few in number, and should be related to consequences for rule followers and rule abusers. A clear-cut rule is easily remembered by students and can work like a charm. The secret is to set up rules and then be consistent in following them. In addition, you might want to establish a special way of getting their attention when you need to. One teacher we know had a little bell on her desk that she would ring when she wanted everyone to be quiet and listen. (Shades of Pavlov and his dog!) Another teacher would clap various patterns and had her class repeat the patterns. By the second pattern, she usually had everyone's attention. Our favorite is the American Sign Language symbol for zero. You basically form a zero with your hand by putting your fingers and thumb together. Then hold your hand high in the air. When students see the signal, they know to make the sign for "zero noise," quiet down, and pay attention. It sure beats flicking off the light, especially if you are in the back of the room.

If you would like to learn more about discipline, take a look in the general methods book that is part of this series.

FITTING TEACHING TECHNIQUE TO MATERIAL

Take advantage of what you have learned about educational psychology. Use some of the tricks of the memory game, showing students mnemonics for things like the color of the rainbow. (You do remember Roy G. Biv, don't you?) You might want to have children shine light through a prism, or even go outside on a sunny day and spray a mist from a garden hose, making a rainbow. The more graphic the lesson, the easier it will be to remember. Sometimes you must get some facts across by standing up in the front, lecturing. This is best done when students have asked you for information; that way, they are automatically motivated to pay attention. If you do lecture, stop the lesson periodically to ask questions and check for understanding. Be sure to keep your lectures short or you risk the chance that students will begin off task behaviors or worse yet, fall asleep!

Another, indirect way to introduce science facts to your students is to weave them into the discussion that follows a science activity. For example, in the science teaching vignette about batteries and bulbs, Ms. Feinstein might have introduced the concept of a complete (versus incomplete) circuit just after Abby mentioned "the circuit is broken and this stops the electricity from flowing." The whole class was tuned in at that moment to what makes the bulb light or why it doesn't light. Introducing complete circuits at that time could have been a "teaching moment"!

Occasionally, sound will provide the best technique to demonstrate something from science. If one of your students plays a stringed instrument, have him or her bring it in. Music is full of science. Let the students feel the vibrations of the instrument as it is plucked or bowed. Have them listen to how the pitch changes when you shorten a string or adjust its tension. Probably the best science teacher in this situation will be the student taking the music lessons! You can provide some of the more scientific vocabulary during or after the demonstration. Maybe the school's music teacher can come in and play a few other instruments so that students can compare how they work and sound.

It is almost always a good idea to ask the students what they know about a particular subject before you really get into studying it. Not only will this help you plan how you want to approach the lessons, it will also point out some of the more interesting ideas children have about the world around them. Some of these ideas, formed through everyday experience, are called misconceptions or, perhaps more politely, naive conceptions. We discussed them briefly in Chapter 2. We will cover them in more detail in the chapters covering specific topics.

After you and the children work on the "What I Know" facts about a topic, brainstorm with your students about "What Questions I Have" about the topic. Each child can do this in his or her own science book (made from folded construction paper). The next section of the science book might be strongly influenced by the local science program: "Observation/Activities to Do" (hands-on activities to find out some answers). Finally, the science book might conclude with a "What I Have Learned" section. Reading, writing, and science are a nice combination!

USING INSTRUCTIONAL MATERIALS

Your choice of how you present a new topic to your students depends on several factors. As we mentioned before, some content areas lend themselves to particular types of materials. It is pretty hard to discuss electricity without letting children have a chance to work with batteries, bulbs, and wires. Similarly, optics without flashlights, mirrors, or lenses can be pretty unexciting. Of course, the overriding factor in your decision is whether you have ready access to materials. Certainly, children love looking at the tiny life forms found in ordinary pond water. But without a microscope or at least magnifying glasses, such a study is quite difficult to carry out. With enough forethought and an understanding principal, you might be able to order equipment or materials. Sometimes you can bring in things that you have at home. (Make sure whatever you bring in is rugged. Although most schools approve of teachers bringing in personal items for class use, few are very excited about replacing those items when they get damaged.)

Probably one of the best ways to incorporate interesting materials into your classes is by having the children bring in their own from home. Egg cartons make great planters for comparing seed growth under different situations. An oatmeal box with holes punched in specific patterns on the end makes a nifty planetarium when a flashlight is placed inside. You can have each child or group make their own constellation and then see if the others can recognize it when it is projected onto the wall. How about having one of the children bring in a family pet (snake, turtle, parrot, hermit crab, or hamster) when appropriate? Of course, you'll need to make sure that science is the topic of investigation (and that none of the children has an animal fur allergy). But with you as a guide, children can learn why snakes shed their skin or what happens to turtles in winter. You can be sure that lessons learned in this kind of actively involving format are not soon forgotten. You might even want to set up a permanent science center in the classroom—with interesting materials brought from home.

Depending on where your school is located, there might be the possibility of exciting science field trips. A zoo or museum is an obvious choice, but don't overlook something as close by as the school play yard or a nearby stream or field. Invite parent chaperones to join you. One of the ideas we want to get across to the children is that science is all around them. Why not show them? If you can't take the children out to the science, maybe you can bring it in to them. You'd be surprised at how many science professionals (sometimes parents) would be willing to visit your classroom and talk to your students about their job and how they "do science."

From earlier discussions, you may have gotten the idea that we don't think textbooks have any place in the classroom. This isn't true. As pointed out before, textbooks should not be a child's only exposure to science. They can be a vital supplement to guided observations. They organize facts and often have excellent photographs or drawings of things that can't easily be seen in the classroom. By all means, take advantage of that! The greater the number of ways you can present information to students, the better the chance that you'll hit just the right way to sneak the material into their heads. (So not only is that the argument for including textbook work in your science lesson, but also the reason why you don't want to rely exclusively on books.) Some students might subscribe to some of the newer science magazines that are now being published for children. If so, have them share them with the class, or even order them for the library. You can find addresses for several of them at the end of this chapter.

Technology

If you have access to a computer in your classroom (possibly hooked up to an overhead projection tablet), you can run all sorts of fun science software. Perhaps your students will get the chance to operate a nuclear power plant or experiment with animal breeding. When the real thing can't be done in the classroom, a simulation on the computer lets students see the major points without most of the difficulties like radiation, expense, or time constraints. Computer software and CD-ROMs have come a long way from simple drill and practice—electronic flashcards. For example, you can take a "computer field trip" to a tropical rainforest and investigate the fragile environment of three of the world's major rainforests—South America, Africa, and Southeast Asia—by using the Sunburst program *A Field Trip to the Rainforest.* Videodiscs can bring practically anything you want into your classroom. The Internet is an exciting tool that we'll mention more about in the next chapter that can offer a multitude of different instructional materials—everything available right in your classroom!

SCIENCE AND THE SPECIAL STUDENT

Today's science classrooms represent a microcosm of society. They are composed of students who are from culturally diverse backgrounds, may be gifted and talented, at risk for failure, and/or have special needs. The federal law, Individuals with Disabilities Education Act, 1997 or commonly referred to as IDEA 1997 provides the legal framework which mandates that students with disabilities be given access to the general education curriculum to the greatest extent possible. Science, because of its hands-on, high interest, engaging nature is perhaps one of the best arenas to include students with disabilities. In all cases, the needs of each learner must be considered before beginning any teaching endeavor. Including students with disabilities in your classroom will require some modifications, but many of your current educational practices will work. The skill deficit and/or the severity of disability— mild, moderate, or severe—will determine when and how you modify and adapt your science lessons.

What does this mean for you as a teacher? The good news is that much of what is addressed in the text will work. There is also a wealth of literature on effective instruction that can be used with most students with disabilities to a high degree of success. *CEC Today* (1997) identifies four key categories that teachers should address when evaluating how to best include students with disabilities in their classroom. These include modifying all or some of the following: the instructional grouping or arrangement, the lesson format, the goals, and your teaching style.

• Changes in the instructional grouping—Students with disabilities can get lost in classrooms. Using cooperative learning and peer partner strategies helps keep students focused and on task. We have already discussed, in this chapter, specific suggestions regarding these techniques.

• Changes in the lesson format—When students with disabilities have an opportunity to be active participants in the learning process, the literature indicates that they will make more progress. Suggestions include hands-on learning, games, simulations, and experiential learning. Pairing disabled students with non-disabled peers when conducting group work is effective. Make sure each student has a role (e.g., recorder, reader, observer, task master, or materials manager).

Find as many ways as you can to actively engage the learner in the lesson. For delivering instruction, the most effective lesson format incorporates these FOUR EFFECTIVE COMPONENTS:

1. Provide a brief description of what the students will learn.

2. Tell the students why they are to learn the information.

3. Explain how they will go about learning it.

4. Let them know how they will be assessed.

When this format is used, students' success is dramatically increased.

If you are conducting a hands-on activity, first introduce the activity, then model the steps—a little role play with another student helps. Give the students a chance to practice while you guide them through the steps—ask questions to check for comprehension (e.g., What are we doing first? What are the rules about handling chemicals? What do we do if?). Finally, let the students work in small groups or independently while you walk around and check to see if everyone is on task.

• Changes in the goals—Decide what you want ALL students to learn from your science unit or lessons. What essential and enduring skills and knowledge will they obtain from your instruction. Depending on the individual student's skill level, you may need to redefine what is taught. Teachers usually think that this means simplifying the material. While in some cases this may be true, there are a variety of ways to teach the same content with modified goals. For example, the sequence of the instruction may be changed or the content may stay the same, but the complexity could be reduced. Doug Carnine (1992) refers to this as teaching "Big Ideas" first and then fitting in more detailed information. Changing the pace of the instruction, breaking it into small sequential steps or delivering several small mini-lessons are other alternatives. Relating the science content to the real world is a technique that benefits all students. Focusing on functional or community-based applications will be a necessity for some students with disabilities. If the vocabulary, terminology or science text poses a potential problem, select those terms that are most important. Find alternative ways to teach the information. Modifying the textbook, putting the information on an audio or video tape, providing guided notes and pairing a non-reader with a reader are some suggestions.

• Changing your teaching style—Although you may be the best teacher in the world, there are a few modifications you can incorporate into your teaching style to increase the success of students with disabilities. Maximizing opportunities for ALL students to respond is one simple, but effective technique. A favorite of ours is Think-Pair-Share. This requires you to ask a question and then, rather than calling on one student, ask the entire class to individually, silently Think of the answer, Pair—turn to a neighbor and take turns comparing answers, and finally, Share—turn to another pair and discuss findings or share with the entire class. A general rule: The more times a student with a disability has an opportunity to respond, the greater his or her retention. Other modifications include giving more prompts or cues, changing the way you ask questions, and providing verbal and written instructions.

In addition to these four key categories, we are adding one more area. Students with disabilities, especially those with visual, hearing, or physical impairments, may require modified equipment and/or materials. For example, a light sensor will help blind students "see" the changes in light by listening to a sound emitted by a light meter which reacts to density of material. Microscopes that project images on a screen not only are useful for students with limited vision, but also for the teacher who is unsure if the students are really looking at what they are supposed to be viewing. Asking students to point to portions of the projected image allows the teacher to check for comprehension—something you can't do with an image on a slide.

The teaching strategies presented in this text are appropriate for learners with disabilities. You will find other suggestions on how to successfully include all students in your science lessons interspersed throughout the chapters. Even though our teaching activities and ideas may or may not specifically mention students with disabilities, try them—they will work! However, remember all students are individuals. What works with one child may not work with another. Also, talk to the specialists in your building or school district. They are living, breathing resources and will help you successfully address the needs of all students.

EVALUATING SCIENCE LEARNING

It has been said that tests drive the curriculum. What does this mean? In most cases, it is meant to be derogatory. Rather than letting the topics and their interrelationships determine what is taught and how it is covered, our instruction is shaped to a large extent by how we plan to evaluate student learning. This may or may not be the case, but it certainly cannot be denied that testing strongly influences student learning! It doesn't take much teaching experience before one gets tired of hearing, "Is this gonna be on the test?" This may not be as severe a problem in the early grades as it is in high school and college, but it indicates student concern with grading and evaluation, nonetheless.

One way to combat this preoccupation with evaluation is to give the students the responsibility for it! If they know exactly what they are to learn and what they have to do to earn a particular grade, the entire process becomes less mysterious and certainly more attainable. It also removes a lot of the subjective judgments required of teachers.

Utilize hands-on assessment and try to make it fun. An interesting part of a hands-on test developed at the University at Buffalo (New York) has students trying to discover the pattern of aluminum foil that connects holes in cardboard. By connecting a battery, bulb, and wires between different pairs of holes, they try to determine the shape of the foil between two sheets of cardboard.

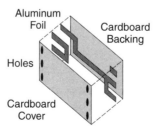

Hidden Foil "Circuits" Sandwiched Between Cardboard

Figure 3–2.   Hands-On Assessment

You can make up several different circuits, let your students work on them for a set period of time, and then let the students take them apart to see if they were right. In other words, the students learn while taking the test. Now, there's a novel idea! (Don't take this to extremes though. Children need to feel free to explore and investigate something without always wondering if they will somehow jeopardize their science grade if they don't find the answer.)

Another example of performance-based assessment, this time at the kindergarten level, would be to allow the child to observe two objects—a marble and a square wooden block. Ask the child, "What is one way the two objects are different?" (If possible, record the student responses.) Then ask, "What is another way the two objects are different?" (Again, record the responses.) You can setup your own simple scoring system and really gain an insight of how different children are performing in science. Most important, too, the children actually enjoy this type of hands-on assessment. Many of these performance-based tasks are referred to as *authentic assessment.* It is a term that describes tasks that try to connect what has been learned in school to the lives and interests of children. An interesting and instructive account of one elementary teacher's experience implementing authentic assessment strategies in her classroom is provided by Kamen (1996). Besides the teacher's new understanding of science teaching, and a shift to a conceptually based constructivist model, a variety of authentic assessment methods are reviewed. It's wise to conduct frequent assessments. This will give you a good indication of what the children have learned. When teachers make teaching decisions based on data rather than impressions, the research shows that students learn more and at a faster rate.

LOOKING BACK

In this chapter, we have looked at what it takes to be a science teacher. It mostly boils down to an openness to try new ideas, a willingness to follow student questions, and a curiosity to seek out answers to interesting situations. You not only need to have materials organized for ready access and plans on hand for presenting exciting situations for study, you must also be prepared to be an example of an interested learner.

SELF-TEST

- Why do some elementary school teachers feel uneasy about teaching science?

- Discuss the following statement: In order to teach about a specific subject, one must know something about that subject matter.

- Compare Mr. Olivere's and Ms. Feinstein's teaching of Batteries and Bulbs. Which science teacher do you relate to most favorably and least favorably? Why?

- It's a month before you begin your first teaching assignment. You're spending the day in your fourth-grade classroom to get organized. What will your day be like?

- Now it's the first day of class. What rules and guidelines have you established to launch the new school year for you and your students?

- How will you introduce rules and guidelines to your class?

- Can you devise a performance-based assessment task for your first graders who are working with shadows?

- Discuss what you can do to increase the success of students with disabilities when you teach science.

REFERENCES FROM RESEARCH

CEC Today (1997). Effective accommodations for students with exceptionalities. *CEC Today, 4*(3), 1, 9, 15.

Hewson, P. and Hewson, M. (1988). An appropriate conception of teaching science: A view from studies of science learning. *Science Education, 72*(5), 597–614.

Jenson, W. R., Rhode, G., and Reavis, H. K. (1993). *The tough kid book: Practical classroom management strategies.* Longmont, CO: Sopris West, Inc.

Kamen, M. (1996). A teacher's implementation of authentic assessment in an elementary science classroom. *Journal of Research in Science Teaching, 33,* 859–877.

Maheady, L., Harper, G., Sacca, K. and Mallette, B. (1991). *Classwide student tutoring teams: Instructor's manual.* Fredonia, NY: SUNY College at Fredonia.

National Center for Improving Science Education, 2000 L St. NW, Suite 616, Washington, DC 20036, (202) 467–0652.

Putnam, J. (Ed.). (1993). *Cooperative learning and strategies for inclusion: Celebrating diversity in the classroom.* Baltimore, MD: Brookes Publishing.

Rowe, M. (1974). Wait-time and rewards as instructional variables, their influence on language, logic and fate control: Part one—wait time. *Journal of Research in Science Teaching, 11,* 263–279.

Scruggs, T. E. & Mastropieri, M. A. (1993). Current approaches to science education: Implications for mainstream instruction of students with disabilities. *Remedial and Special Education, 14*(1), 15–24.

Scruggs, T. E. & Mastropieri, M. A. (1995). Science education for students with behavioral disorders. *Education and Treatment of Children, 18,*(3), 322–334.

Sharan, S., Kussell, P., Hertz-Lazarowitz, R., Bejarano, Y., Raviv, S. and Sharan, Y. (1984). *Cooperative learning in the classroom: Research in desegregated schools.* Hillsdale, NJ: Erlbaum.

Shepardson, D. P. and Jackson, V. (1997). Developing alternative assessments using the benchmarks. *Science and Children, 35*(2), 34–40.

Slavin, R. E. (1991). Synthesis of research on cooperative learning. *Educational Leadership, 48,* 71–82.

Tobin, K. (1984). Effects of extended wait time on discourse characteristics and achievement in middle school grades. *Journal of Research in Science Teaching, 21*(8), 779–791.

Wise, K. C. and Okey, J. R. (1983). A meta-analysis of the effects of various science teaching strategies on achievement. *Journal of Research in Science Teaching, 20*(5), 419–435.

PRACTICAL RESOURCES

Carnine, D. and Kameenui, E. (1992). *Higher order thinking: Designing curriculum for mainstreamed students.* Austin, TX: ProEd.

Doran, R. (1980). *Basic measurement and evaluation of science instruction.* Washington, DC: National Science Teachers Association.

Eisenhower National Clearinghouse for Mathematics and Science Education. (1996). New approaches to assessment in science and mathematics. *ENC Focus, 3*(1), 1–38.

Kids Discover, PO Box 54205, Boulder, CO 80322–4205.

Mastropieri, M. A. and Scruggs, T. E. (1995). Teaching science to students with disabilities in general education settings: Practical and proven strategies. *Teaching Exceptional Children, 27*(4), 10–13.

MECC (Minnesota Education Computing Consortium), 6160 Summit Drive North, Minneapolis, MN 55430-4003, 1-800-685-MECC.

Meng, E. and Doran, R. L. (1993). *Improving instruction and learning through evaluation: Elementary school science.* Columbus, OH: ERIC.

National Geographic World, National Geographic Society, 17th and M Streets, NW, Washington, DC 20036.

Patton, J. R. (1995). Teaching science to students with special needs. *Teaching Exceptional Children, 27*(4), 4–6.

Ranger Rick, National Wildlife Federation, 8925 Leesburg Pike, Vienna, VA 22184. (703) 790-4000.

Shymansky, J. A., et al. (1997). Performance assessment in science as a tool to enhance the picture of student learning. *School Science and Mathematics, 97*(4), 172–183.

Sunburst Communications, 101 Castleton Street, PO Box 100, Pleasantville, NY 10570, 1-800-321-7511.

Vaughn, S., Bos, C. S., and Schumm, J. S. (1997). *Teaching mainstreamed, diverse, and at-risk students in the general education classroom.* Boston: Allyn and Bacon.

ZooBooks, PO Box 85384, San Diego, CA 92186.

WEB SITES

Technology

Assessment and Accountability
http://www.nwrel.org/eval/index.html

Eisenhower National Clearinghouse for Mathematics and Science Education
http://www.enc.org

ERIC Clearinghouse on Assessment and Evaluation
http://www.cua.edu/www/eric_ae/

Improving Math and Science Education
http://www.learner.org/content/k12

An Introduction to Science Portfolios
http://www.gene.com/2ae/21st/TL/

Science Education Resources
http://www.usd.edu/intec/science.html

Teacherlink
http://www.teacherlink.usu.edu/nasa.access/nasa

Teacher's Lounge for Math and Science
http://www.maxis.com

CHAPTER

4 The Science Program

LOOKING AHEAD

You may have gotten the impression from earlier chapters that all you have to do is walk into the classroom and wait for children to ask questions and then start science investigations. Your preparation would just involve knowing where to find information to answer those questions and where to get materials to allow for hands-on exploration to find answers to questions. Actually, that is only partly correct. Certainly you need to be flexible and responsive to the children's interests. That is vital and makes science fun for both student and teacher. Nonetheless, it is equally important to provide all children with a structured program that endeavors to cover the major topics of science in a coherent manner, especially for children with disabilities. This requires planning on a larger scale, not just considering what to teach tomorrow or this week or even this year. The best science programs have come about by careful planning how each grade level's instruction fits together to form a comprehensive program of study. Individual teachers can't really carry out such planning by themselves. They need to work cooperatively with their colleagues in the school so that they don't overlap (except where intended) or miss important science concepts, skills, and attitudes.

Of course, this group planning can generate its own difficulties. Get two science teachers into a room and you will find two different approaches to teaching science. More often than not, you'll also overhear a debate over which program or system is best. This chapter attempts to clarify some of the issues involved in designing your own science program—whether you create it from scratch or closely follow a package made available by a publisher. We will be looking at some things you need to work out for yourself and other things that are best worked out with other teachers and the principal or science supervisor.

CAN YOU?

- Think which of the following is most important in elementary science teaching: the content of science, the processes (or skills) of science, or students' positive attitudes toward science?

- Discuss what features make a good science program?

- Suggest those common features that all science programs should have?

- List the components you will incorporate into your own science program?

- Discuss how you will design such a science program and how you will ensure that it integrates other subject areas.

SOME SCIENCE PROGRAM PHILOSOPHIES

When developing a philosophy of how we want to teach, one place we have to be careful is in the comparison of different ideas. Many logical straw men have been brought into discussions to provide easy targets to tear down. Perhaps by contrasting the extremes of some of the more common debates, you will begin to see that the best course is usually one of moderation.

The all-or-nothing argument: "You either teach them the important facts or they don't learn anything. There's too much fluff in today's curriculum. I've got a lot more experience than children, and I can present science topics to them more efficiently than they can discover these things for themselves."

As is true in most debates, there is some truth in these arguments, which are sometimes couched in "back-to-basics" rhetoric. There is an important body of knowledge that children must learn, just to survive as adults in today's world. There is no denying that the teacher has been around a lot longer than his or her students. It certainly might be more time efficient to hand students lists of facts to be memorized. But the question that remains is, "Will there be greater retention and understanding of the material?" It appears that in science, as in many other areas, less is more. In other words, covering fewer topics—but in greater depth—results in better learning than a cursory overview of many unrelated concepts. It is vitally important to provide a clear picture of how the different topics of science fit together.

The content-driven versus open-ended curriculum argument: "By sticking with an outline of important topics to cover, thorough coverage is ensured. An open-ended approach will almost always miss some of the central facts and principles."

This strict content-oriented philosophy is often tied to the all-or-nothing argument, mostly from an efficiency standpoint. What people need to think about is their definition of *efficient*. If they are considering efficiency of teaching, there is no debate—they win! However, efficiency of learning and retention is another story. Research indicates that children construct their own meanings for concepts based on their prior knowledge. When instruction is designed around this realization, students learn and remember more. When children are given an opportunity to be creative in their approach to learning science, they tend to be more highly motivated, especially if they've been taught metacognitive strategies. Although a well-thought-out plan is of prime importance, flexibility and a willingness to address questions of interest to children is also critical. (Remember the "Questions I Have" section of the student science book from the last chapter?) Of course, a curriculum that does nothing but follow the whims of the students actually does them a disservice. They do need to learn the central concepts of any given area of study. But a curriculum that is so bound to the syllabus that student interests are ignored (i.e., discouraged) might enable the teacher to impart those facts that have been selected as important, but also decreases the chances that the students will ever be interested in learning anything else about the subject!

The textbook/worksheet orientation versus free for all labs argument: "We don't have the equipment or time for hands-on experiments. Besides, it's a waste of time and effort. The children really don't do anything other than play. What if they don't learn the concepts I want them to?"

These are often the arguments of teachers who are unsure of their own science knowledge. The real concern is what to do when something happens that they can't explain. Following the textbook seems much safer. It is important to remember that there is no way that you can know the answer to every possible experimental problem or question that arises. There are too many things that can happen! Instead of trying to be the fountain of knowledge, transfer some of the responsibility for finding the answers to your students. Also, let them design some of the apparatus and experiments themselves from everyday materials. This will quickly get them involved in science, and it reduces the impression that scientific instruments are expensive things kept in the cupboard at school, not to be used (or having any use) outside the classroom. The kind of thinking skills that are encouraged by designing, carrying out, and analyzing experiments are central to science and many other endeavors. Research shows that experimenting skills are closely related to formal thinking abilities. We cannot expect students to do well at skills they have not practiced repeatedly. These basic skills can be taught and readily transferred to new situations.

The content versus process versus attitudes argument: Probably the biggest debate has been among proponents of these three schools of thought. We've already discussed some of the concerns of the content orientation. Other people feel that, at least at the elementary level, time learning specific facts is misspent. Instead, they suggest a focus on the processes or skills of science. Children need to learn how to measure distances and temperatures, isolate and control variables in science experiments, and generally attend to "how science is done" and transfer this information to the world in which they live. The last group feels that what really counts at this age is not science facts or skills, but the development of positive feelings toward science. If all you can do is get children to like science, you will have reached your goal. As you probably expect, a combination of these ideas appears to be the most appropriate. By developing a program that stresses important facts, concepts, and skills (reinforced by extensive hands-on experiences) you also have the best chance of creating positive feelings about science. Whether you expose children to new ideas first and then have them explore or do the reverse is up to you. Try both methods and see which works better and under what circumstances.

IS THERE A *BEST* APPROACH?

With all these conflicting philosophies, is there really any hope of your coming up with a style and program of your own? Each of the extreme points of view has arguments in its favor. Your own program will probably be some combination of parts of all these philosophies. The program you develop will be different than anyone else's. But are there things that different science programs should have in common? Research in classrooms has identified key instructional strategies to help students overcome their naive, inappropriate conceptions and construct strong, correct ideas about science. If teachers, each following different approaches and programs, keep these in mind, their students will be the beneficiaries.

Research indicates that teachers should:

- Diagnose students' thoughts about the topic and help them to clarify what they think.

- Provide a direct contrast between students' views and the desired view, challenging (leading if necessary) students to rethink their existing misperceptions.

- Provide hands-on opportunities to use the desired view to explain a phenomenon, making it more plausible.

Historically Speaking: Post-Sputnik Science Programs

One way to go about developing your own science program is by looking at program packages that have been put together by others. In the 1960s, largely as a national response to the Soviet satellite Sputnik's launch (1957), many groups tried new approaches to teaching science. By briefly examining several of the most popular of these, you might pick up some ideas you can use in your own program. We'll start with Science-A Process Approach (SAPA). As you can guess from its name, it is strongly oriented toward developing the skills of science. (Some have criticized this program, perhaps unreasonably, for downplaying content.) The materials were developed by making observations of working scientists and breaking down what they did into sequences that could be learned by children. Each grade level had about 20 activities. SAPA II, the latest version, has been restructured to allow more teacher flexibility in designing instruction.

SAPA's Basic (K–3) Science Process Skills

- Observe: use the senses to collect data

- Infer: make an educated guess about an event or object

- Measure: use an instrument to collect data

- Communicate: use words or pictures in a description

- Classify: group or order objects or events in categories

- Predict: form expectations of future events from a pattern found in data

---

SAPA's Integrated (4–6) Science Process Skills

- Control variables: isolate and make constant those parameters that might affect the outcome of an experiment

- Operationally define variables: conceptualize variables by how they might be measured in an experiment

- Formulate hypotheses: predict an experimental outcome

- Interpret data: organize data and draw conclusions

- Experiment: include questioning, hypothesizing, identifying, controlling, and operationally defining variables, designing, conducting, and interpreting results of an experiment

---

The Science Curriculum Improvement Study (SCIS) focuses on depth rather than breadth. There are 12 units in this K–6 program, each dealing with a central concept or big idea in science. Each of these units has several parts and carefully integrates process skills with content learning. In the SCIS learning cycle, children generally have some kind of hands-on activity (exploration) before discussing any abstract concepts (invention). Later, children apply what they have learned previously to new situations (discovery). This is similar to the problems approach this book suggests, although it is not as open to what children might bring up and doesn't stress the importance of teachers diagnosing prior knowledge. SCIS II and SCIS III have been restructured and updated, and are available still for student use.

Table 4–1.   The SCIS Program

LEVEL	LIFE SCIENCE		PHYSICAL SCIENCE	
1	ORGANISMS		MATERIAL OBJECTS	
	organism birth death	habitat food web detritus	object property material	serial ordering change evidence
2	LIFE CYCLE		INTERACTION & SYSTEMS	
	growth development life cycle genetic identity	generation biotic potential plant & animal metamorphosis	interaction evidence of interaction system interaction at a distance	
3	POPULATIONS		SUBSYSTEMS & VARIABLES	
	population predator prey community	plant eater animal eater food chain food web	subsystem histogram evaporation	solution variable
4	ENVIRONMENTS		RELATIVE POSITION & MOTION	
	environment environmental factor	range optimum range	rectangular coordinate relative position relative motion	reference object polar coordinate
5	COMMUNITIES		ENERGY SYSTEMS	
	producer consumer decomposer photosynthesis	community food transfer raw materials	energy transfer energy chain	energy source energy receiver
6	ECOSYSTEMS		MODELS: ELECTRIC & MAGNETIC	
	ecosystem water cycle oxygen—carbon-dioxide cycle pollutant food-mineral cycle		scientific model electricity magnetic field	

SCIS Lesson Phases

- Exploration: hands-on activities to examine new ideas

- Invention: students and teachers discuss what they are learning; the teacher imparts new vocabulary

- Discovery: additional experiences to extend and reinforce concepts and skills

---

The Elementary Science Study (ESS) was also developed as part of the nation's response to the launching of Sputnik. There are 41 relatively self-contained units dealing with a wide variety of content areas. Teachers (or schools or districts) decide which sets of materials to use. All the units stress personal involvement: "The child must work with his own hands, mind, and heart." Many of the tasks are open ended and encourage creativity. As children "mess about" with different, interesting materials they are motivated to ask great questions and find their own answers. It is a very teacher-flexible program!

Table 4–2. ESS Program Units and Grade Levels

Growing seeds (K–3)	Colored solutions (3–8)	Match and measure (K–3)
Whistles & strings (4–5)	Mobiles (K–4)	Bones (4–6)
Primary balancing (K–4)	Small things (4–6)	Pattern blocks (K–6)
Earthworms (4–6)	Geo blocks (K–6)	Peas and particles (4–6)
Eggs and tadpoles (K–6)	Batteries and bulbs (4–6)	Tangrams (K–8)
Optics (4–6)	Attribute games and problems (K–9)	Pendulums (4–6)
Spinning tables (1,2)	Microgardening (4–7)	Brine shrimp (1–4)
Senior balancing (4–8)	Printing (1–6)	Behavior of mealworms (4–8)
Structures (2–6)	Stream tables (4–9)	Sink or float (2–7)
Water flow (5–7)	Clay boats (2–8)	Mapping (5–7)
Drops, streams, and containers (3–4)	Heating & cooling (5–7)	Mystery powders (3–4)
Balloons and gases (5–8)	Ice cubes (3–5)	Gases and airs (5–8)
Rocks and charts (3–6)	Kitchen physics (6–7)	

PROGRAMS FOR THE TWENTY-FIRST CENTURY

Don't think that now that the United States has won the space race, whatever that might mean, that science curriculum development has come to a halt. Science education reform includes science programs. There are still many groups working hard at improving how science is taught. Today, a number of new programs have become available to elementary science teachers. These new programs retain many of the strong features of the post-Sputnik programs, build onto others, and introduce new features, including the following:

- topics and activities that have far more personal and social applications;

- integration of more subjects, particularly language arts;

- activities challenging students' misconceptions and allowing time for students to rethink their own ideas and schemata;

- teachers and administrators having more say in the design of the programs, and;

- more prominently featured ways to help teachers teach the program and manage the materials.

A short description of some of these newer, exciting programs follows.

Science for Life and Living: Integrating Science, Technology, and Health

This Biological Science Curriculum Study (BSCS) elementary science program was developed for students in grades K to 6. It is not just biology. "Science for Life and Living: Integrating Science, Technology, and Health" allows children to build their own understanding of an integrated world of science, technology, and health as they work through activities that bring out various concepts and skills. Each grade level has a special theme: Awareness of Myself and My World (K), Order and Organization (grade 1), Change and Measurement (grade 2), Patterns and Prediction (grade 3), Systems and Analysis (grade 4), Energy and Investigation (grade 5), and Balance and Decisions (grade 6). The BSCS curriculum incorporates the following stages to make an instructional model:

1. Engagement—activities that help students to connect to previous knowledge

2. Exploration—students participate in hands-on activities to examine new ideas

3. Explanation—students discuss what they are learning; teacher clarifies students' learning and introduces new concepts

4. Elaboration—students participate in additional activities to increase understanding

5. Evaluation—students and teacher assess what has been learned

Science for Life and Living, through a focus on science, technology, and health issues, nurtures students' natural curiosity and makes them active learners as they construct their own understanding of the world.

The Full Option Science System (FOSS)

FOSS is a program designed to serve both regular and special education students in a wide cross section of schools. Twenty-seven unit modules include science lesson plans in the earth, life, and physical sciences, and extension activities in language, computer, and mathematics applications. Nine of the original SAVI/SELPH (Science Activities for the Visually Impaired/Science Enrichment Learning for the Physically Handicapped) modules are the starting points for FOSS modules. Much care is taken to have a suitable match between activities and students' ability to think at different ages. Further work has been done to make the program easy to instruct and manage. Provisions for preparation time, ease of giving out and retrieving materials, cleanup, storage, and resupply have continually guided program developers. The twenty-seven interdisciplinary, laboratory-based modules are supported by laboratory and tool kits, instructions for building equipment, and correlation tables to aid integration with texts or district science guidelines. FOSS can serve as the science program for grades K–6, or it can integrate with existing programs. FOSS modules include: Animals Two by Two, Fabric, Wood, Trees and Paper (kindergarten); Insects, Balance and Motion, Air and Weather, New Plants, Solids and Liquids, and Pebbles, Sand, and Silt (grades 1–2); Measurement, Ideas and Inventions, the Physics of Sound, Magnetism and Electricity, Earth Materials, Water,

The Human Body, and Structures of Life (grades 3–4); and Environments, Food and Nutrition, Land Forms, Levers and Pulleys, Mixtures and Solutions, Solar Energy, Variables, and Models and Design (grades 5–6).

Improving Urban Elementary Science (Insights)

Insights is a program that targets urban schools and city school children. The program includes activity-based modules that can be used separately within another science curriculum or as a full curriculum within the life, earth, and physical sciences. Activities, often open ended, focus on experiences that draw on the urban environment and that interest city children. Content and process skills are balanced across the curriculum. Material from other school subjects is integrated into many activities to give an overall understanding of how they normally relate. Instructional materials are designed for both the inexperienced teacher and the veteran who seeks innovative strategies to develop critical and creative thinking in urban students.

The Insights units, developed by teachers and tested in urban schools, integrate experimental studies of the natural world with language arts and mathematics, enhancing critical thinking, communication, and problem-solving skills. Currently, the following units are ready for use: Myself and Others, Living Things, My Senses, Moving Things (K–1); Growing Things, Habitats, Liquids, Simple Machines, Sound (grades 2–3); Circuits and Pathways, Bones and Skeletons, Powders and Liquids, Reading the Environment, Changes of State (grades 4–5); and Structures, The Human Body, and There Is No Away (grade 6).

The National Geographic Kids Network

Technology

This program has children gather data on real science problems and then use a computer network to share their data with a scientist and children in other locations. This interdisciplinary, science/social studies/geography program has been an innovator in telecommunications-based curricula. The developer is the Technical Education Resource Center (TERC) in partnership with the National Geographic Society, which publishes and distributes the program. Each of the instructional units is approximately eight weeks long and focuses on a central science problem. Children learn to ask questions and gather data in scientifically acceptable ways. The data are transmitted to a participating scientist who analyzes the data, answers children's questions, and then sends back an overview of all the collected information from cooperating schools. There have been several significant instances in which the children's tests led to the discovery that school drinking water and air pollution standards were not being met! There are seven current National Geographic Kids Network units: Hello, Acid Rain, Weather in Action, What Are We Eating?, Too Much Trash, What's in Our Water?, and Solar Energy are for grades 3–6. These were increased to eleven units for grades 3–9 for the 1997–98 school year and beyond. What Is Our Soil Good For?, Is Our Water at Risk?, How Loud Is Too Loud?, and Are We Getting Enough Oxygen? have expanded this Parents' Choice award-winning program. More than 90 percent of the teachers using National Geographic Kids Network reported that it significantly increased students' interest in science, and that their classes spent almost twice the amount of time on science than they otherwise usually did.

The Life Lab Science Program

This comprehensive elementary science program is founded on its successful garden-based science curriculum, The Growing Classroom. The Living Laboratory, Life Lab's main component, offers a rich context for exploring science. It consists of an indoor center and an outdoor garden area, which can be as simple as a planter box or as complex as an acre farm. In creating an environment, students learn processes and concepts vital in the exploration of the natural world. At the same time, the garden gives them an opportunity to positively affect their surroundings. In short, there's a lot of growing going on!

Life Lab is a comprehensive program for life, earth, and physical science. It incorporates hands-on and multimedia activities in a program that allows students to grow broccoli in varying conditions, analyze nutrients in soil, make compost, or observe garden insects. Concepts studied by students may be directly observed as they occur in nature—life cycles, weather, decomposition, and habitat. Most of the lessons from Life Lab Science units can be done indoors and then applied to the garden. Currently, the following units are available: Great Explorations (K), Earth Is Home (grade 1), Change Around Us (grade 2), How Things Work (grade 3), Interactions (grade 4), and Change Over Times (grade 5).

Science Place

This thematic, core K–6 program offers six complete kits for each grade. Kits offer active hands-on experiences to help students learn how to analyze and use information constructively and to develop an understanding of life, earth, and physical science concepts that explain the world. Each kit includes books, a teacher's *Map to Exploration*, reusable exploration materials, *ScienceMats*, *Assessment Collection*, recording board, *Home Connection Collection*, videotape, description of the *Science Place* program, and a bag. The teacher's *Map to Exploration* provides lesson plans for each book, includes thorough background information and options for exploration, and provides assessment options. *ScienceMats* provides reproducible sheets with pictorial directions for each exploration and a journal format for children to record their observations and conclusions. The *Assessment Collection* includes lesson assessment, baseline and follow-up assessment, a step-by-step guide for using portfolio assessment and performance assessment, observation records, rubrics, and a written test for each unit. The *Home Connection Collection* consists of letters (provided in multiple languages) to go home at the start of each unit to give families a snapshot of the unit explorations and concepts as well as family activities. The videotape features real kids using problem solving to introduce the unit's concepts. Kits include *Human Development, Biodiversity, How Matter Changes, How Telecommunications Works, The Cell, The Universe,* and more! This program was developed through a collaborative effort between Scholastic, Inc. and the nation's leading science museums.

Technology

Super Science: A Mass Media Program

This colorful, year-long, hands-on classroom science magazine is published by Scholastic, Inc. Eight monthly issues enrich the science curriculum with easy-to-do life, earth, and physical science activities and science news, all integrated with language arts and social studies. The Blue Edition of *Super Science* is for grades 4 through 6 and the Red Edition is appropriate for grades 1 through 3. Each colorful issue focuses on one theme and approaches it from several different perspectives, using familiar examples, to give students a unique experience coupled with thorough comprehension. With supporting science software, these publications encourage hands-on, inquiry-based activities, integrating science with other disciplines and stressing applications to contemporary life. This colorful "program" is a nice supplement to your existing science program.

Science and Technology for Children (STC)

The National Science Resources Center in Washington, DC has put together a resource guide for elementary science teachers that was published by the National Academy Press. They also have been working on 24 science units on Science and Technology for Children. Each unit (there are four per grade level, grades 1–6) emphasizes a different, age-appropriate topic in the life, earth, and physical sciences and technology while developing children's critical thinking and problem-solving skills. They are now available from Carolina Biological Supply Company.

The design of the STC program and of individual units is based on a constructivist learning model and on knowledge about cooperative learning and the integration of subject areas. STC units are constructed to be intrinsically interesting and engaging for children and conveniently arranged for teachers. A unit includes a thorough teacher's guide, student activity books, and a kit of materials required for approximately eight weeks of lessons for a class of thirty. The STC program, in its entirety, forms a coherent and fundamental set of science experiences that links science to the broader curriculum through an emphasis on reading, writing, art, and mathematics. Unit titles include: Organisms, Weather, Solids, and Liquids, Comparing and Measuring (grade 1); The Life Cycle of Butterflies, Soils, Changes, Balancing and Weighing (grade 2); Plant Growth and Development, Rocks and Minerals, Chemical Tests, and Sounds (grade 3); Animal Studies, Land and Water, Motion and Design, Electric Circuits (grade 4); Microworlds, Ecosystems, Food Chemistry, and Floating and Sinking (grade 5); and Experiments with Plants, Measuring Time, The Technology of Paper, and Magnets and Motors (grade 6).

Great Explorations in Mathematics and Science (GEMS)

This flexible, integrated math and science curriculum comes to us from the Lawrence Hall of Science (Berkeley, California). There are about forty GEMS units (more are developed every year!) that range from Animal Defenses and Buzzing a Hive to Global Warming and the Greenhouse Effect. Each unit includes a teacher's guide of activities that provides detailed information on the materials needed for the unit, as well as how to prepare for each activity. From a chemical reaction in a polyethylene bag to the blowing of giant bubbles, from a strange green substance said to come from outer space to hands-on experiments in solar heating, the goal of each GEMS activity is to captivate the child's imagination while illuminating essential scientific concepts and developing inquiry skills needed in everyday life. The GEMS teacher's guides integrate math with life, earth, and physical science, fostering a "guided discovery" approach to learning. Materials are usually easily accessible, and lessons are written for teachers with little training in science and math.

GEMS teacher's guides are available for: Animal Defenses, Buzzing a Hive, and Hide a Butterfly (Preschool–3); Liquid Explorations (K–grade 3); Involving Dissolving (grades 1–3); Crime Lab Chemistry, Finger Printing, Hot Water and Warm Homes from Sunlight, Of Cabbages and Chemistry, Oobleck: What Do Scientists Do?, Quadice, and Vitamin C Testing (grades 4–8); Color Analyzers, Paper Towel Testing, Bubble-ology, Earth, Moon, and Stars, and Mapping Animal Movements (grades 5–9); Animals in Action, Convection: A Current Event, More than Magnifiers, and River Cutters (grades 6–9); Chemical Reactions, Discovering Density, Earthworms, Experimenting with Model Rockets, Height-O-Meters, Mapping Fish Habitats, and Acid Rain (grades 6–10); and Global Warming and the Greenhouse Effect (grades 7–10).

Activities That Integrate Mathematics and Science (AIMS)

AIMS is a series (grades K–4; K–6; 5–9) of books (actually a collection of activities for children) that gives children real-life experience in mathematics and science. The emphasis of the program is to integrate mathematics and science in a realistic manner and in ways that are naturally stimulating and meaningful. The rationale for integration lies in the fact that science and mathematics as well as language arts, social studies, and other disciplines are integrally interwoven in the real world. It follows that we should similarly integrate in the classroom, where we are preparing students to live in that complex, real world.

From *Fall into Math and Science* to *Fun with Foods*, each AIMS book offers hands-on investigations that include activities involving questioning, hypothesizing, discovering, and communicating in a more holistic mode of educating students. Kits of materials are available for each series, but materials also can be purchased locally. AIMS program publications include:

Grades K–4 Series

Bats Incredible
Brinca de Alegria Hacia la Promavera
  con las Mathematicas y Ciencias
Caete de Gusto Hacia el Otono con la
  Mathematicas y Ciencias
Fall into Math and Science
Glide into Winter with Math and Science
Hardhatting in a Geo-World
Jawbreakers and Heart Thumpers
Overhead and Underfoot

Patine al Invierno con Mathematicas y
  Ciencias
Popping with Power (Revised Edition)
Primariamente Fisica (Revised Edition)
Priamariamente Plantas
Primarily Physics (Revised Edition)
Primarily Plants
Sense-able Science
Spring into Math and Science

Grades K–6 Series

Budding Botanist
Critters
Mostly Magnets
Principalmente Imanes

Ositos Nada Mas
Primarily Bears
Water Precious Water

Grades 5–9 Series

Down to Earth
Electrical Connections
Conexiones Electricas
Finding Your Bearings (Revised Edition)
Floaters and Sinkers
From Head to Toe
Fun with Foods
Historical Connections in Mathematics,
  Volume I and Volume II
Machine Ship
Math & Science, A Solution

Our Wonderful World
Out of This World (Revised Edition)
Pieces and Patterns, A Patchwork in
  Math and Science
Piezas y Disenos, un Mosaic de Matem-
  aticas y Ciencias
Soap Films and Bubbles
The Sky's the Limit (Revised Edition)
Through the Eyes of the Explorers:
  Minds-On Math & Mapping

Voyage of the Mimi

Technology

If you have access to a videotape or videodisc player, you might want to consider one of the two *Voyage of the Mimi* packages developed by the Bank Street College of Education. The *Mimi* is a research sailing ship with a crew of scientists and children. Many exciting adventures are portrayed in 15-minute video episodes. These are supplemented by video visits to places where "real" science is carried out. There are teacher and student guides, microcomputer-based laboratories, computer software, CD-ROM, and other materials.

Students not only learn science in the *Voyage of the Mimi,* but also see that science is something they can do. They become involved in adventures where scientists are actually role models. During the exciting voyage at sea, students learn about whales, the principles of navigation, how to use maps, how to use the sun to make fresh water from saltwater, and more. Then, after each episode at sea, documentary style expeditions take your students to aquariums, museums, and other places where people are doing interesting scientific work.

The second *Voyage of the Mimi* combines the successful multimedia format of *Voyage of the Mimi* and many of the same characters with a new theme. An archaeological expedition to Mexico City to study the ancient Maya civilization turns into an action packed mystery. All of the same multimedia features of the first *Voyage*— videotape, videodiscs, computer software, CD-ROM, and more are available for the second *Mimi.*

A videodisc player opens up many additional possibilities. One of the more extensive series of video-based science lessons is available from Optical Data Corporation. Their Windows on Science packages cover earth science, life science, and physical science. The materials also include a Resource Binder of lesson plans and unit summaries. The Space Disc packages include the *Voyager Gallery, Planetscapes,* and *Space Shuttle* videodiscs. There are numerous, good videodisc packages on the market. Lists of available products can be found in the catalogs of some of the companies listed at the end of this chapter.

There is a wealth of curriculum materials out there from which to choose. Probably, the school or district where you teach will already have a science program in place. Don't be upset if it is not your favorite one, there is flexibility within all of these curricula to make room for a most important person in the curriculum—you!

INTEGRATING SCIENCE WITH OTHER SUBJECTS

We haven't given much time to discussing how to incorporate science into other content areas and vice versa. It actually isn't difficult if you think about it a little in advance. Even though hands-on ex-

8. Math Games
11:45 Mrs. Halloran
1:50 Music

So far, my regular lens had revealed that, other than the day's schedule, no examples of print produced by the class existed in the room: no wall of words to aid in spelling or decoding, no vocabulary charts, no displays of published work, no charts of content area research or information. I found no indication of science, social studies, or math topics under study. Although I had been told that students have time for independent reading of their own choice on occasion, the day's schedule promised none for today.

Ms. Borders had established routines the class could refer to on the schedule: reading groups named by the basal text they were reading, partner reading, story mapping, math book work, spelling book work, and so on. As well, the class was split into those who had already published their writing and were illustrating, and those who still needed to publish. The girl at the front computer told me she was typing her writing.

What Are the Others Doing?

Having shifted to my close-up lens, I approached Rob, one of the students working independently. He told me they had to write 10 sentences in their composition books about Helen Keller. Ms. Borders had been reading to them about Helen Keller, but they could write whatever they wanted to say about her. Rob sat there, shuffling the book around on his desk but had not written for a few minutes. I asked how he thought of what to write, and he told me he just waited until he thought of something.

Ginger sat down next to me and asked who I was. I told her, and she admired my writing tablet. She showed me her composition book and asked if she had written 10 sentences yet. When I asked her how she could decide, she said she did not know. I then told Ginger to get the book she was reading and she brought over a book about Helen Keller. I turned it to the back cover and asked her to point to the first sentence. She pointed to the beginning of the first sentence in the description of the book. "Where's the end of that sentence?" I asked. Ginger paused, then put her finger on the period at the end of the first sentence. "How did you know?" I asked.

"Because of that," Ginger said, indicating the period.

"Oh, the period?"

She nodded.

"How many sentences are on this cover?" I asked. She counted six. "Now, how many have you . . ." but before I could finish, Ginger returned to her composition book and began counting out 11 sentences. "Then, you've done more than you need to," I said.

"I think I'll keep writing, though," Ginger replied, "because I still have more to say." Before she left, Ginger confirmed for me what I had been told by Kristen's mother about the writing process in Sally Borders's room: Students write in their composition books, they read it to Ms. Borders, she writes it over (a Neat Sheet)

> My bay at hors camp
>
> I rod cuce She has
> a gub Canter not is goD
> as   Cump. we lumt
> a hie   Lumt.
>
> My Day At Horse Camp
>
> I rode Cookie. She
> has a good canter but
> not as good as company.
> We jumped a high
> jump.

**FIGURE 5.1   Kristen's Edited Journal
(Neat Sheet)**

on the other side of the page (see Figure 5.1), and they type the correct version into the computer.

Sally Borders ran a classroom of a type I recognized: the blend of literature-based basals and writing process. I recall Don Graves saying, "American slices are a blend of processed cheeses, too, but are they cheese?" Ms. Borders has traditionally grouped students into three reading groups based on ability, Kristen being in the middle group. Like many literature-based or whole-language educators, she used partner reading and story maps in place of individual seatwork on comprehension questions or workbooks alone.

In Paratore's (1993) terms, the read-aloud supported the writing assignment, and the students did "publish" their writing, although there was no evidence that anyone except the teacher read the pieces. Also, "the writing process" had been reduced to the all-too-common two-draft model, in which students write one draft to an assigned topic, the teacher edits it, and the students copy the edited version as the final product. Students were well-schooled in the routine, but no one spoke of discovery strategies, revision, or audience response.

What Do Reading and Writing Mean Here?

When Ginger returned to her desk, I shifted my close-up lens to the reading group, being careful not to focus too obviously on Kristen, who nonetheless eyed me from time to time as she volunteered an answer or read aloud. Ms. Borders was using a hanging chart to lead a discussion of word analysis. The following words were on the chart:

kind   mild   grind   told   toll
bolt   chill   child   find   roll

She discussed the definition of *toll* with the children. When she asked what *bolt* meant, Kristen explained that a horse can "bolt" or run off fast. Ms. Borders also pointed out that a bolt is like a screw with a nut on it.

The children put the words into sentences, such as *Daniel was a (child) who lived in Tennessee.* In the passage, "Jeff handed Daniel a block of wood. 'This is for you,' Jeff said," Kristen explained that *This* referred to the block of wood.

The group opened its reading books to the story titled "Daniel's Duck" and they read orally, round-robin style, with the teacher or other students interrupting to make corrections of miscues. Kristen tried to help with the word *valley* but missed it. Ms. Borders created a purposefully incorrect "Burgess" summary (Johnson & Louis, 1987) after a couple of pages, and the group gleefully corrected her incorrect insertions of information into the story.

Kristen read a whole page aloud, word by word. She reversed *Daniel said* to *said Daniel,* paused on *winter,* and read *light* for *rights,* but made very few errors, reading as well or better than anyone who read during the lesson. She slowed her pace as she neared the end of the page.

When Ms. Borders asked how Daniel's living room appeared to be the same or different from theirs, Kristen pointed out that both had a fireplace. Ms. Borders asked if the fireplaces were just the same, to which Kristen replied, "Mine doesn't have rocks at the top." She also pointed out that people still use oil lamps when the power goes out. The teacher connected this story to others they had read, and the children eagerly looked through the book for evidence of connections.

"Good reading" in this classroom meant getting the words right and understanding what you read. Students read aloud in the group a story they had already read with a partner, so practice was provided to enhance the oral reading performance. However, readers were merely corrected on their miscues by peers or the teacher, with no effort to elicit strategies for word recognition or to appreciate the expressiveness of the reading. Likewise, vocabulary was taught prior to the reading with sentence completion activities appropriate for reinforcing word knowledge, not developing concepts or highlighting context use strategies.

Sally Borders actively engaged students in understanding the story. Her mendacious summary amused the children, and they knew just how to correct her "errors." Further, she asked them to connect this story to their lives and to other stories, and they knew how to use story structure to skim through the piece for evidence. Except to correct miscues, however, students never addressed each other directly to share information, debate an issue, or connect an experience or thought to a comment by a peer.

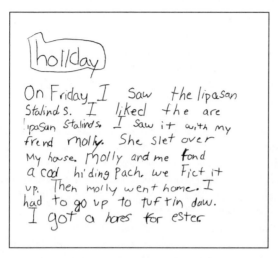

ho11day

On Friday I saw the lipasan
Stalind s. I liked the are
lipasan stalinds. I saw it with my
frend molly. She slet over
My house. Molly and me fond
a cad hi'ding Pach. we Fict it
vp. Then molly went home. I
had to go vp to tuftin daw.
I got a hares for ester

FIGURE 5.2   Kristen's Journal

Is There a Problem?

Kristen's special education team found her to be in a "gray area," not meriting identification as learning disabled but needing support with reading and writing in the classroom. She read a story with her Chapter I tutor, read it again with her partner, and then engaged in the small group reading lesson (as just described), performing as well or better than others in her group. From classroom observation, Kristen and the team's plan seemed to be succeeding.

Evidence from outside the classroom was not so comforting. Kristen's mother said that Kristen did not read at home, cannot read aloud successfully in new material or books harder than Dr. Seuss, and still wrote with mostly invented spelling, even when writing on familiar topics in personal narrative (see Figure 5.2). My further investigation needed to focus on whether the help Kristen had been given so far enabled her to work like everyone else in class but masked unaddressed problems in reading and writing.

CASE REPORT: Good Parts That Do Not Add Up

Background

Kristen attended kindergarten in Hadleyville, where she was assessed with Marie Clay's (1985) Diagnostic Survey. She progressed through the first two levels with 100 percent accuracy and was instructionally appropriate for the level-2 material. She had acquired most concepts about print except that she failed to notice changes in word and letter order; did not know meaning of commas, question marks, and quotation marks; and had trouble with *was*. She was able to use picture clues and predictable text and memory but did not attend to beginning sounds and did not self-correct, often substituting known sight words for the printed word, even when they were not graphically similar. She still reverted to these strategies when reading difficult text. In writing, she was able to get beginning and ending consonants and could spell some family names.

Kristen attended first grade at Round Top School in Wellington, where her first-grade teacher noticed that Kristen's reading skills lagged behind her oral language skills. After assessment, she was given a "modified" Reading Recovery program from an aide, but it was of little help. She read little books in the school tutoring program and then brought them home to read at night. Her mother reported to the school that Kristen had trouble reading them at home, even after three exposures to the story in school. Her folder included a list of 30 trade books used by her reading group with teacher instruction. Books typically used with first-graders such as *Brown Bear, Witches' Brew, More Spaghetti I Say,* and *Rosie's Walk* were included.

In grade 2, Kristen was in a regular classroom with Chapter I help in the classroom and a pull-out Benchmark phonics class. Her mother was concerned that behavior problems of the other Benchmark class members might affect Kristen's learning in this setting. Kristen was reading in the Ginn Silver Burdett grade 2^1 reader, *Garden Gates.* Students would write in a personal journal daily. The teacher read aloud to them, most recently from a book about Helen Keller. The class generated an oral synopsis of the reading, which the teacher transcribed, and then the students drew pictures. The students engaged in partner oral reading of the assigned stories as well as in a reading group for round-robin oral reading. Sustained silent reading time for personally chosen books was provided when other work was finished. Students completed workbook exercises and did dictation for handwriting. An observation of one morning's lesson follows:

Classroom Observation

(See observation section above.)

Assessment History

Woodcock-Johnson Psychoeducational Battery–Revised (January, Grade 1)

Subtest	Standard Score	Percentile
Memory for Sentences	111	77th
Picture Vocabulary	121	92nd
Oral Vocabulary	116	86th
Listening Vocabulary	112	78th
Verbal Analogies	118	88th
*Letter-Word Identification	84	15th
*Passage Comprehension	79	8th
*Word Attack	82	12th
*Reading Vocabulary	92	30th

*These subtests were presented in print; the others were presented orally.

Woodcock-Johnson Psychoeducational Battery–Revised (March, Grade 1)

Subtest	Standard Score	Percentile
Memory for Names	59	0.3th
Memory for Sentences	111	78th
Visual Matching	100	50th
Incomplete Words	96	38th
Visual Closure	93	33rd
Picture Vocabulary	120	90th
*Letter-Word Identification	89	23rd
*Dictation	85	17th
Writing Samples	97	43rd
Science	106	66th
Social Studies	109	73rd
Humanities	108	71st

*Sight vocabulary and spelling tasks require visual memory of word forms.

Wechsler Intelligence Scale for Children—III (March, Grade 1)

Subtest	Scaled Score	Percentile	Difference from Mean
Verbal Subtests			
Information	11	63rd	−0.2
Similarities	8	25th	−3.2
Arithmetic	12	75th	0.8
Vocabulary	14	91st	2.8
Comprehension	15	95th	3.8
*Digit Span	7	16th	−4.2
Performance Subtests			
Picture Completion	10	50th	−1.3
Coding	9	37th	−2.3
Picture Arrangement	16	98th	4.7
Block Design	11	63rd	−0.2
Object Assembly	6	9th	−5.3
Symbol Search	14	91st	2.7
Mazes	13	84th	1.7

*Often associated with reading difficulty.

Lindamood Auditory Conceptualization Test (May, Grade 1)

Total Converted Score   40 K^2 for phonological awareness

Clinical Evaluation of Language Fundamentals–Revised (May, Grade 1)

Subtest	Scaled Score	Percentile
Linguistic Concepts	7	16th
Sentence Structure	10	50th

Subtest	Scaled Score	Percentile
Oral Directions	9	37th
Word Association	14	91st
Receptive Language Standard Score	91	27th

WORD Test

Subtest	Percentile
Associations	18th
Synonyms	98th
Semantic Absurdities	79th
Antonyms	52nd
Definitions	28th
Multiple Definitions	21st

Expressive One Word Picture Vocabulary Test

Standard Score	Percentile
113	87th

Bruininks Oseretsky Test of Motor Proficiency (May, Grade 1)

Subtest	Stanine
Gross Motor	6
Fine Motor	7
Composite	7

Test of Visual-Perceptual Skills (TVPS) Nonmotor (May, Grade 1)

Subtest	Scaled Score
Visual Discrimination	19
Visual Memory	8
Visual-Spatial Relationships	14
Visual Form Constancy	10
Visual Sequential Memory	7
Visual Figure-Ground	11
Visual Closure	9

Visual Motor Integration (VMI) (May, Grade 1)   **53rd percentile**

Durrell Analysis of Reading Difficulty (January, Grade 2)

Subtest	Grade Level
Oral Reading	1 high/2 low
Modified Oral reading	2 mid/low (with prediction and discussion)
Listening Comprehension	4 mid
Listening vocabulary	3 mid

Subtest	Grade Level
Word Recognition	1 high
Word Analysis	1 high
Spelling	2 low/mid
Sounds in Isolation	
Letters	2 mid
Blends/digraphs	3 mid
Phonograms	below norms
Visual Memory of Words	
Primary	2 mid
Identifying Sounds in Words	3 mid

Note: I ignored the grade norms, except as gross, relative measures of strength or weakness.

Summary.   The testing record here was extensive and carefully reported. In general, Kristen consistently showed strong oral language skills but difficulty with print. In particular, she had difficulty remembering the forms of words (word recognition scores, spelling) and remembering and sequencing sounds within words. She did, however, learn well orally and could use her world knowledge to help her understand what she read.

Current Assessment

Reading.   At her home, in her room, Kristen read to me three self-selected passages that she felt were easy, just right, or a challenge. Miscue analyses of her readings follow, in respective order:

Passage 1 (Oral).   *Garden Gates,* "The House That Nobody Wanted," Lilian Moore, Ginn Silver Burdett: 581 words, 91 percent accuracy, 52 miscues, 16 self-corrections, 33 percent self-correction rate

Kristen	Text	Matches Preceding Context	Matches Following Context	Self-Corrects	Preserves Meaning	Corrected or Preserves Meaning
a	an	yes	no	yes	yes	yes
was	had	yes	no	yes	no	yes
there	—	yes	yes	no	yes	yes
get	go	yes	yes	no	yes	yes
white	windows	yes	no	yes	no	yes
they	then	yes	no	yes	no	yes
—	then	yes	yes	no	yes	yes
—	uphill	yes	yes	no	yes	yes
uphill	downhill	yes	yes	no	yes	yes
—	and	yes	yes	no	yes	yes
they	there	yes	no	yes	no	yes

Kristen	Text	Matches Preceding Context	Matches Following Context	Self-Corrects	Preserves Meaning	Corrected or Preserves Meaning
little	—	yes	yes	no	yes	yes
little	—	yes	yes	no	yes	yes
what	with	yes	no	yes	no	yes
green	grass	yes	no	no	no	no
growing	grass	no	no	no	no	no
flowers	gardens	yes	yes	yes	yes	yes
all	—	yes	yes	no	yes	yes
—	it	yes	yes	no	yes	yes
little	—	yes	yes	no	yes	yes
the	their	yes	yes	no	yes	yes
—	house	yes	yes	no	yes	yes
man	woman	yes	yes	no	no	no
with	that	yes	no	yes	yes	yes
white	a	yes	no	yes	yes	yes
and	—	yes	yes	yes	yes	yes
—	a	yes	no	no	yes	yes
flower	fence	yes	no	yes	no	yes
fence	windows	yes	no	no	no	no
—	see	yes	yes	no	yes	yes
—	but	yes	yes	no	yes	yes
the	this	yes	no	yes	no	yes
they	this	yes	no	yes	no	yes
little	time	yes	no	yes	no	yes
after	another	yes	no	no	yes	yes
a	—	yes	yes	no	yes	yes
house	home	yes	yes	no	yes	yes
little	—	yes	yes	no	yes	yes
little	—	yes	yes	no	yes	yes
the	a	yes	yes	no	yes	yes
and	—	yes	no	yes	no	yes
they	there	yes	no	no	no	no
grass	flowers	no	no	no	no	no
—	old	yes	yes	no	yes	yes
man	woman	yes	yes	no	no	no
and the	looked	yes	no	yes	no	yes
outside	out	yes	yes	no	yes	yes
said	asked	yes	yes	no	yes	yes
green	grass	yes	no	no	no	no
as	asked	yes	no	yes	no	yes
man	woman	yes	no	no	no	no
listened	laughed	yes	no	no	no	no
		96%	52%	33%	42%	81%

These percentages, plus her retelling of the story, indicated that Kristen understood the reading but that even this easiest piece was on the difficult side of her instructional range (91 percent accuracy compared to 95 percent for instructional range difficulty versus 90 percent or below for frustration range). However, she showed strong prediction from context (96 percent) and self-corrected (33 percent) enough when her reading did not match the following context (52 percent) in order to preserve meaning (81 percent). Many of the miscues (such as reading *little old man* for *old man* or *and uphill again* for *uphill and downhill again*) indicated that Kristen often read from memory or prediction rather than print.

Passage 2 (Oral). *A Kiss for Little Bear*, Else Holmelund Minarik, HarperCollins: 283 words, 84 percent accuracy, 45 miscues, 18 self-corrections, 40 percent self-correction rate

Kristen	Text	Matches Preceding Context	Matches Following Context	Self-Corrects	Preserves Meaning	Corrected or Preserves Meaning
—	A	yes	yes	yes	yes	yes
—	kiss	yes	yes	yes	yes	yes
—	for	yes	yes	yes	yes	yes
Bear's	Bear	no	no	yes	yes	yes
Kiss	—	no	yes	yes	yes	yes
oh	hello	yes	yes	no	yes	yes
—	Hen	yes	yes	no	yes	yes
—	"Yes, I will,"					
	said Hen	yes	yes	no	yes	yes
was	saw	yes	no	yes	no	yes
for	from	yes	no	yes	no	yes
—	Frog	yes	yes	no	yes	yes
was	saw	yes	no	no	no	no
the	—	yes	yes	no	yes	yes
the	—	yes	yes	yes	yes	yes
sp	spot	yes	yes	yes	yes	yes
—	Little	yes	yes	yes	yes	yes
is	his	no	no	no	no	no
it	—	yes	no	no	no	no
little	good	yes	no	no	yes	yes
good	little	no	no	no	yes	yes
the	—	yes	yes	yes	no	yes
but	do	no	no	yes	no	yes
—	(pages					
	18 & 19)	yes	no	no	no	no
—	then	yes	yes	no	yes	yes

Kristen	Text	Matches Preceding Context	Matches Following Context	Self-Corrects	Preserves Meaning	Corrected or Preserves Meaning
he	she	yes	yes	no	no	no
his	this	yes	no	yes	no	yes
he	this	yes	no	yes	no	yes
a	Little	yes	no	no	yes	yes
kiss	Bear's	no	no	no	yes	yes
for	kiss	no	no	no	yes	yes
Little	—	no	no	no	yes	yes
Bear	—	no	no	no	yes	yes
—	his	yes	yes	no	yes	yes
the	—	yes	yes	no	yes	yes
interesting	indeed	yes	yes	no	yes	yes
he	said	yes	no	yes	yes	yes
kiss	—	yes	yes	no	yes	yes
from	for	yes	no	no	no	no
pretty	picture	yes	no	yes	no	yes
sh	sent	yes	yes	yes	no	yes
gave	gets	yes	no	no	no	no
a	all	no	no	no	no	no
lot	mixed	no	no	no	no	no
skunk	skunk	yes	yes	no	yes	yes
to	a	yes	no	yes	no	yes
a	Little	yes	yes	no	no	no
the	best	yes	no	no	no	no
		75%	50%	40%	56%	75%

Again, these percentages showed Kristen to be a good contextual reader, predicting from context 75 percent of the time and self-correcting 40 percent of the time, especially when the first reading did not match the following context (50 percent). Overall, she maintained meaning at the sentence level 75 percent of the time, and her retell was clear an accurate. She even read the Hen's refusal to take the kiss back to the grandmother with an emphatic, "NO!" and said that the kiss got all traded around and mixed up, even though she had read that phrase incorrectly. She did not use the picture of Little Bear being the best man at the wedding to help her read the last page, however, even though she had been able to do that with the first story. Her word recognition in context (84 percent) was at the frustration level, despite her strong comprehension of the familiar story.

Passage 3 (Oral). *Pony Tails #3*, "Corey's Pony Is Missing," Bonnie Bryant, Bantam: 143 words, 20 miscues, 86 percent accuracy rate, 5 self-corrections, 25 percent self-correction rate

Kristen	Text	Matches Preceding Context	Matches Following Context	Self-Corrects	Preserves Meaning	Corrected or Preserves Meaning
Mr.	Dr.	yes	yes	no	no	no
last	least	yes	no	no	no	no
stack	small	yes	no	no	yes	yes
shouted	sighed	yes	no	no	no	no
called	carried	yes	no	yes	no	yes
pulled	put	yes	no	no	no	no
sure	sensible	yes	no	no	no	no
mom	mother	yes	yes	no	yes	yes
delight	different	no	no	yes	no	yes
could	was	yes	no	no	no	no
picture	packing	no	no	no	no	no
Corey	Corey's	yes	no	yes	no	yes
picture	parents	yes	no	yes	no	yes
was	had	no	no	yes	no	yes
one	only	yes	no	no	no	no
and	a	no	no	no	no	no
show	short	yes	no	no	no	no
painted	spent	yes	no	yes	no	yes
halef	half	no	no	no	no	no
mom	mother	yes	yes	no	yes	yes
		75%	15%	30%	15%	45%

Here, Kristen was clearly reading at her frustration level. She continued to predict words from preceding context (75 percent), but only 15 percent of the time did they fit the following context. Yet, she self-corrected only 30 percent of the time, giving her 45 percent accuracy at the sentence level.

From the picture on the cover and the title, she was able to predict that a girl would lose her horse and go looking for it by riding on the back of her friend's horse. However, those predictions did not help with the early part of the story. She was not able to get the word *divorced* on the second page, for instance, until I asked her where Corey was going for the weekend. She said to her father's. I asked her why a girl would have to go to her father's house for the weekend, but she did not have an answer. When I asked her if she had any friends who spent weekends with one parent and then the other, she said yes, and made the connection that Corey's parents were divorced. Therefore, Kristen had the abilities to (1) predict vocabulary in familiar stories (passages 1 and 2) and (2) use background knowledge to predict vocabulary in new stories (passage 3), but she may not make use of these abilities without prompting.

In this passage Kristen's miscues more often resembled the printed word, at least in the first letter, whereas in the more familiar passages she often substituted a meaningful but graphically dissimilar word. Thus, when context was not available for her to predict print, she more carefully sampled the printed word.

In order to check Kristen's silent reading rate and comprehension, I asked her to read the first few pages of *Frog and Toad All Year* by Arnold Lobel (Scholastic, 1976). She began reading by moving her lips and subvocalizing, then stopped as she became involved in the story. She read 146 words on the first eight pages in two minutes (73 words per minute) and gave a complete retell: "Frog did not want to come out because he had no winter clothes. Toad brought some, and they went sledding down a huge hill." Kristen read slowly but with good comprehension silently in material intended for first-graders. Gilmore and Gilmore (1968) report average second-grade reading speed as 86 words per minute.

When I asked Kristen what she did when she came across a word she did not recognize, she said she tried to sound it out, then she would ask for help. This statement confirmed her performance in the oral reading and in class. In her reading group in class, students read aloud until the teacher or a classmate corrected them on a miscue. Kristen knew when I asked her how to reread a sentence to think what word would make sense (to check for preceding context) and how to read "blank" for the word, go on to the end of the sentence, and then guess (to check for following context), but she did not spontaneously employ these strategies normally taught in Reading Recovery. With longer words, Kristen said she looked for syllables, then tried "to spell it out in my head to see if it's the same as a word I know." In other words, she tried to recall the visual image of a known word and match it to the spelling in front of her. She did not try to think of a word with a same spelling pattern, what sound that makes, and then substitute in the sound (as in the Benchmark program). I also did not see either Reading Recovery or Benchmark strategies practiced or reinforced in Kristen's reading group. In addition, Kristen said that when students read with partners, they did it the same way they did in their reading group with the teacher—taking turns reading orally and correcting each other if the partner noticed a miscue.

Names Test. The Names Test (Duffelmeyer et al., 1994) consists of 35 names (first and last, so 70 altogether) normally used to test second- through fifth-graders' phonics knowledge. Kristen read 18 of the 70 names correctly, recognizing correctly the following percentages of phonics patterns:

Pattern	Percent Correct	Errors
Initial consonants	87	*g/j, B/D, c/s
Initial consonant blends	90	br, sk
Consonant digraphs	67	th, ch, ph
Short vowels	56	a,e,i, o
Long vowels/VC—Final *e*	44	**ate, ale, ace, ane, ade, ene, ine, y, i, o
Vowel digraphs	40	au, ay, ea, oy, oa, oo, ai
Controlled vowels	68	ar, er, aw
Schwa (short *u*)	53	a,o

*C/s and g/j are the only variable consonants; b/d are visual transpositions.
**Phonograms normally taught in the Benchmark program

Initial consonant sounds are normally mastered in first grade, with vowels usually following in second grade. Thus, Kristen appeared to have the decoding knowledge and reading speed of a first-grader and was comfortable with books generally used with first-graders. Significantly, she did not seem to be using phonogram knowledge normally taught in the Benchmark program.

Writing

Selected Writing Samples. Kristen chose three pieces from her writing journal as the three best pieces she had written. The first one ("This Summer at My Grandmother's"; see Figure 5.3) was written on the first day of school. She chose it because, "I like my grandmother, and horses, and my best friend is up there." She said the story was good because it was about her grandmother and horses. She wrote it during the first three hours of the school day, and only had trouble thinking of how to spell words. She told me that the classroom writing procedure was to write a draft on one side of the journal, take it to the teacher, read it aloud while the teacher makes a Neat Sheet (error-free copy), and then type it on the computer. The print-out was stored in the writing folder, but no one had read it. She chose not to read it aloud to me because she wanted to read one she knew "by heart," a similar strategy she used in her reading selections.

Kristen chose as her second-best passage the fourth one in her writing book, a piece about herself in Arizona. She said, "I wrote it when I was freezing cold and it was hot there." She said it only took her "a moment or two" and it had not been published yet. Students decide which pieces are published for their folders, she

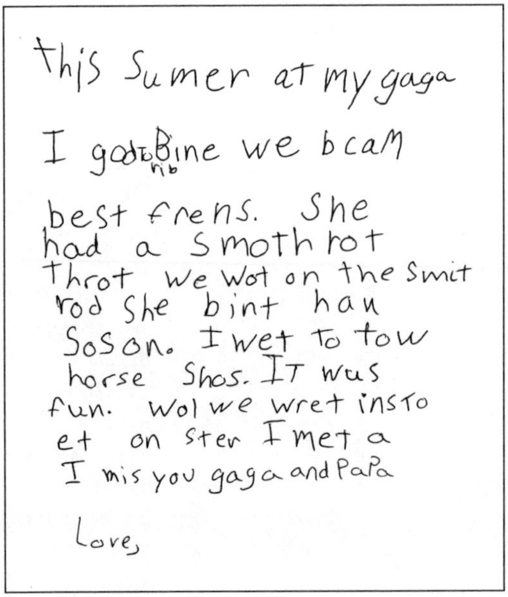
this Sumer at my gaga
I got to Bine we bcam
best frens. She
had a Smoth rot
throt we Wot on the Smit
rod She bint hau
Soson. I wet to tow
horse Shos. IT wus
fun. Wol we wret insto
et on Ster I met a
I mis you gaga and PaPa
Love,

FIGURE 5.3 Kristen's Best Piece

said. She believed the story was good because she liked Arizona and it had horses in it. Nothing was hard in the writing, but she did get help from her mother to spell *Squanto* and *Mickey*.

As her third-best piece, Kristen chose "Three" from her book because I said to get her "third" best one. It, too, took her only "a few moments" to write and is about horses. She had trouble spelling some words, such as *Tonto* and *take*.

Analysis

Kristen valued her writing for its topic, not the quality of the treatment of the topic or the mechanical accuracy. Often, beginning writers will focus on the correctness of the writing, especially in classrooms that emphasize such features. Although Kristen said she received no feedback from her classmates, and only mechanical corrections from her teacher, she still focused on the content of her writing as her measure of quality. Meaning also predominated her thinking in reading, evidenced by her reading what she thought was on the page in preference to what was actually there. In class, she was able to discuss the interior of Daniel's (the main character) house and the similarities it had to her house in some depth. When she read her own writing (see Figure 5.4), she also read what she meant to write, not what was there. Kristen wrote:

> Caring adout horse
> You havd to hus them
> You haf to hid them
> word them give them a home
>   Do all difint tings

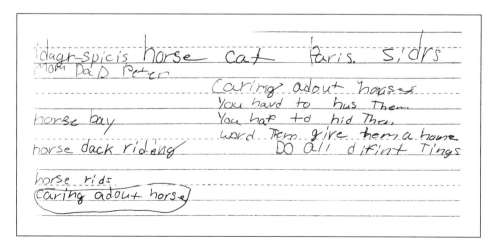

FIGURE 5.4   Kristen's Writing Sample

But Kristen read her writing as:

Caring about horses
You have to breed them.
You have to feed them.
You have to water them.
You have to give them a good home.
You have to do all those good things.

She was able to list nine topics for writing and four titles during our brief brainstorming session. She had no trouble deciding to write directions for the care of horses and did so without delay or requests for help. However, Kristen's lack of requests for help may have indicated that she "doesn't know that she doesn't know"—in other words, that she does not self-monitor her writing performance. In class, both in reading and in writing, the teacher or partner is responsible for finding errors, not the reader or writer, at least in the observations and reports I have seen.

Dictation

As is obvious in the extemporaneous writing sample we have just looked at, Kristen confused *b* and *d* in writing as well as in reading, left off endings, omitted punctuation, confused similar sounds (f/v), and substituted a known spelling word (*word*) for a desired word (*walk*). To investigate her ability to write words when she does not need to concentrate on composing (or creating meaning), I dictated to her the following sentences (see Figure 5.5):

> My friend and I like to go and see the sailboat. It has a blue flag. (Johnston, 1992)

Kristen transcribed these sentences as:

> My friend and I like to go and see the sal bot it has a blow flag

When not using her attention to focus on meaning (her preferred activity), Kristen could spell most beginning sight words well. She had trouble in writing, as well as in reading (see Names Test, earlier) and with vowel digraphs (*sail, boat,*

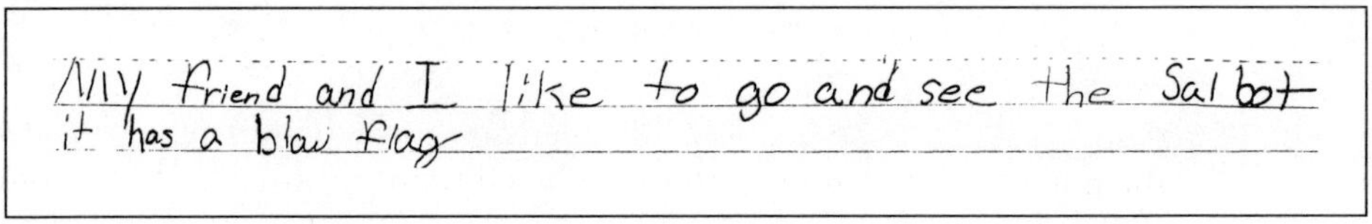
MY friend and I like to go and see the Sal bot
it has a blaw flag

FIGURE 5.5 Kristen's Dictation

blue). She also continued to omit end-of-sentence punctuation, indicating that attention did not affect this mechanical convention. She did not have the concept clearly established in her mind in order to devote attention to it. However, as indicated by the reaction of her classmate to the 10-sentence assignment, Kristen was not atypical of second-graders in this behavior. She used both invented spelling (the nonword *sal* for *sail* and the nonword *bot* for *boat*) and known sight word substitution (*blow* for *blue*).

Current Levels of Functioning

Reading.   Kristen was a second-grader who was able to read material intended for first-graders with comprehension and fluency expected of first-graders. She was currently in a second-grade reader in which she was able to succeed, given the support of partner reading and of Directed Reading and Thinking Activities led by the teacher. However, her lack of automatic sight vocabulary and poorly developed decoding skills (also typical of a first-grader) slowed her reading, made it an unenjoyable task, and drained attention from comprehension in unfamiliar material.

Although Kristen had been tutored in strategy use via Reading Recovery in grade 1, and the analogy approach to decoding via the Benchmark program in grade 2, she showed few signs of using this knowledge in actual reading. She attempted to spell words out letter by letter and match them to known word forms, although she knew rerunning and blanking strategies. However, Kristen did use context to self-correct when meaning was changed. She had a favorite reading series and an active interest in horses and riding on which to build a reading habit.

Writing.   Kristen was able to think of topics about which to write and to think of various types of writing within the topic (e.g., story, description, and directions). She knew her own difficulty with spelling and she could invent spellings and ask for help to solve them, although she had few opportunities to do so.

However, Kristen showed little sense of audience or purpose in writing. To her, a piece was good if she liked the topic. She did not spontaneously self-correct her writing, but read what she intended to write rather than the words on the page. Kristen misspelled 9 of 23 words in extemporaneous composing, but only 2 of 16 in dictation. Therefore, she showed limited attention or memory for word forms, leaving her consumed by the need to construct meaning when she wrote.

Suggested Instruction

Reading.   As noted by the reading specialist, Kristen needed to build her store of automatically recognized words through lots of fluent easy reading. Her current basal placement was too difficult to ensure this would happen. In addition, while the guided reading procedures reinforced Kristen's already strong comprehension skills, the round-robin oral reading served to focus Kristen on word recognition as a letter-by-letter process, in which someone else would quickly tell her if she had made an error. Therefore, Kristen never needed to practice her contextual cross-checking strategies.

Further, the spelling patterns learned in Benchmark needed to be applied daily in connected reading, as well as the process of retrieving the pattern word, applying it to the unknown word, and deriving the correct pronunciation. Her performance on the Names Test indicated that she was having trouble with vowel sounds, the most variable sounds in English. However, vowels are much more regular in phonograms, such as those taught in Benchmark. As the reading specialist noted on the Durrell Test, and as was obvious on the Names Test, many of the words missed are taught by Benchmark. Therefore, Kristen needed this information, was scheduled to receive it, but had not had a chance to practice it in meaningful reading to the point of automaticity.

Writing.   Kristen needed to learn to separate composing from editing and to develop a sense of reader-based prose (Flower, 1990). That is, she needed to make the best use of the short-term memory she had for word forms by learning to edit for spelling after she wrote. This way, she could concentrate on spelling separately from meaning. Current instruction made editing the teacher's responsibility. Moreover, the spelling patterns taught in the Benchmark session needed to be reinforced by use in the writing and editing processes.

Also, Kristen needed to develop a sense of what writing is for—namely, to communicate with a reader. She gave me no indication that she considered a reader when she wrote. Further, she did not indicate that other students read her work in school, that she received any feedback about her writing, nor that she had any chance to accommodate the needs of those readers by revising.

CHAPTER

6 Selecting the Tasks

Principles for Selection

The National Council of Teachers of English (NCTE) and the International Reading Association (IRA) in their *Standards for the English Language Arts* (1996) say the purpose of their standards is "to develop students' knowledge of, facility in, and appreciation of the English language in ways that will serve them throughout their lives" (p. 12). We know we are teaching English well if students know how the language works, can use it themselves, and value literacy as a means for living life fully.

The organizations propose their standards as an interactive model for evaluating language use, as in Figure 6.1. Specifically, the four circles are lenses through which assessors view the learner. Through the content lens, we look for *what* the learner is doing. Considering purpose, we ask *why* he or she is reading or writing. In terms of development, we ask what the reader or writer is *learning* in this instance of literacy. We must also consider the social and cultural contexts surrounding both the learner and the other three dimensions.

In order to meet these social-constructivist standards for language use, we must choose tasks that let us see what the student knows about language, but we must also check why the child reads or writes as he or she does, asking, in effect, what the child conceives to be the purpose of the reading or writing. Since the purpose of all language learning is its appreciation and use throughout the child's life, we will want to ask the student to read or write in ways that he or she is likely to use outside school.

Because we value continued development of readers and writers, we will need to consider how dynamic their language knowledge seems to be. Do they view language as an open set of relationships that can be understood through their own lives and for their own ends? Do they continually reassess what they know about any given text, and text in general, as they read and write more?

Finally, we will want to compare performances by the student in varying social contexts. Does the child read and write differently at school than at home? Does he or she know how to choose among literate registers, so that if home speech is inappropriate at school, he or she can use effective and appropriate forms in each place without shame or confusion? Does the child understand what reading and writing can do for him or her at school, at home, and in the community?

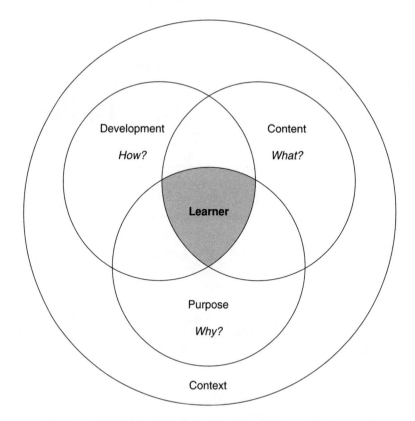

FIGURE 6.1   NCTE/IRA Model of Language Learning

Source: Fig. 1 from p. 13 of *Standards for the English Language Arts* (1996). Copyright by the International Reading Association and the National Council of Teachers of English. All rights reserved. Reprinted with permission.

A Different Set of Principles

Kibby (1995) offers a different view of literacy assessment. In Figure 6.2, we must search long and hard to find the social and cultural context of the literate act. Perhaps it is there under situational "Context Strategies" or "Recognition of purposes of reading" (item 9 under "Aspects of the Reader"). Kibby defines *reading* as a transaction between the reader and the text, listing five categories of reading abilities: "word recognition, meaningful vocabulary, reading comprehension, rates of reading comprehension, and reading study skills" (p. 29). In order to follow Kibby's model when I select tasks, I make sure that I have chances to observe the reader recognizing words, understanding word meanings, and making sense of print. I also check the reader's rate when he or she is reading with comprehension, as well as find out if the student can use reading to study subjects of interest.

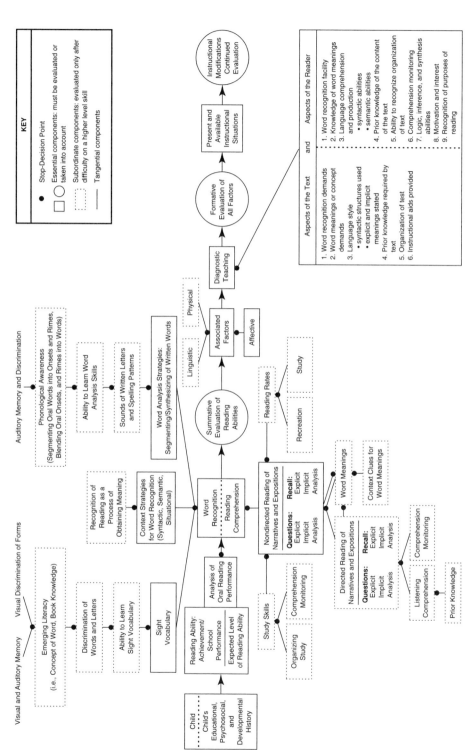

FIGURE 6.2 Kibby's Diagnostic Model

Source: Figure from Kibby, Michael W. (1995). *Practical steps for informing literacy instruction: A diagnostic decision-making model.* Newark, DE: International Reading Association. Reprinted with permission of Michael W. Kibby and the International Reading Association. All rights reserved.

105

I like to combine these complementary philosophical approaches when I assemble an assessment package. The NCTE/IRA standards lead me to include interviews to decide what the reader or writer thinks about literacy. They remind me not only to consider what the context for the reading and writing is but also to observe reading and writing done in a variety of contexts. And most important, these standards keep me focused on how the student's current knowledge is facilitating or impeding continued development of reading and writing abilities.

Kibby, on the other hand, directs me to the page. He reminds me that I do not need to assess visual discrimination or auditory memory as isolated "perceptual skills when a child has already learned even a few of the reading strategies or skills that these perceptual skills are thought to precede . . . they are to be assessed only when a child has absolutely no reading or literacy strategies at all and is unable to learn any single reading strategy with direct instruction—which never happens" (pp. 18–19). Therefore, Kibby directs me to his five central reading abilities observed in as holistic a fashion as possible, then probes to reveal underlying weakness if necessary. Kibby reminds me I am not a medical doctor; I am a reading and writing teacher.

The Problem with Problems

I part company with Kibby, however, at his definition of a *reading problem*. Kibby asks whether a student's current abilities are satisfactory in light of his or her capacity. He critiques the use of IQ measures, listening comprehension, and discrepancy formulas. Discrepancy formulas measure the difference between IQ scores (such as the WISC-III) or listening vocabulary scores (such at the PPVT-R) and reading achievement scores. Kibby concludes that children with low-average, average, or high-average IQ or listening vocabulary scores should be reading at grade level. Discrepancy formulas can be used to decide whether children of above- or below-average potential have significantly divergent reading achievement. We should be careful when applying such formulas to poor children and we should not use them at all with second language students, he says.

First, Kibby's definition of *satisfactory* rests on testing. This book seeks to end diagnosis of reading problems based on tests that require little if any reading. Second, *reading at grade level* means many things, from the ability to score near grade-level norms on a standardized test, to the ability to get satisfactory grades in a class with same-age cohorts. Third, the emphasis on *problem* is misguided. All the students I see either think they have a reading or writing problem or have parents or teachers who think that they do. In any of those cases, I would maintain there is a problem.

The important question is: What is the nature of the student's reading and writing abilities? When I ask the descriptive question, not the comparative one, I start to generate useful information. Kristen, for instance, did not have sufficient discrepancy scores to warrant being labeled as learning disabled, nor did she appear to be unable to participate in her second-grade basal reading group. However, she had not learned enough of the alphabetic nature of English to allow her to use that knowledge strategically when reading unfamiliar text or when composing pieces to be read by others. She did not voluntarily read for comprehension. Worse, her knowledge seemed to have been stalled for two years, indicating that she had not learned enough to facilitate further development, in terms of the NCTE/IRA standards. I needed to begin assembling reading and writing tasks that would illuminate her knowledge, facility, and appreciation of English, not compare her to a linguistically impoverished norm.

Inviting the Student to Select the Texts

As noted in Chapter 1, tests do little to simulate reading done outside of school or, in fact, outside the testing room. Tests choose the reading material, whereas the individual chooses his or her own books, magazines, or newspapers when not being tested. Therefore, I begin by asking students to choose what they will read with me.

After my initial conversation with the parent or guardian, I send home a request for information and help (Figure 2.1). I ask for all educational and testing records the parent has or can get copies of, but I also ask that the student choose three pieces of reading to read with me: an *easy* one, a *just-right* one, and a *challenging* one. These terms, which come from Leslie Funkhouser's second-grade classroom at Mast Way School (Hansen, 1987), demonstrate that readers can decide for themselves what they can read on their own (easy), with help (just right), and with a good deal of difficulty (challenge).

Other reading educators have used similar concepts for decades to describe the span of children's reading abilities. Clay (1993) calls them *easy* (accuracy of word recognition in oral reading of at least 95 percent), *instructional* (accuracy between 90 and 95 percent), and *hard* (accuracy less than 90 percent). Johnston (1992) uses *easy, learning,* and *hard.* More traditional terms are *independent, instructional,* and *frustration* (Betts, 1954), but the percentages are the same, or nearly so.

Corresponding percentages for successful comprehension vary more across the reading community, but Barr and associates (1995) take a middle view. They suggest 90 percent as appropriate for independent or easy reading, 75 percent for unprepared reading of instructional text, and 50 percent as indicating frustration with text that is too hard. Naturally, the use of percentages implies a system based on prepared questions with scorable answers.

Informal reading inventories (IRIs) are created from basal reading systems with designated books for specific grade levels, or from passages evaluated by one or another of the readability formulas, to produce a set of passages ordered in increasing levels of difficulty. They include questions or guidelines for scoring retellings. The examiner's copy of the passage is generally double-spaced to allow interlinear notes of deviations from print.

I have used IRIs for decades with thousands of students. I have gotten better information from them than from standardized test scores. I can see, for instance, some patterns of word recognition, the balance between word recognition and comprehension strengths and weaknesses, and perhaps even the rate of reading, although the passages are pretty short for that. Perhaps they are best as quick screening devices to find the five or six children in my class who cannot read anywhere near grade level. Of course, last year's teachers can tell me that. Perhaps they also serve as quick measures of growth; in September, Toby could read only with 95 percent accuracy and 90 percent comprehension in grade-3 material, but now he can read with the same percentages in grade-5 material.

I admit that IRIs are convenient alternatives to opaque test scores. However, I agree with Weaver (1988) that the passages are too short, the questions are often not dependent on a careful reading of the text, and questioning itself fails to recognize that readers often get very different but equally valid meanings from the same passage. Many newer IRIs have responded to such critiques. The *Bader Reading and Language Inventory,* second edition (Bader & Wiesendanger, 1994) includes both questions and guidelines for retells. The *Analytic Reading Inventory,* fourth edition (Woods & Moe, 1989), includes a miscue analysis sheet. Leslie and Caldwell (1995) in the *Qualitative Reading Inventory—II* include both these features. No IRI, however, allows a reader to choose the passage read.

Running Records Allow Reader Choice

Running records of children's oral reading, as demonstrated by Clay (1993) or Johnston (1997), allow the teacher to sit next to any reader and obtain the same information about word recognition in context that IRIs allow. I stood next to the ladder going from the floor to the top bunk of Kristen's bunk beds as she read *A Kiss for Little Bear* (Minarik, 1968). She sat on a step of the ladder and held the book while I looked over her shoulder. The tape recorder sat nearby on her desk. Kristen was in charge of what she read and where she read it, and the conditions could not have been more different from the classroom we had just left.

However, Kristen's reading strategies were the same. She predicted heavily from context in familiar text but seldom self-corrected from print. In class, for instance, she misread *Daniel said* as *said Daniel* and read *light* for *rights*. At home, she self-corrected as many as 40 percent of her miscues in the familiar *A Kiss for Little Bear* when over half of them made sense anyway, but only 30 percent in new reading (*Corey's Pony Is Missing*) and only 15 percent preserved meaning. In class, she read publicly and was corrected by others when she miscued, but she had prepared by reading the story with a tutor and a partner. At home, she read in private, was not corrected, and read both prepared and new text. In both cases, she used familiarity with the meaning to guide her word recognition, but she could not use word recognition to generate useful context on her own, even given the privacy of her own room and a new book from her own bookshelf.

Running records, then, allow us to follow the child, not the dictates of the testing format. We are doing what Vygotsky urged in *Mind in Society* (1978): allowing our questions to determine the method of investigation, not the testing method to dictate the questions. In Kristen's case, I changed the social context of the reading and the familiarity of the text, and I found that text familiarity, not the social conditions, controlled how Kristen reads. Therefore, I knew I needed more information about her word recognition abilities.

Finding the Range of Success

Weaver (1988) emphasizes analyzing miscues from instructional material, not from material that is too frustrating, since we want to see what children know when they are making meaning. But I still like to determine whether any text is easy for the student. Kristen, for instance, initially read "The House That Nobody Wanted" for me with 91 percent accuracy, making 52 miscues in 581 words. She had already read this piece with a tutor in class, and 91 percent was at the lower end of the instructional range. I had her select another familiar piece, *A Kiss for Little Bear*, but she read this with only 84 percent accuracy, although she understood the story. Her mother had already told me that no reading other than Dr. Seuss books was easy for Kristen and that she did not read voluntarily. These performances confirmed that, even in familiar material, Kristen's word recognition was not automatic, so she had little, if any, easy text. With support, she was able to read materials appropriate for her grade.

Mike, on the other hand, brought with him a book appropriate for fifth grade, *The Whipping Boy* (Fleishman, 1986), but he labored through the first two pages of Chapter 18 with 87 percent accuracy and 22 miscues. His retell lacked detail and he followed the pictures more closely than the story, so I asked him to choose from a selection of beginning chapter books. He selected *Nate the Great and the Boring Beach Bag* (Sharmat, 1987) and read with 97 percent accuracy and only 5 miscues. His retell was somewhat inaccurate due to trouble with pronouns, but Mike clearly had more automatic word recognition than Kristen, and therefore a wider instructional band of material in which he could succeed.

Analyzing Miscues for Strategies

I can learn much more from a child's oral reading than simply how difficult the text is for him or her. As Weaver (1988) and Johnston (1997) point out, not all miscues are equal and not all indicate weaknesses. I need, as much as possible, to find out what the child is thinking as he or she reads. For instance, I ask the child why he or she chose the piece to read to me. Andrew chose the article on the Red Sox because he liked sports and he was interested to know if the Sox might do well on their West Coast road trip. Tara picked the story about the giant because her class had read it earlier in the year and she had done well on it. She also brought an American Girl Doll series book, *The Christmas Surprise*, because she had an American Girl Doll of her own. Both these readers had reasons connected to their lives and interests for their selections.

Jason could not recall a book he wanted to bring, so his teacher gave his mother one to bring with him that she knew he had read during the school year. Mike brought the book he was currently reading in school, although it was clearly too hard for him to read comfortably. Neither of these boys chose to read; Jason could not think of books by name or story, and Mike apparently did not know that some reading can be easy, as indicated by his choice of *The Whipping Boy* as his easiest piece.

It is important that our observations seem as little like tests as possible. Weaver (1988) suggests we tell the reader that we will be taking notes of the reading and that the child is to do what he or she does when no one is around to help with an unknown word or a confusing part. Johnston (1997) stresses that we should sit next to the child, with our writing hand as far away from the child as possible to reduce distraction. However, we should explain that we will be putting a mark for each word the child says and that we are willing to discuss our marks or ideas any time the child has a question. I find that all readers, but especially those for whom reading is difficult, respond well to this sharing of information and intentions. No longer is the "testing" a mystery. Also, no longer does every mark I make indicate a mistake by the reader. When I used only IRIs, I found my students quickly learned to listen for marks and responded with flinchs.

Counting the Miscues

Johnston (1997) counts omissions, insertions, substitutions, and words the teacher helps the student with as miscues. He does not include repetitions, self-corrections, hesitations, or ignored punctuation in the miscue count. Not only do I agree but I also follow Johnston and Weaver (1988) in their advice not to count the same miscue repeated, nor each word in a whole line skipped (just count it as one miscue and delete the number of words over that from the total count of the passage), nor a series of miscues tied to one original misreading. However, I do take note of all these other behaviors as signs of dysfluent reading and I begin to question a student's sight word recognition or sense of how text should sound if too many of these occur. Like Andrew, students may overcorrect and lose overall meaning by paying too close attention to surface accuracy.

The aim is to find what the student can do comfortably enough from which to learn. I recall sitting with my alto recorder in front of my Trapp family instructional book with a friend, trying to pick out the fingerings and notes in a Christmas tune. I got my fingers in the right place but I must have been playing gibberish, because she stopped me, said, "Listen to this," and proceeded to play an enchanting little melody I can recall to this day. The next time I tried the fingerings, my ear led my fingers to smoother movements. A student may be able to read with adequate accuracy, by gross miscue counts, but he or she may need a little choral reading with someone whose ear is more tuned to the sounds of print.

During the reading, then, I intervene as little as possible. When I do, I follow Johnston's (1997) advice and say, "Try again," since that indicates that the student did not know that she or he did not know. As well, I mark when the child asks for help and when I finally tell him or her the word. (I will discuss lengthier interventions in the dynamic assessment section later.)

Like Weaver (1988), I list all of the student's miscues on a chart and compare them to the text (see Mike's case report at the end of this chapter). Next, I ask if the word matches preceding context. Weaver suggests that readers succeeding with an instructional-level text should be predicting correctly from context 60 percent of the time; in Mike's *Whipping Boy* passage, he achieved 55 percent. Weaver also suggests that successful readers match following context 60 percent of the time, as well; Mike's miscues only fit 27 percent of the following sentences. This means that Mike's guesses at unfamiliar words fit syntactically about half the time with what he has just read, but only fit one-fourth of the phrases coming up. Worse yet, the predictions only work semantically (meaning preserving) 18 percent of the time, or less than once in five chances.

In Johnston's (1997) terms, Mike is predicting from syntax, which is a strength, but he should also be correcting from meaning, since the predictions were not working out. However, although he corrects 36 percent of the time, better than Weaver's 30 percent minimum suggestion, Mike's resulting comprehending or process percentage is only 50 percent self-corrected or meaning-preserving. Since his retell is also spare and confused on many details, following the pictures more closely than the text, we can see that his product or comprehension score was less than adequate.

By contrast, Mike made 8 self-corrections, 2 of them completions of partial words, 2 of them graphically the same but semantically inappropriate (*judgler* for *juggler* and *listing* for *listening*), and 4 semantically appropriate but graphically dissimilar (*you* for *me, enormous* for *immense, haul* for *hauling,* and *let* for *let's*). In other words, he corrected most often from print, not context, just as 19 of his 22 original guesses resembled the target word in spelling. So, he attempted to sound out words, as he had been taught, but did not use all of the language systems to crosscheck the logic of his guesses.

Synthetic or Analytic Phonics?

Barr and colleagues (1995) further analyze decoding strategies in oral reading, asking about errors in content words if the reader employs letter-by-letter synthesis, analogizing, or contextual guessing. For instance, Kristen made 72 substitution miscues in three oral passages. Of those, 29 matched context but not print (*was* for *had* or *fence* for *windows*). The bulk, 41, matched the initial or initial and medial sounds (*get* for *go, growing* for *grass,* and *pulled* for *put*), but only two matched the spelling patterns typical of analogy methods, or analytic phonics (*his* for *this* and *is* for *his*). Even these two miscues could be considered basic sight word confusions instead of analogizing.

Kristen, remember, had been taught a "modified" Reading Recovery and the Benchmark program. However, in oral reading she did not integrate reading strategies in a way typical of Reading Recovery teaching, nor did she use spelling patterns emphasized by the Benchmark approach. Perhaps her failure to benefit from instruction can be explained in part by the fact that in class she only read out loud, round-robin style, with corrections, not strategic questions, being offered.

Retellings, Not Questions

Once the reading is finished, Weaver (1988) and Barr and colleagues (1995) suggest having the reader retell as much as possible from the passage, then following up with questions to probe for any aspects not covered, at least asking, "Is there anything else you want to tell me or can remember?" I ask younger students, or ones who have never been asked to retell a passage in their own words, to retell the piece as if to a friend who is not there. Weaver reminds us to avoid questions that can be answered *yes* or *no* and to be careful that our questions do not frame insights we desire from the reader. She suggests we ask if any parts were troublesome. I also follow Rhodes and Shanklin's (1993) suggestion and observe, "You seemed to be thinking hard at this point (point it out). What were you thinking?"

Weaver (1988) uses a seven-point holistic scale (1 = poor, 3 = adequate, 5 = good, 7 = excellent) to rate the retell, allowing a midpoint of 4, but setting "adequate" below the midpoint. I prefer a four-point system (1 = poor, 2 = OK, 3 = good, 4 = excellent), since it eliminates the midpoint. I must choose twice between better and worse: 1 or 2 = among the worst I have heard or would expect; 3 or 4 = among the best. Then, 1 = the worst of the worst, while 2 = the best of the worst; 3 = the worst of the best, while 4 = the best of the best. Retells scored 1 or 2 show a weakness comprehending the passage; 3s and 4s indicate strength.

I follow Weaver's (1988) suggestion and have students who cannot successfully retell or discuss any passage read orally to read silently and then retell. The student who recalls more fully after silent reading may be devoting more attention to word recognition in order to read orally. I then check silent reading speed against the Gilmore and Gilmore (1968) chart to see if silent reading speed is slow, possibly due to lack of automatic word recognition (see Table 6.1). I look for further corroboration of instant word recognition in word-by-word or dysfluent oral reading, miscues on basic (Dolch) sight words, or spelling difficulty. As Barr and colleagues (1995) point out, there is no sense teaching comprehension skills to someone who comprehends well when he or she does not need to decode the words.

Look-Backs

Never assume a reader did not remember a detail simply because he or she did not say it in his or her unprompted retell. Even good readers will leave out information they feel to be either trivial or obvious. Even when a reader fails to respond to one of my questions, I give the passage back and ask him or her to look for the answer

TABLE 6.1 Gilmore and Gilmore's (1968) Reading Speed Chart

Oral Rate		Silent Rate	
Grade Level	Words per Minute	Grade	Words per Minute
1.8	30–54	2	86
2.8	66–104	3	116
3.8	86–124	4	155
4.8	95–130	5	177
5.8	108–140	6	206
6.8	112–145	7	215
7.8	122–155	8	237
8.8	136–157	9	252
		12	251

(Paratore & Indrisano, 1987). The student who knows just where to look, such as Andrew with the word *herbology*, has demonstrated a working knowledge of text structure. If the child still cannot find the desired information, I generally direct him or her to the section; if the child is still confused, I point to the exact sentence(s).

Mike (see the case report in this chapter) was confused about who did what in *Nate the Great and the Boring Beach Bag*. Mike said that "he" lost his beach bag, but there are two boys in the story. I asked him to look back and find out who had lost the bag. He found a picture of Nate swimming with his dog and said, "Him." I asked if he meant Nate, and Mike looked more closely at the picture and saw another boy following Nate. He realized that Oliver had been following Nate in the water and that it was Oliver who had lost the bag. Mike's speech and language testing revealed a weakness with pronouns, and the pictures here helped him overcome this weakness. Paratore and Indrisano's (1987) progressive look-back strategy helped me see both Mike's weakness with grammar in action and his relative strength with text structure.

Vocabulary Probes

Barr and associates (1995) probe vocabulary knowledge before deciding that a student has difficulty comprehending text due to other factors. In Mike's case, he had miscued on a number of important content words in his passage from *The Whipping Boy* (see the case report in this chapter). Barr and colleagues suggest listing the key content words missed and asking the student to try again. I point the word out in the text and ask for a retry, since I want to see how the student recognizes or attempts to recognize new or difficult words in context. Mike had said *cobballed* for *cobbled* and guessed the same when I pointed the word out after his reading. I broke the word into two parts: *cob-* and *-bled*. But he still made the same guess. I pronounced it for him, and he still did not know what it meant. Clearly, it was a new word for Mike. He had the same trouble with *turf,* although he guessed it meant "somewhere or a place." When I pronounced *fowl* for him, he said he knew about "foul language" but he could see that did not make sense in the sentence in question.

Mike recognized the other miscued content words (*immense, banners, copper, battered, pump,* and *crowd*) when asked to look back, although *pump* took some work. At first, he could not say it. I showed him *pumpkin* and he got it with that analogy. However, the sound did not produce retrieval of the meaning. When I gave him the meaning, he recalled seeing a pump on a class trip to a colonial village.

Mike had trouble understanding this passage because of difficult vocabulary in three of nine cases, but five of the words he had in memory yet failed to decode, and another he could not connect to his experience even when he heard it. Mike would benefit more in less frustrating material, practicing skills he already had, than from direct instruction in comprehension strategies he applied when not overloaded by word recognition.

Scoring and Analyzing Retells

When I finish observing how a student works with words in oral reading, I ask the reader to retell the piece as he or she would to a friend who has not read it. Of course, I cannot score a retell without guidelines, at least general ones, in mind. I ask the student to choose passages *before* meeting with me, then I ask the parent to send the passages to me so that I may prepare for the reading. With stories, I can write out a story ladder (Johnson & Louis, 1987) or list of story grammar elements (characters, setting, problem, and attempts at resolution). A story ladder is simply a five- or six-sentence summary in which the second half of each sentence is left off. In class, students would read or listen to complete them. In my case, I listen to see if the retell completes it.

Rhodes and Dudley-Marling (1996) mention six guidelines for scoring re-tellings, including evidence of story structure or logic, the amount retold, evidence of inference, extra or false information, evidence of prior knowledge, and the degree to which the details are connected to the main idea. I can remember a short list such as this one without having to resort to a checklist in front of the reader.

None of the students in this book was able to think of material he or she wanted to read with me early enough for the parents to copy it and send it along. However, I taped the sessions, asked follow-up questions at the time, and checked the retells in depth afterwards. Sadie (see Chapter 2), for instance, chose an easy story about a cat and a mouse that go fishing. She chose this passage, as she did all her selections, because it was short and it dealt with animals. She predicted that the mouse would be better at fishing because books sometimes have surprise endings. After reading, she noted that her prediction had not come true, for both the cat and the mouse had made mistakes and fallen into the water.

I chose not to pursue her retelling with a comprehensive list of questions and answers. Sadie's prediction had focused her reading and she had attended to details enough to draw a conclusion ("they both made mistakes") and to invalidate her prediction. She showed me that she sets purposes for reading by having preferred subject matter (animals), knowing how stories work (sometimes the opposite of what one would expect happens), and predicting based on the details of the story (a small mouse and a large cat) and her knowledge of literature (the smaller sometimes wins). Moreover, she read to confirm or reject her prediction (they both erred and fell overboard) and revised it as needed. Despite her word-by-word reading, Sadie did what good readers do.

Retelling Informational Text

Andrew selected an informational article to read in his career interest area—physical training and health. Not only did he choose a piece related to his interest and prior knowledge but he also had a good sense of what would challenge him. He predicted the reading would be hard because it had technical vocabulary.

I observed Andrew as he found the article in the magazine, *Let's Live*. He used the cover of the magazine to find the subject of the article he planned to read (mushrooms), used the table of contents to find a related title ("Medicinal Mushrooms, Part I: How Mushrooms Fit the Mold for Health and Healing"), and turned to the appropriate page (page 78). From the title and headings, Andrew predicted the article would be about mushrooms and how they are nutritious. He said he expected to learn about different types of mushrooms, but admitted that he never ate mushrooms and did not know much about them.

"You never had a mushroom on a pizza?" I asked, since he delivers them.

"Never tasted one. Well, maybe I had one when I was a kid, but I didn't like it, so that's why I don't eat them," he explained.

"Never went back, huh?"

"Nope. Never."

Andrew also did what good readers do. In this case, he used the parts of the magazine to locate information and to use the graphic displays to focus on the purpose of the reading. He predicted what he might encounter and alerted himself to new terms and information that could arise.

After reading the passage with 94 percent word recognition accuracy, he summarized the section as follows:

> They're not just for cooking anymore. They're used for medical reasons, to kick up the immune system on such things as cancer and AIDS and the flu. And there are lots of different kinds, like the miatic (maitake) and the tiakay (shiitake) and some other long names. They have been used in Japan and China and a study called, some -ology (looks back)—it was right up here . . . herbology (explains it is the study of herbs and what they can do for you and what is in them). It

said there were more than two hundred varieties. Pretty much it. They're used for illnesses. How Americans are trying to bring up their health and study for that.

Using the text structure of a generalization passage (Cook & Mayer, 1988), we can see that Andrew gave a retelling of the major idea (mushrooms are used medicinally as well as nutritionally) and some of the most striking details (they kick up the immune system against cancer, AIDS, and the flu; Americans are eating for health; many varieties are from China and Japan). He was able to find the technical word *herbology* after reading in order to complete his retelling and he used his knowledge of suffixes to figure out the meaning. He did not pick up the details of technical vocabulary, and misread "200 varieties of mushroom formulations for ailments" as "200 varieties of mushrooms." Overall, Andrew scored perhaps a 3 on my four-point scale. Unlike Sadie, Andrew read the passage fluently (except for the chemical and mushroom names), but his comprehension was limited by his access to technical terms. In more detailed reading, especially for study purposes, it is likely that Andrew will have trouble.

Being Dynamic

When I probed how Mike understood important content words or how Andrew knew *herbology,* I was practicing dynamic assessment. Traditional testing pretends to be objective, presenting the stimulus but offering no feedback or help with the response. Writers such as Paratore and Indrisano (1987) and Carney and Cioffi (1990) show how to offer suggestions as a means to see what the reader can do with help as well as to find out what help works.

For instance, Andrew predicted his Red Sox article would be about their most recent game. When I asked him why he thought so, he said he saw a play from the game pictured next to the article. I knew the article was about their upcoming road trip compared to an earlier, successful one, so I directed him to the headline ("Sox Look for More West Success") and the subhead ("First Trip Was Great but AL West Teams Playing Better Now"). He changed his prediction to finding out how the Sox hope to win in the West, even though the western teams are playing better than when the Sox beat them earlier. I learned that Andrew did not necessarily use heads and subheads to guide his reading for information but that when helped to do so, he could make proper use of the information. With his change in attitude and medication, he was able to profit from study skills tutoring.

Carney and Cioffi (1990) list ways to aid students in recognizing printed words. For instance, since Mike had read *crown* for *crowd,* I wrote both words on a piece of paper and showed Mike what he had said (*crown*) and what the word is as printed (*crowd*), and he understood. Dividing *cobbled* into parts did not help Mike, but then I found that was because he did not know the word. When I compared *pump* to *pumpkin* for him, he was able to sound out *pump.*

Jason also benefited from dynamic intervention, a method practiced by Reading Recovery teachers. When Jason could not read *pal,* I asked him how he knew to figure it out, but no ideas came to mind. I suggested he try the sentence from the beginning, and he got the word, showing me that he had trouble maintaining context in mind as he tried to recognize words. He could, however, regenerate context and try again. (He also demonstrated he knew how to find the beginning of a sentence, as we will see later in this chapter.)

When Jason read *The van has no gas* as *The van is out gas*, he matched the number of words and tried to put the phrase into more natural language. I covered the words around *no*, focusing him on the print he was ignoring. He read the sentence correctly. Jason showed that he either had strategies and knowledge that did not come to mind or that he could learn how to apply them in context with appropriate support. Clearly, an integrated, supported reading model such as Reading Recovery would be more helpful than continued drill in isolated sight words and single-letter phonics patterns and copying of dictated writing.

Phonological Recoding Knowledge

Most of the students I see have trouble with decoding and spelling. They have been taught and tested, but, in general, they do not recognize nor produce print effectively under the stress of assigned reading nor automatically enough to make reading and writing enjoyable and voluntary.

Having read their records, then, I still needed to see what they had learned from the single-letter phonics method (Jason) or the workbook approach (Sadie) and how they applied that knowledge in authentic reading tasks. Of course, miscue analysis shows me a great deal about strategies in context, but in brief readings, miscue analysis cannot offer comprehensive information about phonics knowledge. On the other hand, most of these students were tested with isolated synthetic phonics tasks. (Say the sound /cr/ makes. Say the little word *at*. Say what they say together.) Readers do not need to blend isolated word fragments into nonsense words in actual reading, of course. Alternatively, I can substitute low-frequency real words for the nonsense words, thereby nominally preserving the meaning-making aspect of phonics in use.

I prefer the Names Test (Duffelmeyer et al., 1994), since it is a list of 35 names (first and last names produce 70 examples) that can be analyzed to show knowledge of the spectrum of sound-letter relationships in English. With young or struggling readers, such as Kristen, Sadie, or Jason, I suggest putting the names on index cards to avoid overwhelming them with unfamiliar print.

Mike and Andrew demonstrated strengths with word analysis across settings. Mike scored in the 44th percentile on the Woodcock Reading Mastery Test (WRMT) word attack subtest (synthetic blending of nonwords) and in the 55th and 49th percentiles, respectively, on his second- and fourth-grade Stanford Achievement Test word study skills subtest. Mike generally produced miscues similar to the target words in graphophonic content and he self-corrected most often from print.

Andrew scored at the 12.9 grade level on the WRMT word attack in grade 10 and read the Names Test with 98 percent accuracy. In addition, Andrew self-corrected 60 percent of the time and produced 12 of 17 graphophonically similar substitution miscues. Although he scored only 7.5 grade level on the Morrison McCall spelling task in grade 10, he wrote extemporaneously with 96 percent spelling accuracy on a self-selected topic with me.

Jason could respond to only 4 of the 35 names on the Names Test, so I stopped the procedure with him. Sadie and Kristen also had much difficulty with the task, but I begged them to try it for me, giving them all the time they wanted. I found Sadie's results particularly useful.

Sadie had been tested in grade 3 with the WJ–R and scored in the 23rd percentile for sight word and decoding ability and in the 13th percentile for spelling and mechanics dictation. Although she did poorly on the Names Test as well, I knew a lot more about her decoding ability when she finished. Sadie knew most of the consonant sounds (92 percent) and consonant digraphs (80 percent), sounds usually learned in first grade. She did less well with vowels: short (50 percent), long (43 percent), digraphs (60 percent), *r*-controlled (68 percent), and schwa (33 percent). She also recognized only 63 percent of the consonant blends.

Despite her grade-level score of 2.5 on the WJ-R, these results look like a first-grader's knowledge of phonics to me. It is also interesting to observe that the lowest scores (schwa, long, and short vowels) came on the most irregularly spelled sounds in English. Combined with her low spelling scores and her consistent but mostly invented spelling, these results describe someone who understands the concept of phonics but has such disorganized information about sound-letter relationships and poor visual memory for word forms that she tires rapidly when processing print and applies her knowledge sporadically.

Older Emergent Readers

Readers such as Jason, despite their age, can best be understood as emergent readers. I use the term *emergent reading* rather than *reading readiness* because I read the work of Harste and colleagues (1984) and Ehri (1987) and I realize they ask different questions, the former being, "What *do* emergent readers know about print?" and the latter, "What *don't* they know?" Author Jane Hansen once responded to a draft of mine by writing and underlining in the margin of one page, "Jay, emergent readers don't *pretend* to read. They *READ!*" Hansen, in her quiet, subtle way, reminded me to look at what children were doing, not what I thought they should be doing.

Jason's mother was not willing to give up on his reading. His Reading Recovery teacher told her it would be a slow process. Most children take a few years to become fluent with a variety of texts. Patience and a search for effective methods are attitudes we would consider appropriate with 5- and 6-year-old emergent readers. Once we think of Jason as an emergent reader, we can investigate his knowledge of print as we would with a younger person.

For instance, Jason read controlled, familiar text haltingly and with many miscues. He tried to pronounce only four names on the Names Test. Perhaps I needed to know more about his phonemic awareness. I could have used the Yopp-Singer Test (Yopp, 1995), but I was engaged in helping Jason write about the story he had just read, so I tried to assess his phonemic segmentation ability using Elkonin boxes (Elkonin, 1973) (see Appendix C) as I assisted his invented spelling. He decided to write *It's Pat's ham*. He did not know how to start on *It's*, so we drew a box for each sound. He was then able to say the word, push in a coin for /i/, and make the sound for /s/, but he did not feel the /t/ as he said the word. When I pronounced it slowly, he heard it, pushed the coin into the box under the space for *T*, and wrote *T* in the second box, then *S* in the third.

Notice that Jason was not able to produce the medial sound /t/ and hear or feel it at the same time, but he could hear it when I pronounced the word for him. He could then segment the sounds mentally as he wrote them. So, the concrete movement of the coin into the box facilitated the hearing of the sound, the hearing of the sound facilitated hearing and saying the sound, and the combination facilitated the mental reproduction of the sound and the letter in the final writing. This also showed me that Jason was capable of segmenting the phonemes of English.

Selecting Tasks for Emergent Readers

When working with emergent readers of any age, I want to know the following:

- What they think reading and writing are (interview)
- What they know about the procedures and artifacts of literacy (concepts about print)
- How aware they are of phonemes within words (phonemic awareness)
- What letters they recognize (letter knowledge)
- What words they know how to read or write (dictation and sight word lists)

Following the advice of Goodman and associates (1987), I ask emergent readers what they read and write, why they read or write, what makes a good writer or reader, how to help someone be a better reader or writer, and what goals they have in reading or writing. I probe to find the names of their favorite books or authors as well as what they do when they do not know how to read or write a word. I ask when and where they read and write and who they know who reads or writes. If they have observed people, I might ask what they have seen the people do.

Concepts about Print

Clay (1993) provides an array of tasks appropriate for emergent readers and writers as well as norms for interpretation of the performances. I will show how I use the writing activities later, but for now, we will look at Johnston's (1997) more informal version of one of Clay's reading assessments, Concepts about Print. Johnston gives general guidelines for observing readers as they approach books that cover many of the topics discussed in Clay (1993). Simply put, we offer a child a book and see what he or she does with it. Does the child know which way is right way up? Front and back? Does the child know where to find the book title? The author's name? The illustrator's name? Does the child know how to find the title page? The first page? The first line? Do the child's eyes or finger or reading go left to right and stop at the last word? Does his or her reading acknowledge the difference between pictures and print? Show that each spoken word corresponds to a printed word? That book language is sometimes different from spoken language?

When I gave Jason the book his teacher had provided, I slid it across the table to him cover down. He flipped it over, turned it right side up, and flipped to the first page. I try to intervene as little as possible, and many of the preceding concepts can be observed as the student reads, especially if I do not structure my questions or situation so that I have made decisions I want the reader to make—which way is right side up, for instance.

I noticed that Jason read the last page, "The pals can gab and gab" as "they have ham and jam." The illustration showed the two rats eating sandwiches in the parking lot of the store. When I asked Jason to point to *jam*, he showed me *gab*. Here, he showed me that he expected the print to match the picture and that he expected the last word in his oral sentence to be the last word on the page.

Phoneme, Letter, and Word Knowledge

Since phonemic awareness has been shown to correlate strongly with reading success (Yopp, 1995), I use Yopp's 20-word survey to assess readers' awareness of and ability to segment the phonemes in words. Clay (1993) and Johnston (1997) provide letter inventories and dictation tasks that we can use to see if students can write letters in isolation, can find them in printed matter, and can transcribe dictated language. Clay shows how to give credit for the phonemes correctly transcribed and has norms for young writers.

Sight words are the high-frequency words accounting for most of English text, such as the list of 200 most frequent sight words in children's literature (Mason & Au, 1990). I agree with Taylor and colleagues (1995) that oral reading provides the best measure of sight word knowledge. Consequently, I note confusions with such words as a student reads or writes.

Interviewing Other Readers and Writers

Many experts who advocate that readers and writers should choose their own material suggest teachers interview students to ascertain their habits, preferences, and conceptions of reading and writing (Graves, 1994; Atwell, 1998; Rief, 1992; Weaver, 1988; Rhodes & Dudley-Marling, 1996). Some (Atwell, 1998) employ a formal, lengthy set of questions. I prefer to ask a few general questions and pursue the student's response with follow-up inquiries. I want to know what the child thinks reading and writing are: their uses, their requirements, and the feelings associated with them. Weaver (1988) asks, "What is reading?" "What do readers do?" "What is good reading?" and "What do good readers do?"

I want to know what connections reading and writing have to the child's life: collections, favorites, routines, plans, history, friends or relatives who read or write, and so on. I want to know how the child thinks of himself or herself as a reader and writer: competence, preference, aversion, need, and habits. Weaver (1988) asks, "What do you do when you don't know?" "How would you help someone?" "What would you like to do better?" and "Do you think you are a good reader?" Rhodes and Dudley-Marling (1996) include similar questions about writing as well as ones about favorite books and writers, favorite places for reading, preferred topics, and pet problems.

Only one of the students in this book was currently reading a book when I met her. Tara was reading *Where the Red Fern Grows* because her parents required her to read one-half hour per night at home. She was the only one with a favorite book, *Little Women,* which she read last year. Tara also considered herself a good reader and was interested to try the beginning of *The Great Gilly Hopkins* because her friends had read it and recommended it. Andrew did not consider himself a reader, even though he voluntarily read the sports page and wanted to get better at reading technical books for his career area of physical fitness and training. Kristen and Sadie had interests, Kristen in horses and Sadie in animals, but neither chose to read about them.

All of the students stressed accuracy at the word level as the hallmark of a good reader or writer. Jason said a good reader reads the words right, and he's not a good one because there are only a few books he can read. A good writer, he said, is one who practices writing words correctly. Mike also said a good reader gets all the words by sounding them out, but that he's not very good because he loses track of what he's reading when he tries to get the words. Mike's idea of a good book was a short book. Tara said she can be a good writer if she takes her time, because when she rushes her writing gets sloppy—poor handwriting, spelling, indentations, capitalization, and punctuation.

Their impoverished views of reading and writing showed when they tried to choose pieces to read. Only Andrew could find a selection to read that was not a school assignment (his Red Sox article from the local paper). Sadie, Kristen, and Tara chose stories read in school, and Jason read what his teacher had sent in for him. Mike brought his in-class reading book, but it was clearly too hard for him.

I am concerned that these students who have had difficulty learning to read and write do not know how to find effortless pleasure reading (what one of my colleagues calls "beach reading"). Sadie and Kristen were in classrooms using literature-based basals, anthologies of quality children's literature—stories written as literature, not as instructional material. Yet, when asked to find easy reading material, they could only find stories from their textbooks, not from a collection of children's literature on their bookshelves. And the bookshelves are there. The parents of each of the elementary students (everyone but Andrew) made a point of telling me that they had bought lots of books for their children. Still, books for fun were missing from their lives.

From 1978 to 1991, I taught English at Oyster River High School in Durham, New Hampshire, with Liz Whaley, coauthor of *Weaving in the Women* (1993). I knew that as an English major at Bowdoin College in the late 1960s, where no women attended or taught and where literature in translation only appeared in drama class, I had missed a few writers. Liz introduced me to the work of Alice Munro, Bobbie Ann Mason, Nella Larsen, Tillie Olsen, Marge Piercy, Doris Lessing, Maxine Hong Kingston, Margaret Atwood, Paule Marshall, Sheila Balantyne, Anne Tyler, and Kate Chopin. My literary studies had been incomplete to say the least.

But when I left high school teaching to enter a third-grade classroom, Liz and her coauthor, Liz Dodge, made me an even more significant present—several paperback books by Sue Grafton and Sara Paretsky. Liz and Liz, my literate friends, changed my reading habits by connecting me to easy reading—not books that are likely to replace Toni Morrison's *Beloved* as my choice for greatest American novel—but exactly the kind of reading that I, as an English major—as well as Sadie, Kristen, Jason, Mike, and Tara, as problem readers and writers—had no network to connect us to—easy, pleasure reading.

The Interview Portfolio of Writing

I use the reading interview and the selection of pieces to be read as occasions to discuss a student's ideas about reading and its place in his or her life. I do the same with writing, asking parents and children to collect three best pieces, much as the Vermont Writing Assessment (Rothman, 1988) or the National Assessment of Educational Progress (NAEP) (Gentile et al., 1995) have done. Only three of these students could comply with my request. Sadie had selected three pieces from her classroom folder—a computer-published research report on killer whales and two unedited classroom stories. Kristen brought her writing journal home with her— a daily notebook kept from the beginning of second grade with her entries, some of which had been edited by her teacher. Tara had two social studies tests and a poem about trees written in class to the prompt, "Look out the window and describe the tree. Use six descriptive details and no sentence beginning with *the, it, a,* or *this.*" None of these selections could be called rich collections of student work indicating deep engagement in reading and writing communities.

Andrew's mother had found a few papers, but one turned out to be his sister's and another he did not recall writing at all. We were left with an English assignment on Hugh Hefner to discuss. Mike's mother had found no current examples of writing he had done on his own. Jason, of course, dictated stories and copied the adult transcriptions. When I showed him a copy of the poem about the graveyard for which he had won an award, he initially did not recognize it.

The Piece, the Classroom, the Values

I asked each student to tell me which work was the best and why, how it was written, and what he or she learned about himself or herself as a writer from writing it. I repeated the process with each of the pieces. Mike, of course, had nothing to discuss, but Jason said his poem was good because he was able to think of it. I had already learned from his classroom aide that once Jason got an idea, he was hard to stop. He generally dictated his whole story onto tape without a break. Also, he did no actual composing of print (rather, he just copied the aide's transcription, and he neither read it over nor took suggestions from other writers who listened to the aide read it in workshop time). Therefore, Jason only did two things when he wrote: He thought of ideas and copied print. I would say he chose the most logical strength for his poem.

Interviewing the other students told me not only how they wrote the pieces but also how they were instructed and what attitudes they had picked up about writing (Graves, 1994). Andrew did not think his piece was good, since the only reason he had written it was to get it done. He chose Hefner, whose name he did not recognize, from the remaining two on the list of assigned research topics. He found a magazine article in the school library and watched an HBO special, took notes, and wrote the paper the night before it was due. His mother typed the pages as he finished them, and he tried to say what he thought the teacher wanted to hear. He quit when he reached the required number of pages.

I had not learned much about Andrew's knowledge as a writer, but I had learned a good deal about how he was taught (or not taught) to write. In reporting on the results of the 1992 NAEP portfolio assessment of writing, Gentile and associates (1995) found that fourth- and eighth-graders who used more "process strategies" received higher ratings on their narrative and informative writing. In general, two or more strategies were needed to make significant differences. The researchers counted the following classroom procedures as process strategies: "pre-writing, peer-conferencing, teacher conferencing, use of resources, revising, peer editing, teacher editing, and publication/sharing of a final product" (p. 88). I guess the magazine article and HBO count as "use of resources." If so, most classrooms probably teach the writing process. Such a general counting of writing practices as "process strategies" probably explains why three-fourths of the teachers polled by NAEP reported using the writing process, but the "process approach" was not associated with any better performance. Andrew's writing process was equally devoid of thoughtful content.

I needed to write with Andrew to find out if he had topics about which he thought he could write. I needed to show him how I brainstorm ideas and focus on subjects, since he had never had demonstrations of how writers work. Also, I needed to observe if Andrew was able to evaluate his writing in progress in terms of his purpose and then realign his goals or revise his product.

Strengths, Problems, Help, and Duration

Sadie, Kristen, and Tara offered me more chance to learn about their attitudes toward writing because they actually had classroom writing that they, their teachers, or their parents had saved. Rhodes and Dudley-Marling (1996) ask students about how they got ideas, how they wrote the piece, what problems they had, how they rate it now, and what they might do next. Graves (1994) reduces this list for the purpose of on-the-fly classroom conferences to: "What's up? How'd you get there? What's next?" I ask the same questions in diagnostic conferences.

Sadie told me she chose the killer whale piece as her best because it was exciting to write about. "I like how they survive in the cold ocean, and I wanted to learn more about them," she told me. Sadie valued the piece because of its subject, not its execution, indicating her writer-based, not reader-based, values (Flower, 1990). Since her peers did not share their work in workshop groups, I am not surprised that Sadie had little concern for her audience, beyond the direct address in the first sentence, "I am doing the killer whale."

When my son Zack was in second grade, he told me that his story, "Mr. Carrot," was good because it was funny and had a good ending. He knew this, he said, because his classmates laughed and were surprised that the little girl who found Mr. Carrot sleeping in her doll house ate him, "CRUNCH," at the end. Zack's reader-based attitudes developed in a reading and writing community, not on some developmental train track. Sadie also had developed attitudes we would expect in a classroom in which children do not share or respond.

Her prose also seemed typical of third-graders. She arranged attributes of the whale hierarchically (Newkirk, 1987), with physical description, team work, hunting, echolocation, and reasons for being hunted separated into paragraphs. The last details seemed randomly added, although her earlier paragraphs followed a logical order from general to specific information.

Sadie also typified young writers in her focus on the surface features of print and information during the writing process. She said she spent four or five days "cruising around," looking in books, and typing on the computer. She added that she had trouble finding the keys and spelling and that she got help from her mother and the writing program. In school, where these aids were not available, Sadie sounded out words, asked for help, or found "something else to write."

Collaboration and Intertextuality

Sadie showed me she was typical of third-grade writers when she discussed her other two writing choices. They were written in class, each during one writing time, and were written collaboratively with a friend. The first one was about a key she tried to make like her friend's story and she included her friend Caroline in the story. The story about the *Titanic* was written as a class extension activity following viewing a film about the ship, and she "did it with [her] friend." I have found that third-graders routinely use writing to form and negotiate friendships (Simmons, 1996) and that their standards for good writing often have more to do with the context of the writing than the features of the product.

Sadie also said she got the idea for her key story by "remembering exciting stories and mixing them together." Jenkins (1996) stresses intertextuality in her assessment of children's writing and writing growth, showing that her subject, Shane, developed his stories using books by Beverly Cleary and Matt Christopher, TV shows, and movies. My third-graders used all of these sources to script their stories, as well as dolls and action figures, each other's stories, newspaper articles, curricular subjects, and school and home routines.

Gardner (1982) says that children adopt popular superheroes as characters in order to exercise control over the world around them and that children demonstrate cognitive growth when they combine elements from different stories to create new ones. Sadie had done just this by using "Black Beauty"; *The Secret Garden;* trolls, goblins, and unicorns from fairy tales; and alligators in the sewer from TV cartoons. Moreover, she was aware she had done so, and she valued the "mixing" as a strength of the story.

Write with Me

I needed to observe writers such as Tara, Mike, Kristen, and Andrew as they wrote and to discuss their process with them, since they had limited products and classroom experience to consider. I have combined brainstorming, title writing, and discovery drafting from Murray (1985) into a 15- to 30-minute activity that combines demonstration, observation, production, and reflection. I call it "Write with Me" (see Figure 6.3).

I explain to the child that he or she and I will write together but on our own pieces. I will do each thing along with the child and I will share what I have written as we go along. I also explain that we will take about three minutes or so to do each part, so we probably will not be finishing the piece, just getting started.

FIGURE 6.3 Write with Me

---

1. Explain that you will be asking the student to write with you to begin a piece of writing but that you probably will not finish it. The whole process will take no more than 15 minutes.
2. Ask the student to list, as quickly as possible, people, places, or things he or she cares about and knows about. Explain that you will be doing this, too. (Allow about 3 minutes.)
3. Stop the student and share your list. Ask if he or she would like to share. Discuss at least how you would group your list into sets of items that go together. Allow about 3 minutes for the student to do this, too.
4. Ask the student if he or she would like to share his or her groups. If not, share yours and pick one to write about. Think of one or two titles that might work for a piece that includes those ideas, and share the titles with the student. Allow the student about 3 minutes to write as many titles as possible. You write, too.
5. Share your titles with the student and ask him or her to share, as well. Pick one you might write about and share your reasons. Ask the student to select one and think of why.
6. Take 3 minutes to write a fast draft on that title. (Try to observe the student as you write.)
7. Share your draft and talk about what you might write next, if you were to continue it. Ask the student what he or she might do next.

Source: Adapted from Murray (1985).

Finally, I explain that we will list things we know about, write some titles, and begin a piece. I try to observe the student as I do my writing, making brief marginal notes that I can expand on later.

When I asked Andrew to think of people, places, and things he knew about and cared about, he quickly listed the seven in Figure 1.1, focusing them on the subject of health. Mike and Tara each listed seven ideas, Kristen listed nine; only Andrew focused on a single topic. The younger children, not surprisingly, included family, school, and hobbies.

Andrew wrote four titles, as did Kristen, Mike developed six, and Tara could think only of two. Andrew associated different purposes with each of the titles. "Get Fit," for instance, connoted training for him, whereas "Shape Up" included both training and diet. Mike (see Figure 6.4) wrote six titles, three seemingly narrative ("The Roler Blads," "The Kid with Roler Blads," and "The Roler Blading Kid") and three informational ("My Roler Blading," "My Bast Fruids Roler Blads," and "All about Roler Blads"). Kristen's titles (Figure 5.4) all related to informational pieces ("Horse Bay [Day]," "Horse Dack [Back] Riding," "Horse Rids," and "Caring adout Horse"), although the last one is clearly instructional. Tara (Figure 7.2) could only think of "Playing the Piano" and "The Piano." She also wrote an instructional piece, even though she started off with her opinion that playing the piano is easy.

Despite the fact that I explained we would just start writing, not actually finish a whole piece so quickly, all of these students chose to write essays, not stories. In my research (Simmons, 1990, 1992), elementary and middle school writers most often included narratives in their portfolios of classroom pieces or wrote narratives given an open topic during timed writings. Students in districts I sampled had longer to work on pieces (two weeks in grade 5 and a month in grade 8) than Sadie, Mike, and the others here, indicating a less teacher-controlled process than the two-draft, one-day procedures reported by Tara and most teachers in the most recent NAEP study (Gentile et al., 1995).

I find it interesting that the NAEP students more often included informative than narrative pieces in their portfolios of classroom work, but achieved fewer low ratings on the narrative pieces. That is, when asked to create portfolios of their best work, they included more of what they did less well. Perhaps they had been convinced that writing for teachers, as all assessments arguably are, means writing to display knowledge, not to entertain an audience or tell a story. Certainly, my readers and writers who have had difficulty chose to write pieces focusing on "you," not on themselves. Tara, who said stories are easier to write, chose to write an informational piece when we wrote together. In any case, when these students write, teachers call the shots.

Such lack of control matters. Mike should know more about "my roler blading" than "all about roler blads," yet he chose to write the more academic piece. Kristen started writing straight off and never stopped to ask for help, indicating that it was not her job to know when she did not know how to spell something—rather, a teacher would tell her. Tara, seeing that her titles could lead to stories or essays, asked if she should write a story. "What do you think you should write?" I asked her in return. She started off with an opinion but quickly slipped into giving directions. These writers did not own their writing, and therefore were not fully engaged in it.

Attitudes of Writers

I wrote alongside these writers and stopped to share my developing stories and essays. I discussed my plans and my options, and they were able to do so, as well. When I wrote with Andrew, I brainstormed nine titles for this book, one being "Get Real: Useful Evaluation of Reading and Writing Problems." I told him I liked it because it was like Dallas Cowboy Quarterback Troy Aikman's commercials for football gear and sounded tough and angry—reflecting how I felt about the status of reading testing. It did not sound too professional, however, and not everyone is a football fan. Andrew was also able to critique his possible titles. In addition, he was able to assess his beginning efforts to complete his task and to plan what he would have to do next—a far cry from filling a page with what the teacher might want to hear.

When I wrote with Mike, I chose "newspapers" from a list of 11 things I knew and cared about. I generated 12 titles, from "At the Courthouse" (my column) to "Xmas Eve on the Beat" (a story about spending Christmas Eve at work with a photographer covering a human-interest story in the neighborhood of the editor-in-chief). I began writing, "The photographer was running between the houses firing flashbulbs. He was so overweight . . ." I went back and inserted *fat* before *photographer*. I continued writing, ". . . so overweight I was afraid he'd have a heart attack, but he came puffing back to the camera tripod where I was standing, just as the drunk guy came up and flashed a picture of the street.

" 'What are you doing?' he screamed at the drunk.

"Jerry and I had been . . ." I stopped and crossed this out, continuing the conversation between Jerry and the drunk for two more paragraphs, then explaining what Jerry and I had been assigned to cover that night.

" 'I'm taking a picture on my own front walk,' " the man replied huffily.

" 'Well, you just ruined 30 minutes work!'

"Jerry and I had been assigned to cover the neighborhood tradition of setting out candles to light the way to the Christ child . . ."

Mike, too, stopped several times during composing, not to fix spelling but to shift direction. He started to write, "First you put on your ro . . ." but crossed out *ro-* and wrote "nee pads . . ." He continued with ". . . and then you put one your rolerblads and you strap them on. a . . ." He stopped and wrote "Then" the *T* over the *a*, and went back and put a period before the new sentence. He continued with, "Then you put your hallmit on . . ." but stopped and crossed out *on* and wrote "and elpobads . . ."

Mike is doing just what I am doing, listening to the text as it comes out, realizing that the kneepads must come first or that the *on* would sound better after *the elbowpads* so as not to repeat.

With Tara, I had begun a piece on "Kicking the CD Habit," about having to resign from several music clubs while I still had a credit rating—the kind of piece Don Murray might write in his "Over 60" column in the *Boston Globe,* a piece that starts with a quirky personal situation that gets you to realize some deeper truth about yourself that you are going to have to learn to live with, possibly willingly. By the time we stopped, I had written a page and a half explaining how I had gotten the CD player, but had only two CD sets. I knew that soon I would have to get into how I had decided to enroll in music clubs to build a collection fast. Still, I liked the mock humor and round-about presentation of information in the beginning.

Tara, too, had reasons for liking what she had written: A reader could learn what songs you could play. She also knew what she needed to do next: Focus on how to learn to play the songs. All of these students, then, despite the lack of writing instruction in their histories, had demonstrated the ability to learn from meaningful demonstrations the habits and attitudes of writers.

Dynamic Observation

Tara had told me earlier that her problem with writing had to do with thinking of what to write as she was writing, although she was able to think of ideas before writing. In fact, when Tara listed ideas to write about, she was the only student of the six in this book who began associating words during listing. After writing (see Figure 7.2) "social studies, reading, playing piano, socer, comperts," Tara went back to the idea of "playing piano" and extended her list with "keys" and "sound." Given her definition of good writing as good spelling, punctuation, capitalization, and indentation, and her record of poor spelling, I suspected Tara had trouble remembering her ideas while she tried to get the surface features right. When Tara told me about her piano lessons, I made notes and gave the notes to her before she started writing (see Figure 7.3), following Graves (1994) in helping a student know and use what he or she knows to write.

While I write, I also try to observe the student at work, which is quite easy because we sit side by side at a table. Tara positioned the paper on the desk appropriately and held the pencil properly, if a little tightly. She wrote small, tight letters, referring back to the list of notes as she wrote. She did not erase or cross out at all. After writing one paragraph, she flexed her hand as if it were tired and reread what she had written. All in all, Tara wrote 68 words, spelling all but three correctly (*socer* for *soccer*, *comperts* for *computers*, and *rember* for *remember*), and missing only one comma (after an introductory adverbial clause) but six possible capital letters in song titles.

I could see that Tara wrote as she said: She concentrated on the appearance of her writing and tried to produce correct forms the first time through. She did not stop to ask for help, and the list of notes made before writing (accessible information) was useful during her writing.

Varying the Conditions of Writing

Tara learned that she could think of what to write before composing. She made notes and then referred to the notes as she wrote. She did not have a short-term or long-term memory problem, nor did she need to practice automatized retrieval. She simply used the capacity needed to retrieve ideas as she focused on spelling and other mechanics. Therefore, varying the retrieval conditions makes the capacity she has sufficient.

Jason, as well, was overloaded when trying to compose and to produce correctly spelled text. When I asked him to write a sentence about the book he had read, he first copied the title—just the technique he had been taught in school. When he tried to write, "It's Pat's ham," he was not able to retrieve the spelling information and the syntax information at once. He said, "It's Pat's ham," but he wrote, "Pat its ham"; thus, he recognized correct syntax in speech but not when producing print. Elkonin boxes enabled him to hear, reconstruct, and write "it's."

As we saw in his case report in Chapter 4, I asked Jason to write all the words he could think of, in order to separate the writing from composing syntactical sentences. However, he could write only his first name. When I dictated a sentence to Jason, he heard and wrote several initial consonant sounds. He also separated each word in space and represented each word in the message. He relied on visual memory and articulatory cues. Jason substituted basic sight words for each other and used a letter name to represent a word, as emergent writers often do. Therefore, sound, graphics, letter name, and sight word strategies were available to Jason in memory, although not reliably. He had learned some of what he had been taught, but he had not yet developed cues to tell him when to use his knowledge.

Redundancy and Triangulation

Some may argue that my analyses of the preceding examples are too detailed and lengthy to be expected of any classroom teacher. I think not. First, the lessons I have been taught by Donald Graves, Jane Hansen, Nancie Atwell, and others have been learned in classrooms. They, their graduate students, or cooperating teacher-researchers have observed "teachers and children at work" (Graves, 1983). Jenkins (1996), while following Shane through several years of classroom instruction, shows that we must corroborate one finding with another. It is not sufficient that I guessed that Sadie became tired from decoding words in my initial assessment of her in her special education room. She could merely have been frustrated with the school texts, the setting, or the length of the school day. When she repeated the pattern of reading behavior at home, with her mother and with self-selected, personally owned books, I could more justifiably conclude that her difficulty was with the print, not the context.

I was also able to triangulate data from several sources when working with Sadie. Her spelling showed me that she had poor visual memory of words but a sense of how the alphabetic principle works, since her spellings were readable if wrong. Moreover, Sadie's mother confirmed that Sadie could not use the spell-checker effectively since she did not recognize the correct spelling when it was listed. Thus, the demands of composing did not merely block retrieval. Sadie, apparently, did not have the word forms in memory to retrieve in the first place.

Such redundancy of data about the state of Sadie's word knowledge allowed me to suggest that she needed multisensory code instruction. She had experienced literature-based and workbook phonics instruction, but neither exposure to the words in reading nor paper-and-pencil drill in generalizations had created a schema into which Sadie could file new word knowledge. Given performance data across settings and her instructional history, I could new design new instruction that might work.

Good teachers notice such patterns of behavior all the time. They keep track of what they have tried and they confer with former teachers about their students. I have only made such procedures explicit and connected them to current research, theory, and best practice.

Mike, whose case report follows, avoided standardized testing during most of his schooling. His parents were concerned about his inability to read aloud accurately, to write with reasonable mechanical accuracy, or to enjoy reading at home. In fifth grade, Mike found it harder and harder to do what the others in his competitive classroom were doing, but he had virtually no record of careful examination of his reading and writing under various conditions.

CASE REPORT: Counting the Pages

Background

Mike was a 10-year-old fifth-grader who had attended a Montessori school since second grade. He attended first grade at the Skillings Elementary School, where he was recommended for retention for young behavior, including impulsivity and trouble staying seated. He received supplemental reading help four times weekly for 25 minutes in a group of three. He was taught word recognition through flash cards, tactile approaches, and finger spelling. The group reviewed vocabulary and reread stories, and Mike was reported to have enjoyed books.

In second grade, Mike's teacher reported that his reading problems continued, especially when many symbols appeared on the page. In grade 3, his report card indicated he was able to apply phonics, word recognition, phonetic spelling, and grammar. His Stanford Achievement Test was *read to him* and his scores were as follows:

Total Reading	27th percentile
Total Language	19th percentile
Comprehension	14th percentile
Spelling	13th percentile
Vocabulary	48th percentile
Listening Comprehension	48th percentile
Word Study Skills	55th percentile
Language	27th percentile

Evidence of classwork in the first two grades included many examples of dictation of vocabulary, spelling and grammar, and punctuation rules. He wrote from dictation (apparently) a book about Mt. Rayburn, and on his own a book called *The Bad Guy*, with 100 percent spelling accuracy and two run-on sentences. The characters were "the man," "the wife," and "the police." Mike also completed a word study book with alphabetic lists, parts of speech, and vowel sound groups.

His composition book included punctuation rule dictation, cursive practice, and science and social studies fact dictations.

The grade 4 Stanford Test was also read to him, yielding the following results:

Total Reading	33rd percentile
Total Language	25th percentile
Comprehension	22nd percentile
Spelling	8th percentile
Vocabulary	51st percentile
Listening Comprehension	62nd percentile
Word Study Skills	49th percentile
Language	58th percentile

Mike's teacher reported that although Mike's energy level was "exhausting to watch," he was able to memorize challenging vocabulary with 100 percent accuracy. Spelling miscues included *raenforest, lags (legs), bittig (biting), amphibinians,* and *trapal (tropical).*

His fifth-grade teacher reported that Mike could not read directions on his own, yet he continued to work at copying from the board. Misspellings included: *yester day, i, strit, rad (red), pooem, rat (wrote), wath (what), dadelen (dandelions), yello, fello, dicidid, tastid, pesis (piece), tost, (toast),* and *chicen.*

Current Assessment

Woodcock Reading Mastery Tests

Subtest	Percentile
Word Identification	26th
Word Attack	44th
Word Comprehension	29th
Passage Comprehension	32nd

The word attack score here compares to the Stanford score in grade 4, whereas the vocabulary score is much lower (29th vs. 51st percentile), probably because the test was not read to him and because the Woodcock Test consists of analogies rather than mere sentence or passage completion. The word recognition score (credit is given if the word is pronounced, regardless of knowledge of meaning) on the Woodcock was also in the 29th percentile, indicating his problem with the vocabulary was attributed more to word recognition than to word knowledge. His comprehension score on the Woodcock was actually higher than on the Stanford (32nd vs. 22nd percentile).

Reading for Meaning

Mike read a 164-word passage from *The Whipping Boy* by Sid Fleishman (Greenwillow Press, 1986). He said he read a chapter a day in class and tried "to get all the words" by working with his teacher who "tells me to sound it out." He told me he had trouble remembering the story when he read it, so his teacher would help him by explaining the words and by asking him at the end of every page if he knew what he had read about.

Mike said the book is about a boy who is whipped in place of the prince when the prince gets in trouble, because a prince cannot be whipped. He said the two ran away because the prince had no friends and then "those two" got them, and they tried to escape. He had trouble finding the page where he had left off, and said that this was a harder chapter because it was 10½ pages long. He expected the chapter to be about the pair catching up to the coach, and the two guys come back and chase them, and they help the carriage, and the guy is going to a fair, and going to the "hot potato guy." He found the picture of the wagon and "hot potato guy" and the fair.

This book, appropriate for fifth grade, is obviously too hard for him to profit by reading from it daily. His miscues are tabulated here:

Passage 1 (Oral).   *The Whipping Boy,* Sid Fleishman, Greenwillow Press: 164 words, 22 miscues, 87 percent accuracy rate, 36 percent self-correction rate

Mike	Text	Matches Preceding Context	Matches Following Context	Self-Corrects	Preserves Meaning	Corrected or Preserves Meaning
cobballed	cobbled	no	no	no	no	no
enormous	immense	yes	yes	yes	yes	yes
above	aboard	no	no	no	no	no
con	contrast	yes	no	yes	no	yes
barns	banners	yes	yes	no	no	no
the	a	yes	yes	no	yes	yes
smaller	seller	yes	no	no	no	no
flower	fowl	no	no	no	no	no
judgler	juggler	no	no	yes	no	yes
Bessly	Betsy	yes	yes	no	yes	yes
came	come	no	no	no	no	no
let	let's	yes	no	yes	no	yes
crown	crowd	yes	yes	no	no	no
popper	copper	no	no	no	no	no
bettered	battered	no	no	no	no	no
haul	hauling	yes	no	yes	no	yes
off	out	yes	yes	no	yes	yes
listing	listening	yes	no	yes	no	yes
stom	stomach	no	no	yes	no	yes
you	me	yes	no	yes	no	yes
pun	pump	no	no	no	no	no
I	eh	no	no	no	no	no
		55%	27%	36%	18%	50%

This pattern of miscues further illustrated the difficulty of such a passage for Mike. He made less than 60 percent usage of preceding context to predict words, instead focusing on sounding them out, as he has been taught. When only 27 percent of the guesses fit the following context and even fewer (18 percent) preserve overall meaning, he corrected only 36 percent of the time. Therefore, Mike focused on word-level information, not constructing sentence-level context to help him match the sounds to a known word, or, as he said, building context to remember.

Mike retold the passage as, "They were in the carriage going to the fair." When asked, he could not recall where the fair was, but looking back, he found it was in the city. He could not find out what happened when he looked back. When asked specifically what Captain Nips was going to do, he said, "Give them hot potatoes." He explained that Petunia was a dancing bear, but when he read over the sentence, "Come along, Petunia. Let's fetch us a crowd and earn a copper or two," he read *crown* for *crowd,* as he had in the original reading. When asked to look at the word again, he corrected himself. When asked what it means to "fetch a crowd," Mike said, "to get a crowd to watch," and he was able to explain that "earn a copper or two" means "to make some money."

Mike had trouble with other vocabulary in the passage. When asked what *banners* were, he said they hung from walls and said things like "Happy New Year." When I pronounced *fowl* for him, he could only define it as "foul language," but he knew that was not the right usage here. When I asked him what *battered* meant, he said "bent or broken." Overall, the vocabulary items were as follows:

Word	First Try	Retry	Help	Problem
cobbled	cobballed	cobballed	syllables	new word
immense	enormous	immense	none	word recognition
turf	somewhere	don't know		new word
banners	barns	hang from walls		word recognition
fowl	flowers	foul language		new word
copper	popper	money	look back	word recognition
battered	bettered	bent, broken		word recognition
pump	pu	pun	pumpkin	retrieval, recognition
crowd	crown	crowd	look back	word recognition

Of the nine words that he did not know, only three were new to Mike, whereas five he knew when he got the sounds. In the case of *pump,* he got the sound from the pattern in *pumpkin,* but he did not recognize it until I explained the meaning, then he connected it to a class trip to a colonial village. Thus, retrieval of meanings for orally recognized words was present but seemed less important than retrieval of words from context and partial phonetic information.

Passage 2 (Oral). *Nate the Great and the Boring Beach Bag,* Marjorie Weinman Sharmat, Dell, pages 7–11: 165 words, 5 miscues, 97 percent accuracy rate, 2 self-corrections, 40 percent self-correction rate

Mike	Text	Matches Preceding Context	Matches Following Context	Self-Corrects	Preserves Meaning	Corrected or Preserves Meaning
detetive	detective	no	no	no	no	no
Ohliver	Oliver	no	no	no	no	no
pet	pest	no	no	yes	no	yes
the	this	yes	yes	yes	yes	yes
I	It	yes	no	no	no	no
		40%	20%	40%	20%	40%

When I covered the syllables in *detective,* uncovering them one by one, Mike was able to decode *detective*. When I asked Mike why *Oliver* might begin with a capital letter, he realized it was a name and knew that "Oliver" was the name of a play.

Mike retold the passage as, "They were swimming and he lost his bag with his shoes and his seashells." He said that Nate lost his bag. When I asked him to look back, he looked at the picture of Nate swimming with his dog. I asked Mike who that was and he said, "Him." "Nate?" I asked. Then, realizing that Oliver had been following Nate and his dog, Mike was able to clarify his confusion. With questioning, Mike told me that Oliver had lost the bag and wanted Nate to get it. He explained that Nate did not look for seashells because he was a detective and they looked for clues. He explained that Oliver was the one who lost the bag, and Nate was the great detective, so Oliver needed Nate to find the bag. He also guessed that Oliver might have just dropped the bag or that someone could have picked it up.

Mike obviously understood this passage well, except for the confusion over names. He said it was easier because it was shorter, but, in fact, the passage was one word longer than the earlier one. It seemed shorter because he recognized more words immediately and knew more of the background concepts. He still did not make good use of context nor did he self-correct even when meaning was altered, and he still had trouble with sentence-level comprehension, such as recognizing who is meant by *he*.

Interview Data

I asked Mike what advice he would give a first-grader who wanted to be a good reader. He replied, "Don't skip over words. Sound them out. Try as hard as you can. If you have problems, come to me or ask your mom." Clearly, these are the strategies used by Mike. He never skipped words, even when that strategy might have helped him. For instance, when reading *The Whipping Boy,* Mike did not understand *turf*. When I asked him to reread the sentence and think of what word might fit there, he said, "A place?" Therefore, he could make use of context, but he did not realize that it could help him nor did he have practice in doing it.

When I asked Mike to describe himself as a reader, he called himself a "beginner" because he had a "hard time getting words I don't know" and "I don't remember" what was read. He said his teacher had him recall at the end of each page, and he believed he could practice doing that for himself. However, we must note that he recalled quite well in *Nate the Great,* when word recognition did not consume his attention.

Writing

Since I had no current samples of Mike's independent composing, I asked him to write a brief piece along with me. Together, we listed things we know about and care about. We shared our lists and then wrote titles for possible pieces we might write on from one of the topics we know about. After we talked about what the pieces with those titles would probably be like, we then wrote the beginning of our piece for a few minutes. Mike produced the writing shown in Figure 6.4.

He listed seven topics he knew about and cared about: soccer, math, skiing, skateboarding, Rollerblading, Mom, and Dad. He chose Rollerblading for his topic, although he could not explain why. He wrote six possible titles for pieces, the first

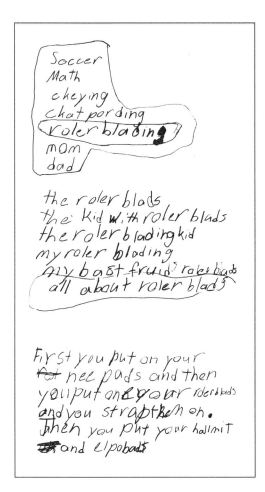

FIGURE 6.4 Mike's Writing

three being fictional in nature ("The Roller Blades," "The Kid with Rollerblades," and "The Rollerblading Kid"), while the others seemed to be nonfiction and/or expository ("My Rollerblading," "My Best Friend's Rollerblades," and "All about Roller Blades").

Of the titles Mike might have chosen, he probably knew more about his or his best friend's Rollerblades. In fact, he was able to describe for me his pair well enough that I recognized them as the same brand my son had owned, although neither of us could recall the exact name. Still, Mike chose to write on "All about Rollerblades."

He wrote 26 words in two sentences, telling how to get dressed for Roller-blading in a four-step process. He spelled 21 of 26 words correctly, and corrected 2. He began to write, "First you put on your rollerblades," but changed that to "kneepads and then you put on your rollerblades," indicating that in self-selected writing, he was able to monitor his meaning (what do I want to say first?) and his spelling at the sentence level. His misspellings reflected the same phonics general-izations he had trouble with in reading: silent *k; c* as /*s*/ or /*k*/; vowels, including silent *e* and final *y;* and consonant blends, especially those with transposable let-ters, such as *pr/p/pl, b/d, d/dr,* and *b/br.*

Summary of Current Abilities

Mike was able to read narrative material intended for second-graders with 97 per-cent accuracy and good comprehension and word skills. He could not successfully read materials intended for use with fifth-graders, probably due to lack of instanta-neous word recognition, lack of context-facilitated, automatic decoding, and lack of strategies to integrate vocabulary knowledge, context clues, and structure of text.

Mike's standardized testing placed him in the average range for his age in decoding skills and vocabulary knowledge when the words are presented orally (Stanford Achievement scores). When he had to recognize the words himself, he scored in the 25th to 30th percentile range. His listening comprehension consis-tently fell in the average range, but his silent comprehension fell in the 14th to 32nd percentile range. The latter higher score came from the Woodcock, which uses shorter (1- to 2-sentence) passages with a word missing that must be filled in, which he was able to read aloud to himself. The Stanford passages are longer and require multiple-choice recognition of answers to questions.

Since Mike could read with comprehension when he recognized more than 90 percent of the words without decoding, we can assume his comprehension dif-ficulty derived more from lack of available attention for comprehension than a lack of comprehension skill. On the other hand, Mike did evidence trouble with pronouns in his own speech and in text, not always realizing to whom or what they referred. This confusion was connected to his lack of use of sentence-level context to recognize unfamiliar words. For Mike, reading was a word-by-word process; he needed to learn to chunk print in larger units and to bring his knowl-edge to bear on the tasks made difficult by his lack of visual memory for word forms.

For instance, Mike's classroom records clearly showed that his spelling and copying deteriorated when cursive writing was introduced. On the Woodcock test, as well, he had difficulty only with letters presented in cursive writing. Therefore, it would seem that when new visual and/or motor demands were placed on Mike, his performance declined, not from lack of knowledge but from lack of attention available to apply the knowledge.

In the area of reading, the strain that visual processing or print placed on Mike's attention made it impossible for him to sound out each word *and* attend to meaning. Therefore, Mike needed to recognize more words immediately (without conscious attention) and to develop more flexible fix-up strategies when sounding out did not work.

Instructional Suggestions

Attention/Impulsivity.   Mike was able to concentrate on reading and writing during our two-hour session with three breaks. I therefore concluded that when the instructional setting was not emotionally threatening to Mike (as a classroom setting with his peers might be), there was no indication of lack of ability to attend to academic tasks, unusual impulsivity, or immature behavior. I did not find him to be overly active or unable to stay on task during the lengthy session.

Easy Reading.   Mike exhibited difficulty with visual memory of print—for instance, the confusion of *p/b/d,* the lack of instant word recognition, the poor spelling, and the reluctance to use cursive. Mike, then, needed more exposure to print, not less. Mike needed lots of easy books to read—ones in which he could recognize more than 95 percent of all words on sight. Continued reading of grade-appropriate material would only further reduce his exposure to meaningful print, while concomitantly requiring inefficient reading techniques due to the word recognition demands. Research clearly indicates that wide reading of easy material most reliably increases sight recognition of high-frequency words.

Based on their study of a summer reading program for students in grades 3, 4, and 5, Carver and Leibert (1995) question the usefulness of easy reading to improve reading ability. The authors provide pre- and posttesting of both vocabulary and rate gains, and find no evidence of improvement for those using easy text. However, there was no attempt to determine whether those reading easy texts needed to consolidate their sight word recognition in context, nor did the authors attempt to match the book to the reader in terms of difficulty. Rather, the authors used publishers' ratings of text difficulty, measured growth with brief computerized assessments, and randomly assigned "easy" books to readers with no reference to reading behavior.

Knowledge of Text Structure.   Mike needed to strengthen his knowledge of language structure at the sentence and text levels. First, I would suggest work on cloze (deletion of key words in passages) exercises, in which Mike is asked to read over the whole sentence or passage and figure out what word goes in the space.

He would need to be shown how to use syntactic markers; anaphoric relationships such as synonyms, parallel construction, and pronouns; as well as initial consonant clues to derive the word. Second, I would show Mike how to predict what will happen in a passage based on its structure: story grammar, comparison/contrast, sequence, chronological order, cause/effect, and generalization/example. Paratore and Indrisano (1987) provide a good source for this procedure. Also, Savage (1998) provides a compendium of literature-based methods for teaching context use and text structure awareness.

Strategic Reading.   Finally, Mike needed to go beyond "sound it out" as a strategy for fixing reading problems. Periodic stops to check recall (which he was already practicing with his teacher) were a good start. Combined with increased knowledge of sentence-level relationships and text structure, Mike would have a way to fill in gaps in his recall. However, he needed more options.

First, Mike was able to predict what a reading would be about; thus, the next step would be to use the prediction to check his understanding. The Directed Listening/Thinking/Reading Activity mentioned in Savage (1998) would help here. Reciprocal teaching or KWL (also in Savage) would also be helpful with expository material.

Next, Mike needed to learn to finish reading a sentence, saying "blank" for the unknown word, and to guess from meaning what might go in "the blank," then add to that his sample of print features. Alternatively, he could reread the whole sentence, regenerating context to facilitate the word recognition.

In order to make better use of Mike's existing strength in word attack, I would suggest using the word building or analogy approach (see Gunning, 1996). Letter-by-letter phonics is too attention consuming for Mike to use successfully with lengthy text. Additionally, vowel sounds are more regular in high-frequency phonograms (*-ake, -ead, -est*) than by isolated rules. Finally, I would stress the use of open and closed syllables to guess at the short or long sound, and to show Mike how to be flexible, sliding short or long guesses into the known word that fits the context.

Overall, the rote memorization and copying practice of earlier years' instruction took Mike as far as they could go. He now needed daily practice in manageable material (not frustratingly hard material) and demonstration and practice in strategic use of information he already possessed about language.

Writing.   Given Mike's lack of reliable visual memory for words, I believe he needed to be shown how to edit for spelling after he composed. Clearly, he needed to learn how to gauge how much he knew about a subject before he wrote, and to decide what sort of writing task best fits his knowledge. If his classroom used a workshop approach, Mike would benefit from learning how to incorporate the feedback of others into his rewrites.

Since the generation of conventionally spelled and punctuated print was a challenge for Mike, I would suggest he learn to type and use a word processor. Then, text would be more malleable and he would more easily be able to rewrite for surface features as well as for meaning.

7 Recommending Instruction

Multiple Frameworks to Analyze the Data

Johnston (1997) suggests evaluating a student's progress from several reference points: theory, the child, and the context. In order to follow Johnston's advice, we must choose or construct a theory of literacy. As discussed in Chapter 3, most reading experts currently propose some interactive model of reading (Adams, 1990; Kibby, 1995)—one that is neither top-down reading for meaning alone nor simplistic bottom-up addition of information and skills. Most practitioners also advocate using as many approaches as possible within a classroom in order to meet the learning needs of all students.

I combine a skills approach, exemplified by Barr and associates (1995) and Kibby (1995) (see Table 3.1); Johnston's (1997) constructivist definition of skills; a data-processing model that combines the interactive processor (described in Adams, 1990) (see Figure 3.2) with the Lahey and Bloom (1994) limited-capacity processor (Figure 2.5); and the Weaver (1988) model of reading as a sociopsycholinguistic process (Figure 3.1).

Skills

Barr and colleagues (1995) suggest diagnosing a person's reading needs by examining three layers of the process: word recognition, vocabulary knowledge, and comprehension. If a person reads a passage silently but is unable to retell it clearly and with sufficient detail for another person to understand the basic idea and main details of the piece, we might conclude the reader has a comprehension problem. Perhaps we would then teach the person comprehension strategies, such as thinking of what he or she knows about the subject before reading, predicting what might occur or be discussed, generating some questions to answer, and checking to see if the predictions or answers appeared. Our student then reads another passage on the same subject, but is still unable to discuss the reading with any comprehension or recall of main points.

Barr and associates (1995) suggest we have neglected to find out if any key vocabulary for understanding the passage is unknown to our reader. Our student may know how to understand passages but be unable to do so when too many new words appear without clear context for understanding—as it might in a piece on neurological disorders read by a lay person.

Sometimes we may have a student who knows all the key vocabulary when we discuss the words with him or her, but spends too much time figuring out what the individual words are, often getting them wrong. Then he or she cannot devote attention to understanding the meaning or retaining information. Here, Barr and associates (1995) tell us that word recognition prevents comprehension, and word recognition needs to be addressed before we know if our reader has a "comprehension problem." Kristen (see the case report in Chapter 5) scored in the high first-grade range for oral reading (which emphasizes correct word identification) on the Durrell, but, when similar passages were read to her, she scored in the fourth-grade range for listening comprehension. When she read the beginning of *Corey's Pony Is Missing,* she could not get past the word *divorced,* yet she knew that some of her friends had divorced parents and that they alternated weekends between their parents. She had the concept and the ability to use the idea to understand the text, once she had recognized the word *divorced.*

Strategic Use of Knowledge

Kristen's problem with the word *divorce* illustrates why I integrate Johnston's (1997) constructivist definition of skills with the Barr (Barr et al., 1995) model. We know that she has trouble with word recognition; in the passages that she chose to read, she correctly recognized 91 percent of the words or less in context, putting her on the borderline of frustration, at best. She also read only 18 of the 70 names on the Names Test correctly, and had not even ventured a guess on *divorced* before I intervened. We can be confident that Kristen needs to develop more instantly recognized sight words and better decoding ability. Over the past two years she was tutored with methods adapted from Reading Recovery and the Benchmark word analogy approach, yet she continued to have difficulty. We know what Kristen knows, and what she has been taught (loosely), although I am suspicious of any "modification" of Reading Recovery that involves teaching done by any person less experienced and knowledgeable than a Reading Recovery teacher. Kristen's program had been run by a teacher's aide.

We do not know how Kristen constructs meaning from her knowledge, and it is here that Johnston's (1997) framework helps. Kristen recognized *divorced* after I discussed with her what she knew about her friends who spend alternate weekends with their parents, had her recall that their parents are divorced, then had her go back and rerun the sentence. The first two passages Kristen chose to read were stories she had read before, and she often read words that made sense in context but did not match the printed word too closely. Therefore, Kristen was able to predict words from context, but in less familiar material where the word recognition demands were greater, she could not automatically integrate what she knew as she read. She simply waited to be told.

Kristen's Sociopsycholinguistic Process

Weaver (1988) describes reading by means of four circles (Figure 3.1). In the center are two circles, the text and the reader, that intersect in a transaction. Kristen reading *Corey's Pony Is Missing* is such a transaction. She brings to the text knowledge of horses and divorce, but her knowledge of graphophonemics is limited.

The reader and the text are surrounded by the immediate social context. Kristen and I were in her room in her own house, she perched on the ladder to her bunkbeds, me standing next to her, balancing a notebook to keep a running record of her reading. We had just come from her broader social linguistic context (Weaver's outermost circle), her classroom reading group. There, she sat in a semi-circle with her teacher (Ms. Borders) and 11 classmates, who volunteered to read aloud until they got stuck or misread a word. Immediately, a classmate or Ms. Borders would offer a correction.

With a full view of Kristen's reading experience, we can understand how she reads. Regardless of how much information on strategic reading she acquired from her Reading Recovery-type tutoring, she was getting precious little opportunity to practice "being strategic," as Johnston would say, in her reading group. Worse, her partner reading later in the day worked exactly the same way: Read aloud until your partner corrects you.

Since I was ostensibly a teacher judging her reading, she waited for me to tell her the word. Enough bad news. The good news is that when I showed her how to recall what she knew about kids of divorce, she could apply that knowledge to this difficult context and get the word. The traditional round-robin reading group actually prevented her from using what she had been taught.

Pedagogenic Disorders

Iatrogenic diseases are diseases or conditions caused by doctors rather than cured by them. If a doctor misprescribes medication, and I take it and damage my liver, for example, that liver condition is an iatrogenic disease. Even without a mistake, as in the case of certain heart disease medications that can cause impotence, the treatment causes the new disorder.

If we follow Johnston (1997) and evaluate a student's reading and writing through multiple frames, we see that Kristen has word identification problems (skills theory from testing results) but that she can apply context to word recognition in familiar text (self-referencing Kristen's performance). We can also see that her classroom reading instruction (the larger social context, from sociopsycholinguistic theory) actually creates part of her reading problem.

Kristen is not alone in this negative effect of schooling. Andrew (Chapter 1), for instance, reads the sports pages (like his father) but slowly (like his mother), so he has no reading problem at home (the larger social context). In school, however, he reads more slowly than most of his peers (115 words per minute versus an average of 251 words per minute in grade 12 [Gilmore & Gilmore, 1968]).

Therefore, he cannot finish assignments geared for the average reader. Andrew has a reading problem in school, but not at home—thus, we see the importance of *context* in defining a problem.

New problems arise from the interaction of Andrew's reading speed, his personality, and the schedule of his school assignments. Given his habit of not trying when he cannot succeed, Andrew does not read his school assignments, thereby denying himself the chance to build technical vocabulary, awareness of expository text structure, self-monitoring skills in text reading, background knowledge for further reading, and fluency. In this manner, his new reading problems can be considered *school created,* or *pedagogic,* whereas his reading speed simply became a problem in the context of school.

Planning from Principles, Not Packages

In order for Andrew to improve as a reader, he must read. His new medication for attention made it easier for him to keep at it; witness the fact that he read and wrote with me for an hour and a half. He also had new motivation for reading textbooks; he wanted to pursue a career in physical therapy, so he planned to take a course in anatomy in his next school year. So, Andrew had more attention to give to reading and more reason to give it, but he was unlikely to have more manageable assignments. The class proceeds at the pace the teacher has set for it. Andrew chose not to be involved in the special education program in high school, so there was no modification of the class assignments as a result of a team planning session. Andrew had to learn how to change his schedule to succeed at school on the school's terms.

Specifically, Andrew was tutored in study skills through middle school, but he showed no signs of using this package of skills in his first three years of high school. Rather, he stopped off for breakfast instead of being on time for class. He tried to write down what the instructor put on the board, instead of prequestioning himself to set a purpose for his listening based on his reading. He seldom set aside time for homework.

This is the same young man who attended school regularly, was a linebacker on the football team, and delivered pizzas. Both he and his mother testified that his employer found him a reliable, hard worker, but his mother added that she suspected he succeeded with pizzas because there was always a change of pace and a chance to move around. Now the time had arrived for Andrew to plan his anatomy reading sessions in manageable sizes and establish the times he would do them. He had already demonstrated that he knew how to set purposes for his reading, to preview text, to learn technical vocabulary from reading, and to check on his predictions as he read. He now needed to learn to time himself reading a section of the text, to calculate his minutes per page, and to plan how much time will be needed for a given reading assignment.

As a linebacker, perhaps Andrew would like to be able to bench-press 400 pounds, but he is unlikely to get there by loading up the bar and struggling to budge it off the standards. It is better for Andrew to add 5 pounds every time the repetitions become easy—achieving little stages of success. In the same way, four 20-minute sessions with his anatomy book will not only complete the assignment designed to be read in 45 minutes by the average reader but this schedule will also provide Andrew with four successes to make his next effort more likely, as well as practice in productive reading habits, rather than cut-and-paste techniques designed to allow him with his slow speed to read the assignment in the same time or less as his classmates.

In middle school, Andrew had not been diagnosed with an attention deficit and treated with the appropriate medication. Because he could not attend to the average assignment long enough to succeed, his fear of failure drove him to flee the reading act rather than apply the package of study skills he was taught. Now that the principle that a person needs attention and motivation to master a skill has been attended to, Andrew can benefit from study skills instruction. He and his parents now planned to hire a tutor for his senior year to work on this issue and to help him prepare for an untimed administration of the SAT 1.

Packages but No Practice

Andrew had been taught both decoding skills and study habits in his middle school special education classes, and his initial testing showed needs for both sets of instruction. However, his individual education plans indicated that he continued to use the same levels of the same phonics programs even after his test results showed he had reached middle school level mastery of word attack. Worse, he was taught study skills before he had the attention or the motivation to use them. It was no wonder that Andrew decided to try high school on his own.

Kristen, on the other hand, had taken both the Observational Survey of Marie Clay and standardized testing. Both methods found her to need more knowledge of sound-letter relationships as well as practice in using what she knew. Accordingly, she received Reading Recovery-type teaching of word recognition strategies using context and sound-letter relationships as well as pull-out tutoring in the Benchmark program, which teaches the use of phonograms or spelling patterns to help students sound out unfamiliar words.

One problem with pull-out programs (Cunningham & Allington, 1994) is that they often place the most challenging learners with the least trained professionals. Kristen experienced this problem with the Reading Recovery program taught by a paraprofessional. Another shortcoming of pull-out models, according to Cunningham and Allington, is that students seldom practice in their regular classes what they learn in their special classes. Kristen's round-robin reading of literature-based readers in a teacher-led reading group or with a partner prevented her practicing either the rerunning or blanking strategies (which she said she remembered) or the spelling patterns (which she never mentioned as an alternative). Thus, good diagnosis and prescription are foiled by lack of practice.

Kristen's parents reported that she was likely to be placed in the class of a very knowledgeable third-grade teacher who allows students to read a variety of material of their own choice, while providing instruction and practice in word recognition strategies for those who need it. Although not identified by the special education system in her school, Kristen had been monitored by it and perhaps would finally be getting the coordinated instruction she needed. Sadie and Jason's schools, as we will see in the next section, had to go outside themselves for expertise, but they were willing to do so.

Phonics or Whole Language?

I do not allow my teacher-in-training students to ask the question of whether to use phonics or whole language. It assumes a battle between straw figures. No responsible whole-language educator recommends keeping children ignorant of decoding principles, nor forcing readers to use whole-word memorization as the sole means of reading. At the same time, no reasonable code-emphasis teacher contends that readers learn better without reading whole books or writing extended pieces in order to communicate with other people they know and care about. Mills and colleagues (1992) show that whole-language teachers help children learn how to decode words. They draw readers' attention to the internal structure of words and they help students learn sound-letter correspondences in English. At the same time, Adams (1990) advocates that reading and writing be learned through wide reading of quality literature and that children write often and for a variety of purposes.

When I realized that Sadie (see the case report in Chapter 2) recognized few words instantly and struggled to decode or spell, I asked not only if she had ever been taught to do so but also how. It turned out that Sadie's learning center had used a collection of worksheet phonics packages along with a basal reading textbook graded above her instructional level. She had not learned with these methods, but her current classroom placement also used a literature-based basal series above her instructional level.

Since Sadie could read few names on the Names Test (Duffelmeyer et al., 1994), I decided to recommend thorough and systematic decoding instruction. Reading Recovery and some form of Orton-Gillingham multisensory instruction came to mind. Sadie already applied a number of reading strategies to recognize print and construct meaning. She reread sentences to regenerate context, read "blank" for the unknown word to check following context, asked herself what would make sense in the spot, and sampled print. She did not seem to need the integrated strategy instruction of Reading Recovery, but she did need to develop more detailed awareness of sound-letter relationships, and no multisensory approach had been tried. I suggested that some form of Orton-Gillingham instruction be taught by a trained teacher and that Sadie be placed in a class in which she could read books at or below her instructional level in order to develop fluent word recognition at sight.

Sadie's district hired an Orton-Gillingham trained tutor to work with her three times a week. Her school, however, had adopted a literature-based basal system in every classroom, so she continued to be placed in a grade-level reading book, with grade-appropriate ancillary texts to read "if they get the time." They never do. I fear that the best multisensory decoding training will wither if Sadie never uses these skills in an abundance of easy, meaningful reading.

Enough Single-Letter Phonics

Jason (see the case report in Chapter 4) knew few words at sight, and at the beginning of fifth grade he could barely read a simple linguistic reader. He spelled less regularly than Sadie, but he, too, had been taught for years with isolated drill in sound-letter relationships. In his case, Jason pronounced letters and blends when the cards were flashed for him, and he combined the letters to make words, which he then pronounced. Alternatively, he separated the words into their cards and made the sounds for the letters. Jason sat at a low table in the special education teaching area while the teaching aide flashed the word and letter cards for him, or asked him to read a list of basic sight vocabulary, drawn from the Dolch Sight Word List, off the board from bottom to top. He never got more than eight correct.

Following the word recognition practice, he would read a short, controlled vocabulary book with the aide. *Pat's Jam* was one such book, 61 words long, telling the story of two rabbits, Pat and Pam, who drove a van to the store to buy jam. The book helped students practice decoding short /a/ words. Despite the fact that Jason had read the book several times during the school year, he read it for me during the summer with 21 miscues out of 61 words.

Single-letter phonics and isolated sight word practice did not work for Jason. Most of his miscues preserved meaning, but Jason was able to retell the story before reading it, clearly able to read from memory and the pictures more than print. Of the 21 miscues, 16 involved basic sight words, indicating that practice reading lists from the chalkboard did not improve his reading in context.

When he tried unfamiliar text ("One red bottle, one rubber band," from *I Spy*), Jason read, "Two red blocks, two red . . ." but could not guess the next word. Notice that he confused the basic counting words, correctly read *red,* but misread *rubber* as *red,* predicting from context and the first letter. He also predicted the word *blocks* from the picture and the first letter but had trouble with the blend.

Jason could write only his own name from memory but was able to take dictation, using the same strategies (confusion of sight words and first letters) as well as letter name (*c* for *see*) and vowel place holders (*boe* for *big*). In addition, Jason learned how to separate his name into syllables when I showed him how to beat out the parts of words, how to use Elkonin boxes to segment the phonemes in words he wanted to spell, how to rerun a sentence in order to regenerate context after identifying a tough word, and how to rearrange word cards from a sentence he had written to make his sentence again.

In other words, Jason showed me that he could do the things that Reading Recovery teachers often ask their students to do, and that these activities drew his attention more closely and actively to the internal structure of words and the syntax of sentences. But he did none of these things independently nor in his class-room using books on tape or recopying his own dictated stories. I suggested that the school hire a trained Reading Recovery teacher for Jason.

Jason demonstrated knowledge and strategies typical of an emergent reader, not some aberrant combination of information and habits. He guessed words in reading and writing by first (and sometimes last) letter, used context and pictures to predict words, used the sound of the letter name to write words, and memorized a few sight words. He confused basic sight words, probably because they were presented in isolation, with no meaning attached to them, and he did not integrate his phonics and context clues reliably in reading.

Therefore, the strategic lessons of integrated reading and writing of whole texts included in Reading Recovery should help him. Moreover, the gradually increasing difficulty of the little books used in the program should provide regular practice in meaningful, not artificially controlled, reading.

The Language Experience Approach (Van Allen & Allen, 1966) would also likely help Jason, since it would allow him to read meaningful text on subjects of his knowledge and experience. Unfortunately, his special education teacher said she had tried it with him but had quickly given up. Since his classroom teacher was not likely to incorporate such a technique into the classroom in such a way that Jason could do it with dignity, pull-out tutoring seemed to be the best option for this boy in this school.

Writers Need to Write for Engaged Readers

Only one of the students in this book was part of a writing workshop class. Jason dictated his stories in fourth grade to a teacher's aide, then he copied her transcription, and finally she read it aloud in his writing group. She said Jason never took the group's suggestions for change. Small wonder, since Jason had no responsibility for producing his piece, beyond the initial brief dictation. He could not even read his own story. His modifications in regular classroom practice were intended to allow him to take part in class, yet they gave him precious little practice in what writers do. At least, however, he thought of ideas and heard what his classmates said about them. But since he could not "write" in the first place, how could he rewrite given their response? He was not part of a writing community.

Sadie, identified as learning disabled, learns in both tutorial and full-class settings. Kristen, although not labeled learning disabled, is tutored outside her regular second-grade class and is in the middle reading group within her class. Andrew and Tara were formerly identified, but they and/or their parents have chosen to stop the special teaching. Andrew is attempting high school classes in the two least academic levels on his own, and Tara attends parochial school. Terry has moved from a project-based public school class to a more traditional fifth-grade classroom, and Mike continues in his Montessori school. Only Sadie was able to present me with pieces she wrote on topics of her own choice over more than one class period. None of the students shared their pieces with other students, published the pieces for inclusion in the classroom library, or received anything but mechanical editing feedback from their teachers.

I would argue that none of these children should have been candidates for assessment in writing disability. They were never taught to write. They were assigned to write and they had their print corrected, but they never learned to do what writers do: to discover what they have to say, to consider what audience might be interested in their piece, to find information and to compose language that accomplishes that purpose for that audience, to try out the creation on the audience and observe the reaction, and to reshape the piece as needed to produce the intended effect.

These students came from public and private schools, from traditional approaches and from innovative classrooms calling themselves "literature based," "progressive," or "project based." They wrote in elementary schools and high schools, in special education resource rooms, and in inclusionary classrooms, yet their writing experience was so similar that their teachers could have been using the same manual.

Making Do While Schools Change

All students, not just those with reading and writing difficulties, need better writing instruction. If three-quarters of this country's fourth-graders and half of eighth-graders (Gentile et al., 1995) cannot write clear, logical essays, current methods not only fly in the face of common writing sense but also produce terrible results. Large-scale reform of general writing instruction is beyond the scope of this book. Perhaps if enough principals attend enough special education planning sessions in which teachers and specialists tell stories such as those I have shared with you, principals will instigate change. Until that time, we need to teach students how to survive in bad situations or to find better situations in other schools.

Unfortunately, pull-out tutoring will not provide a writing community. Isolating all students who have difficulty writing will only leave them without proficient role models close to their ages, interests, and stages of development. Some classroom modifications, however, can be relatively painless.

For instance, Sadie's mother, Virginia, told me (see Chapter 9) that teachers in Sadie's school regularly selected student papers for printing in a newsletter to go home. Meanwhile, Sadie had been learning better spelling and decoding through Orton-Gillingham tutoring. "She would rather do anything than practice Orton-Gillingham," Virginia stated.

"I'll bet she'd use that new knowledge to edit, if she were publishing in the newsletter," I naively suggested.

"Oh, her papers never show up there," Virginia countered. "I can predict the kids I'll see there each month. You know—perfect spelling, no errors. Sadie's idea is that I should hire her a secretary or editor."

"You said she's able to read names off the movie credits. (*Note:* Sadie was able to read almost none of the names on the Names Test a year ago, nor could she find correct spellings on a spell-checker list of options.) How's she do with the spell-checker now? Does she still word-process with you? Can she now pick out the correct spellings?"

"Oh, yes, she's doing much better with that."

"Then have her word-process and spell-check her pieces before turning them in for consideration for the newsletter. Get *that* into her IEP (individual educational plan)."

Edited for spelling and punctuation, Sadie's writing is as good or better than that of her peers (see Figures 2.2, 2.3, and 2.4). This simple change in classroom routine made Sadie eligible for the same writing motivation the other students received without requiring her teacher having to change her attitudes or knowledge.

When Instruction Is the Problem

Tara (see the case report at the end of this chapter) suffered more directly from misguided instruction. Her teacher required mechanical accuracy on every piece (as much as possible on the first draft), responded to little besides the mechanics, and assigned writing as tests of what Tara had learned in social studies or English.

Consequently, Tara could only find worksheets and exercises as favorite pieces for her portfolio. Do not blame this result on the parochial school system. I have collected portfolios from students in grades K–12 in public and private schools and found many who feel worksheets are their best writing, if not their only writing, because they got good grades on them.

Tara came to me because she had trouble thinking of what to write. "I can think of it in my head," she said, "but not on the paper." She meant that she could not concentrate on writing the words and thinking of ideas at the same time. In her standardized testing, Tara consistently scored better on items requiring general or academic knowledge, a wide listening vocabulary, good listening comprehension, or good oral expression. When she had to process print, she had difficulty.

But both Tara and her teacher defined good writing as correct spelling, punctuation, and neatness. When I asked her if she had any problems writing, Tara first said that when she went too fast, her handwriting would get sloppy. She defined good writing as neat handwriting and good spelling, with proper indentation, capitalization, and punctuation. She chose her best pieces because they were not messy, she could explain and give descriptive answers, she used good handwriting, and she used complete sentences. Her one creative piece was an assignment to describe a tree with six details and no sentence beginning with *the, it, a,* or *this.*

These criteria focus on the mechanical and literal details of writing and comprehension. Such standards forced Tara to perform the language tasks she found most difficult—recall and reproduction of written language forms—under conditions least conducive to success. She was not allowed to draft her ideas first without regard to mechanics, simply to collect ideas and retain them for shaping into meaningful and accurate form. She was not allowed to talk about her ideas first, in order to use her speaking facility to produce language she could then transcribe. Rather, she had to retrieve, hold in memory, organize, and reproduce language simultaneously on subjects about which she was hardly expert.

The Limited Capacity Processor

Lahey and Bloom (1994) explain that human language processing runs on a limited capacity. That is, attention is finite in amount and is required for all literate functions. I cannot talk about an idea that I cannot hold in mind, and I cannot hold it in mind if I cannot build a mental model of the idea. I cannot build a mental model if I cannot retrieve information from which to construct it, and I cannot retrieve information if I do not first have a schema, or filing system, to organize in memory. When more than the usual attention is needed for one of these steps, less than usual is available for the others. Anything I can do automatically—steering my car, for instance—requires no attention, so I have more attention available for tuning the radio and drinking coffee as I drive.

Tara could not spell nor recall words automatically, as evidenced by her slow reading speed and poor scores on spelling and writing mechanics. These tasks required more attention, draining capacity from her mental processes (or using more random access memory [RAM]), so that less attention was available for building that mental model, holding it in memory and writing, speaking, or thinking about it. Tara could "think of ideas in my head, but not on paper."

Because Tara was able to write along with me when I showed her how to brainstorm ideas, jot them down, and then refer to her notes as she wrote, I suggested that she needed a writing workshop model of writing instruction. Tara's mother pointed out that she and her husband were considering shifting Tara to the public middle school the next year. The assessment gave them a model of writing instruction to look for in the public school (if the current parochial school had no such teacher of writing in sixth grade).

In the meantime, Tara could learn to separate editing from composing. Even in class, if she wrote in pencil, she could spell to the best of her ability, perhaps making a check above a word when she was not sure, but then quickly going on. Once she collected her ideas, she could go back and focus her full attention on the form of the checked words. She could also skim over her writing *backwards*—that is, starting from the bottom of the page, moving up, going from right to left. This technique prevents comprehension and focuses attention solely on the form of the word, thereby permitting Tara to make best use of the attention she had for the functions that required it most.

When finding likely candidates for misspelling, Tara could further focus on the suspicious area (say, the middle of *speSHal*) and think of what else might work. She could even write down these notes (*spessal* or *spechial* or *special*), eventually guessing and inserting the right one. Often, but not always, these steps focus the imperfect, but not absent, visual memory of students with graphophonemic writing problems. Tara could become her own spell-checker.

CASE REPORT: **Worksheets Are What I Do Best**

Background

Tara was a 10-year-old fifth-grader attending parochial school in a suburb of a large northeastern city. She took the National Achievement Test of the American College Testing Comprehensive Assessment Program and scored as follows:

Subtest	National Percentile	National Stanine
Vocabulary	24th	4
Comprehension	35th	4
Spelling	17th	3
Mechanics	15th	3
Expression	23rd	4
Reference Skills	40th	4
Social Studies	59th	5
Science	79th	7

These scores indicated Tara had acquired as much or more information than most fifth-graders in social studies and science, typically subjects in which information can be learned independent of reading skills. Further, the testing format did not require writing to demonstrate that knowledge. In contrast, Tara's spelling and mechanics scores fell into the below-average range. These testing tasks require recognition of spelling, capitalization, and punctuation errors by checking printed samples against visual memory. The average scores in comprehension, vocabulary, and expression derive from tasks involving more context in the examples.

When Tara was a third-grader, she was tested with the Durrell Analysis of Reading Difficulty (third edition), scoring the following grade levels:

Subtest	Grade Level
Oral Reading Rate	Low second (comprehension very good)
Silent Reading Rate	Low second (comprehension very good)
Listening Comprehension	Fourth
Listening Vocabulary	Sixth
Word Recognition	Below second
Word Analysis	Mid-third
Spelling	Mid-third
Visual Memory	High first
Sounds in Isolation	
Blends/Digraphs	Mid-third
Phonograms	High second (with self-correction)

As in the fifth-grade testing, Tara performed better on tests measuring her comprehension of language presented orally, rather than tests of her visual memory of word forms. Her decoding and spelling had either not yet fallen behind her peers or were more advantageously measured by the individual test.

Tara was also tested by the school district psychologist with the Wechsler Intelligence Scale for Children (WISC-III), scoring as follows:

Verbal Subtests	*Scaled Scores*
Information	10
Similarities	12
Arithmetic	12
Vocabulary	14
Comprehension	13
(Digit Span)	15

Performance Subtests	*Scaled Scores*
Picture Completion	12
Coding	5
Picture Arrangement	14
Block Design	8
Object Assembly	12
(Symbol Search)	7

IQ Scores
Verbal   113
Performance   99
Full Scale   107

The examiner noted Tara's strength in defining words presented orally, as well as her ability to recall orally presented strings of numbers. High scores in Picture Arrangement often indicate good attention to detail, logical planning, and ability to see whole patterns from a collection of parts. These results seemed to confirm Tara's well-developed oral language ability and her ability to derive phonics patterns. She also had considerable difficulty with scanning and matching symbols. Low scores in the Coding task sometimes indicate an overconcern with exact reproduction of the symbols, thus slowing the test time. This concern seemed typical of Tara's writing as well.

During the same month that the WISC-III was administered, the resource teacher tested Tara with the Woodcock-Johnson Psychoeducational Battery, generating the following scores:

Cognitive Factors	*Standard Score Range*
Long-Term Retrieval	91–99
Short-Term Memory	95–105
Processing Speed	89–99
Auditory Processing	115–125
Visual Processing	102–116
Comprehension Knowledge	117–125
Fluid Reasoning	101–107

The examiner noted weaknesses in long-term retrieval and processing speed. These scores are based on two tests each that involve decontextualized memory and matching of words, pictures, and numbers. Short-term memory, by contrast, is based on repeating orally presented sentences, a more contextual task. Tara's strengths were in comprehension knowledge, measured by picture vocabulary and oral synonyms, and in auditory processing, measured by blending sounds into words or identifying missing sounds in words presented orally.

These same tasks are recombined to generate predicted aptitudes and compared to achievement measures. The reading score is based on recognition of letters in isolation and in words, as well as the ability to supply a missing word in passages one to three sentences long. The writing tasks involve using correct mechanics to write answers to questions or to compose descriptions with provided words. Tara's scores showed the following:

Scholastic Aptitude	Standard Score Range	Actual Score Range	Standard Deviation Difference
Reading	108–114	93–99	−1.24
Math	105–109	92–100	−0.84
Written Language	114–120	104–110	−0.39
Knowledge	106–112	120–128	1.68

Given that the subject and some vocabulary for the brief writing tasks were supplied, it is not surprising that Tara did relatively better on the writing portions than on the reading portions. With the need to think of ideas removed, she could probably concentrate more fully on the mechanics of the writing. However, reading the incomplete passages would be more difficult, given her underdeveloped visual recognition of words.

Based on these results, the school district developed an educational plan that involved Tara continuing to attend Assumption School, while receiving tutoring from the resource teacher two and one-half hours per week. The plan indicated work on decoding, reading rate, and editing in writing. Tara's parents decided to discontinue the tutoring after fourth grade because much work was repetitious and was not coordinated with the work at Assumption. Tara confirmed that she recalled doing certain worksheets more than once.

Current Assessment

I met with Tara and her mother in my office one afternoon to examine what they both described as a difficulty with writing. Tara's mother told me that Tara wrote slowly and had trouble with mechanical accuracy. Tara said that if she wrote too fast, her handwriting became sloppy. She defined good writing as neat handwriting and good spelling, with proper indentation, capitalization, and punctuation. She could not think of any easy parts in writing, saying at different times that her social studies work or writing stories was easy because "you can make it up."

The hardest parts of writing, according to Tara, were when she had to write long pieces and when she could not find an answer. She said she could think of the answer in her head, but not on paper. Her most recent writing was the questions at the end of her social studies chapter. Currently, she was working on a story for social studies, in which a Quaker girl whose mother has died now had a sick father. The doctors did not know what was wrong. Tara explained that she was still working on the ending but she could not recall the name of the main character.

Writing Samples

Tara chose three pieces of her work to discuss. Her best was a social studies test done in class. The four pages included two multiple-choice or true/false answers and two short-answer responses. She said it was her best because of the way it looked (not messy) and that she could explain it. Her third choice was also a social studies test chosen for its good handwriting. She said she gave descriptive answers in complete sentences. The test included three pages of letter response questions and one page of short-answer responses.

In each of these papers Tara used the strategy of repeating the question stem in order to write her answer. In addition, the key words in the questions had been highlighted for her. In response to "What is the title of this table?" for instance, Tara wrote, "The title of this table is Colonist's Relations with the Indians." In general, although she wrote quite compactly, Tara had more to say than she could fit on the lines provided. The teacher had responded to the writing with correct spellings written over or under the misspellings and one request for more information.

Tara's second piece (see Figure 7.1) was a poem entitled "Trees," written in class to the prompt, "Look out the window and describe the tree. Use six descriptive details and no sentence beginning with *the, it, a,* or *this.*" She chose this piece because the handwriting was good and she liked the description of the bark as "frozen waves." None of Tara's pieces took her more than 90 minutes.

Tara described her classroom writing procedure as follows: Students write a rough draft and correct it for spelling, punctuation, and capitalization. The teacher checks it and the student recopies it on a different piece of paper.

Writing Together

Tara and I wrote together (Murray, 1985) for about 30 minutes on topics of our own choice (see Figure 7.2). I asked her to write down (brainstorm) things she knew about and cared about, and she listed: social studies, reading, playing piano, soccer, computers, keys, sound. After I shared my list with her, I asked her to write as many titles as she could about one subject from her list. She chose *playing the piano* as her subject and wrote "Playing the Piano" and "The Piano" as possible titles. I asked her how writing about the two titles might be different. She said that "Playing the Piano" might talk about the songs you could play, but the "The Piano" would not be about playing, maybe just describing a piano.

Tara asked me if she should write a story, and I replied by asking her if she wanted to. She was unsure if she wanted to write a story, so I asked her how she might start. As she told me about her lessons with her teacher, I made notes and gave the notes to her before she started writing (see Figure 7.3).

6 descrip delcils
No sent begins
with the, it, a, this

Trees

Trees are beautiful Thier bark is like frozen waves
Trees are brown and light red. Trees are bare in the
winter, But they are as mighty as a lion. Trees are like
mighty Kings when they swing and sway in the breze.

FIGURE 7.1 Tara's Second-Best Piece

Social Studies
Reading
playing piano
socer
comperts
keys
sound

playing the piano The piano

I think playing the piano is easy.
All you have to do is rember
the right keys. If you learn
all the right keys you can
learn songs like Christmas song,
Amazing grace,
Mary had a little lamb colors of
the wind, Heart and Soul
Tom Tom, Twinkle Twinkle little
star. Row Row Row your boat
and othe songs like that.

FIGURE 7.2 Tara's Writing Sample

lessons
Mrs. Murphy
$\frac{1}{2}$ hours
every week
her house
not big, not little, medium

Christmas
Amazing Grace—favorite
Mary Had a Little Lamb
Colors of the Wind
Heart & Soul
Tom Tom
Twinkle, Twinkle
Row, Row, Row

FIGURE 7.3   My Notes for Tara

   She positioned the paper on the desk appropriately and held the pencil properly, if a little tightly. She wrote small, tight letters, referring back to the list of notes as she wrote. She did not erase or cross out at all. After writing one paragraph, she flexed her hand as if it were tired and then reread what she had written. When I asked her if she liked it, she responded that it was pretty good because it told you what you can learn. I asked if the paragraph had been difficult to write and she said no. I then queried her as to what she would write next, if she were to continue writing, and she said she would write about how she learned these songs, but she would concentrate on directions, not how she did it, so that a person who liked the songs could learn to play them. All in all, Tara wrote 68 words, spelling all but 3 correctly (*socer/soccer, comperts/computers, rember/remember*), and missing only one comma (after an introductory adverbial clause) and six possible capital letters in song titles.

Knowledge about Writing

Tara defined writing as neat handwriting and accurate mechanics. She had received feedback on her written responses to reading and brief writing assignments in the form of editing for mechanics, with an occasional comment on content. There was no evidence that Tara had participated in a reading/writing workshop. In such a classroom, the teacher demonstrates how to get ideas, select useful information, make decisions while writing, and edit after writing. The students confer with the teacher and each other about subjects on which to write, about the effectiveness of the piece, and about strategies for improvement. In addition, students share their work orally and publish their writing for others to read.

I tried these techniques with Tara and she responded well. She was able to produce a short list of ideas for writing, indicating that with practice her brainstorming ability would improve. Also, in a classroom in which students are expected to come to class with ideas for writing *each day*, they develop the habit of thinking about subjects outside of class, thereby developing both a store of topics as well as a retrieval system for getting at them when the need arises.

Tara had more trouble focusing on an aspect of a subject for a particular purpose; she generated only two titles, for instance, and had no sense that her personal experience in learning to play the piano would be instructive to others, as well as a subject on which she was an expert and had the most information. Academic writing of the type in evidence in Tara's writing folder generally requires students to write on subjects in which they are far from expert for a reader who is looking for errors. Tara's writing habits indicated that she had learned these lessons, but that they did not help her develop ideas for writing and may have been one of the sources of her "writer's block."

Tara wrote the most fluently when she referred to notes we had made before writing. Since her testing record and her own assessment indicated that spelling was a challenge for her, most of her attention during writing was consumed by the generation of accurate print. Consequently, she either forgot what she wanted to write about or was unable to find information to begin writing. Once she began, Tara could write for a focused purpose, as indicated by her ability to plan how she would continue the piece she had started. Moreover, she reformatted the questions to begin her answers on worksheets in much the same way, using the question as notes from which to "jump start" the production of accurate print connected to what she knew about the subject. Once the connection was made, retrieval of additional items became easier.

Reading for Meaning

I asked Tara to bring three pieces to read aloud for me—an easy one, a just-right one, and a challenging one, I recorded her oral reading, asked her about the passages, and analyzed her miscues. For a piece to be easy (or at her independent level), she should read it with 95 percent or better accuracy and be able to retell and discuss the reading. For material to be "just right" for instruction, she should read with 90 to 95 percent accuracy and be able to retell and discuss most of the ideas in the passage. Frustrating material generally produces less than 90 percent accuracy and an inability to preserve meaning while reading the print. The results follow:

Passage 1 (Oral).   *People Need People,* "The Giant Who Didn't Win," Elizabeth Levy; Holt, Rinehart and Winston, pages 92–95: 361 words, 6 miscues, 98 percent accuracy rate, 3 self-corrections, 50 percent self-correction rate

Tara	Text	Matches Preceding Context	Matches Following Context	Self-Corrects	Preserves Meaning	Corrected or Preserves Meaning
of	from	yes	no	yes	yes	yes
how	who	yes	no	yes	no	yes
towns	town	yes	no	no	yes	yes
the	a	yes	yes	no	yes	yes
book	books	yes	yes	yes	yes	yes
there	here	yes	yes	no	yes	yes
		100%	50%	50%	84%	100%

These numbers indicated that Tara read comfortable material, predicted unfamiliar words 100 percent of the time from preceding context, and preserved the essential meaning 84 percent of the time. Adding her self-corrections (50 percent of her chances), she preserved meaning 100 percent of the time. Therefore, Tara was a good contextual reader, using meaning both to predict and to signal herself to self-correct when the meaning of her guess failed to make sense.

She was able to evaluate the actions of the giant and the townspeople in the story and to reformulate her predictions as she went along in the reading, indicating strong inferential and evaluative thinking during reading. However, Tara did not read even this easier passage fluently, indicating that her tested weakness with visual memory for word forms caused her to pause to recognize many words that would be recognized automatically by a fluent reader.

Passage 2 (Oral). *The Christmas Surprise,* American Girl Doll series, pages 1–2: 307 words, 25 miscues, 92 percent accuracy rate, 5 self-corrections, 20 percent self-correction rate

Tara	Text	Matches Preceding Context	Matches Following Context	Self-Corrects	Preserves Meaning	Corrected or Preserves Meaning
at	that	yes	no	no	no	no
—	little	yes	yes	yes	yes	yes
Oliver's	Olav's	yes	yes	yes	yes	yes
rice	ice	no	no	no	no	no
bread	beard	no	no	no	no	no
winter	winter's	yes	yes	no	yes	yes
there	here	no	yes	no	no	no
—	in	yes	yes	no	yes	yes
a	the	yes	no	no	yes	yes
snow	snows	yes	yes	yes	yes	yes
—	the	yes	yes	no	yes	yes
it's	it was	no	yes	yes	yes	yes
smiled	smelled	yes	no	no	no	no

Tara	Text	Matches Preceding Context	Matches Following Context	Self-Corrects	Preserves Meaning	Corrected or Preserves Meaning
common	cinnamon	no	no	no	no	no
and	—	yes	yes	no	yes	yes
tried	tied	yes	no	no	no	no
doesn't	won't	yes	yes	no	yes	yes
cup/board	cupboard	yes	yes	no	yes	yes
raisin	risen	yes	yes	no	no	no
a	the	yes	yes	no	yes	yes
smell	smells	yes	yes	no	yes	yes
spice	spices	yes	yes	no	yes	yes
wisped	wiped	no	no	yes	no	yes
—	here	yes	yes	no	yes	yes
our	the	yes	no	yes	yes	yes
		76%	64%	20%	64%	68%

Tara read this book, commonly read by students in grade 3 or higher, with instructional range accuracy (92 percent) and good comprehension. She failed to take into account, however, that the family might not have the money to buy the presents Kirsten might want, an idea implied in the conversation. Her miscues also indicated that she predicted less from context (76 percent), self-corrected less (20 percent), and preserved meaning within the passage less (68 percent). These percentages were all acceptable, given her ability to retell and discuss the material; however, they indicated that as more words appeared that were unfamiliar at sight, Tara's strong contextual reading ability had less attention to use because of her need to recognize words.

Passage 3 (Oral). *Reader's Digest Condensed Books* (Vol. 1), "The Chamber," by John Grisham, page 9: 49 words, 7 miscues, 86 percent accuracy rate, 2 self-correction, 28 percent self-correction rate

Tara	Text	Matches Preceding Context	Matches Following Context	Self-Corrects	Preserves Meaning	Corrected or Preserves Meaning
discussion	decision	yes	no	no	no	no
doom	bomb	yes	no	yes	no	yes
raydical	radical	no	no	yes	no	yes
teached	reached	no	no	no	no	no
operaytive	operative	no	no	no	no	no
technology	territory	yes	yes	no	no	no
pattriot	patriot	no	no	no	no	no
		42%	14%	28%	0%	28%

I stopped Tara's reading here because she was clearly frustrated by the print, although she did an admirable job decoding difficult words such as *radical* and *doom*. From our discussion prior to the reading, it was clear she had no depth of prior knowledge about this subject or this type of adult book.

Passage 1 (Silent).   *The Great Gilly Hopkins,* Katherine Paterson, Harper and Row, pages 1–2: 222 words, 2 minutes, 111 words per minute

Tara was able to discuss the passage accurately after reading, indicating she was reading for meaning. However, her reading speed was appropriate for a second-grader (Gilmore & Gilmore, 1968) and much slower than most fifth-graders (177 words per minute). This relative slowness in silent reading confirmed earlier indications that Tara's poor visual memory required her to slow down due to lack of automatic word recognition of common words. She probably needed extra time to finish reading assignments. Her difficulty with recall of detail and with writing accurately while remembering information are also connected to this pattern.

Phonics Knowledge

Tara read the 35 names on the Names Test (Duffelmeyer et al., 1994) with the following results:

Phonics Category	Errors	Accuracy Rate (percent)
Initial consonants	2/37	95
Initial consonant blends	0/19	100
Consonant digraphs	2/15	88
Short vowels	3/36	92
Long vowels/VC—Final *e*	3/23	87
Vowel digraphs	0/15	100
Controlled vowels	3/25	88
Schwa	2/15	86

These results indicated relative weaknesses with vowel sounds and consonant digraphs. Vowel digraphs (as in *Joan, Loomis,* and *tweed*) are strong, however, indicating Tara could benefit from instruction in phonograms for both word recognition and spelling. Vowel sounds are much more regular in phonograms, and she already stated that she looked for known words inside unfamiliar words as a strategy when she reads.

Current Levels of Functioning

Tara, a 10-year-old fifth-grader, was able to read grade-appropriate material slowly but accurately and with good comprehension. Her lack of automatic word recognition may have prevented her from retaining details or thinking fully about reading with many new or unfamiliar words. She generally had strong decoding skills and checked her predictions against context. She could become stumped on words, pausing a very long time or asking a nearby adult for help.

Tara was able to write short answers to questions required for tests and homework by restating the question in her answer and relying on her strong reading comprehension for information. She had more trouble with longer writing assignments and with creative writing assignments in which the topic and format were not dictated by the teacher. Although she tested poorly in spelling, she misspelled few words in self-selected writing assignments, probably because by focusing on spelling before meaning, she wrote only the words she knew how to spell.

Strengths

Tara was a bright, enthusiastic girl who liked to succeed in school. She listed social studies as one of the things she knew about and cared about. She also enjoyed learning outside of school, listing soccer and the piano as two of her interests. She demonstrated a history of excellent oral language ability and knowledge about academic subjects such as science and social studies.

As a reader, Tara was able to name books that she enjoyed and had reasons for choosing the book she was currently reading. Her generally strong phonics skills and contextual reading allowed her to read successfully grade-appropriate material. As a writer, she knew how to respond to classroom tasks and placed emphasis on the surface features of print stressed by her teachers. She knew what parts of writing were difficult for her and planned appropriately by using words she knew how to spell and by using print available on the test sheet to help her.

Weaknesses

Tara's weak visual memory made spelling difficult and reading slow. In addition, as she allocated attention to spelling or word recognition, she was unable to locate, retain, and orchestrate information for analyzing more challenging reading or for composing longer and more independent writing. Tara had few strategies to facilitate the recall of words or information during reading and writing, and could get stumped and be unable to move forward. Finally, the lack of practice with easy, informal reading and writing probably contributed to the lack of fluency in reading and writing.

Suggested Instruction

Reading.   Tara needed to increase her reading speed. She currently read grade-appropriate material at 111 words per minute (with the average sixth-grade reading speed at 206 words per minute). Therefore, assignments aimed at the average student would take Tara twice as long—a tedious prospect at home and likely an impossible one in class.

Automatic word recognition (and hence fluency) is enhanced by two activities: previewing and predicting before reading, and frequent reading of *easy* books. Tara needed to be taught and to practice how to activate her memory banks of concepts and words prior to reading with such techniques as KWL, Directed Listening/Thinking/Reading Activity, SQ3R, advanced graphic organizers, or word webbing. Research indicates that when students think about ideas that may come up in the reading before they read, they more quickly call up from memory the target words during reading.

Reading of easy books promotes fluent reading habits and reinforces the visual memory of commonly encountered words. People with poor visual memory need more exposures, not fewer, to the same words in order to reinforce their impressions in memory. For example, challenging books such as *Little Women* may be read too slowly and infrequently to produce the instant recognition that five *Boxcar Children* books will. Finally, practice with spelling patterns will reinforce attention to the internal structure of words, heightening automatic word recognition, giving more strategies for decoding in reading, and improving spelling automaticity as well.

Writing.   Tara needed instruction in and practice with the writing process. Specifically, she needed to see (by demonstration), to practice, and to learn how to choose techniques for generating topics and information *prior* to composing. She also needed to learn how to guess what information her reader already knows, needs to know, and wants to know. She needed to see (by demonstration) and to practice techniques for holding information in note or schematic form to refer to while she composed. Separating the composing process from the editing process would allow her to spell the right word as best she could while composing, and then to fix its spelling after composing. Finally, Tara needed to learn purposes for writing other than to demonstrate the acquisition of content material on tests, worksheets, or artificial writing exercises.

Tara's current forms of writing instruction actually reinforced her weaknesses in writing by requiring her to get the surface features correct with no chance for revision. They provided artificial writing tasks in which she did not have to generate a topic connected to her experience or in-depth knowledge, thus activating those parts of her memory before writing, and they did not allow her to use notes and organizers to reduce the attention drains on her while composing. If more process-oriented instruction is not available in Tara's school, I would suggest trained tutors who can work with Tara.

CHAPTER

8

Assessing Culturally and Linguistically Diverse Students' Literacy

BY MILEIDIS GORT

Oxford and colleagues (1981) report that the school-age population of children with non-English backgrounds is expected to continue growing into the twenty-first century at a pace exceeding the growth of the general population at large. These culturally and linguistically diverse (CLD) students have the right to useful, fair, and valid assessment services. Traditionally, CLD students have been assessed either with English instruments designed to work well with middle-class monolingual students or have been exempt from testing because of English language limitations. There are problems related with both of these practices. The first practice ignores the cultural and linguistic differences of these students by giving equal weight to test scores of monolingual and CLD students alike. The second practice ignores CLD students' educational progress altogether (LaCelle-Peterson & Rivera, 1994) and does not account for their learning. Assessment of CLD students' literacy must be done with respect to their general ability to read and write as well as their ability to read and write in specific languages (Brisk, 1998). The challenge faced by assessment specialists and educators is to explore and understand how cultural and linguistic factors influence assessment (Duran, 1989), rather than to deny the existence of such influences. The challenge, then, is to understand both the strengths and limitations of different assessment tools and practices for CLD students.

Formal Measures of Reading Assessment and CLD Students

Historically, low-income African American, Latina/Latino, and Native American students have not performed as well as their European-American middle- and upper-class peers on formal assessment measures (Garcia & Pearson, 1994). *Formal measures of assessment* refers to those tests that are based on or strongly influenced by the standardized testing paradigm. They include commercial early reading tests, standardized reading achievement tests, domain-referenced/basal reading tests, and new statewide reading tests (Garcia & Pearson, 1991).

Early Reading Tests

Edelsky and Harman (1988) discuss problems with reading readiness and early reading measures in the assessment of CLD students. First, a subskills approach to reading is implicit in both types of tests. Many of the skills tested are not needed for reading and the emphasis on recognition tasks provides no information as to how students operationalize these tasks when they are read. In addition, children's prereading potential is often based on the identification of unfamiliar pictures or second-language (L2) vocabulary, or on their pronunciation of standard English. Because of linguistic differences or literacy experiences, CLD children are often placed in transitional kindergarten and first-grade programs where they are not exposed to the types of literacy activities that are thought to help promote emergent literacy (Garcia & Pearson, 1991).

Standardized Reading Achievement Tests

Cummins (1984) and Ascher (1990) believe that standardized achievement and aptitude tests developed for middle-class monolingual students are of very limited value for CLD students. Cummins says that it takes "at least five years, on the average, for immigrant students to acquire peer appropriate cognitive/academic proficiency in English . . . [so] low verbal ability scores should be considered an underestimate of students' potential until at least five years of exposure to English in an academic context" (p. 185). However, it is important to understand how CLD students perform on reading achievement tests and how their performance is related to their literacy development, since schools often use these tests for assessment and placement. One criticism of standardized reading achievement tests is that they obscure rather than confront the influence of students' prior knowledge, reading strategies, and reasoning strategies (Johnston, 1984a). Further, although few second-language researchers have looked at the role of prior knowledge in L2 children's reading, native-language (L1) reading studies have indicated that prior knowledge of passage content is a variable that can account for differences in children's reading test scores (Johnston, 1984b). Thus, differences in prior knowledge or cultural schemata may negatively affect the reading performance of CLD children as compared to that of Anglo children (Garcia, 1991).

Sanchez (1934) and Duran (1983) warn against testing Spanish-speaking children in English without first assessing their familiarity with the L2 test vocabulary. Garcia (1991) discusses several researchers who have pointed out that difficulties with key text vocabulary seem to hinder reading comprehension of second-language learners more so than that of first-language readers. For example, Garcia (1988, 1991) states that Latino/Latina students' test performance is negatively affected by limited prior knowledge, poor performance on implicit questions, unfamiliarity with vocabulary terms used in the questions and answer choices, and a tendency for literal interpretations of the test questions. In some cases, the children showed that, although they had understood the test passages, problems with vocabulary did not allow them to comprehend the questions and answer choices. The students' lower performance is consistent with other researchers' findings that the standardized test performance of CLD students is negatively affected by their limited knowledge of test vocabulary and test topics (Garcia & Pearson, 1991).

The historically weak performance of CLD students on standardized reading tests has also incited complaints of cultural test bias that may occur when the test procedures and test content confound dominant cultural knowledge with students' reading test performance. To test this notion, Richard-Amato and Snow (1992) counted the percentage of biased test items in three widely used tests of reading comprehension: the Canadian Test of Basic Skills (a revision of the Iowa Test of Basic Skills for Canadian use), the Gates-MacGinitie Reading Test, and the Stanford Diagnostic Reading Test. They found that between 7 and 16 percent of the test items were culturally biased, a percentage high enough to have a marked effect on scores. Since reading comprehension scores from such tests are often used to determine levels of reading competence, biased results most likely lead to incorrect diagnosis of reading difficulties, inappropriate teaching, and possible misplacement.

Moreover, Garcia (1991) reports that CLD students' test performance may be affected by differences in their knowledge of testing procedures, test anxiety and test wiseness, perception of questions and answers, and differences in the characteristics of the testing event itself. She discusses second-language research that has shown bilingual speakers take longer to process either of the two languages, tend to read at a slower rate in their second language, and develop L2 receptive competencies more rapidly than productive competencies.

Domain-Referenced/Basal Reading Tests

Many of the same criticisms of standardized reading tests apply to domain-referenced or basal reading tests because of their format and content emphases. Specifically, the inherent assumption that children taking these tests are familiar with the test content and format poses a problem for second-language learners who are transitioned out of bilingual classrooms into monolingual L2 classrooms (Garcia & Pearson, 1991). Although children from the bilingual classroom may have acquired the comprehension strategies needed to read, they may not have developed the vocabulary or background knowledge required to perform well on basal tests.

Statewide Tests

Finally, new statewide tests have been developed in an attempt to reflect current reading research (Wixson et al., 1987). They assess prior knowledge, inference and knowledge of text structure, awareness of reading strategies, and attitudes and interests in reading. These tests attempt to avoid a common criticism of traditional standardized tests—that brief and contrived test passages only simulate reading (Edelsky & Harman, 1988) and do not show what students can do with real-life literacy tasks, by providing children with longer, noncontrived passages. Although these changes clearly represent an improvement over formal reading tests, they are still product measures based on mainstream reading performance and are subject to the same complaints of bias that plague standardized tests (Garcia & Pearson, 1991). The extent to which these tests help explain the relationship between CLD children's reading test performance and literacy development has not been explored.

The Role of the First Language in Second-Language Comprehension Tasks

Valdes and Figueroa (1989) define *bilingualism* as the condition of knowing two languages rather than one. Thus, individuals who are bilingual to any extent have two language systems that both overlap and are distinct, and that are relied on in numerous ways depending on different linguistic and communicative demands. Research suggests that CLD students perform at higher levels when allowed to use L1 in L2 comprehension tasks. Garcia (1991) finds that Latino/Latina students who had problems with vocabulary in comprehension test questions were able to correct their answers when the questions and the answer choices were translated into Spanish. Although the students had understood the test passages, unknown L2 vocabulary in the comprehension questions and answer choices negatively affected their scores.

This finding is consistent with second-language research that uses the recall task to measure L2 reading comprehension. Lee (1986) finds a significant difference in the language of recall. Specifically, recall was significantly better when done in the subjects' native language than in the target language (L2). In contrast, Connor (1984) explored the differences between first- and second-language readers' comprehension of an English text. Native English speakers were able to recall 72 percent of the text, whereas English language learners were able to recall only 49 percent of the information when doing the recall task in English. Brisk (1998) suggests that literacy testing to determine general ability does not have to be done in one particular language. Further, CLD students "write better in the language they know best or in the language in which they have learned a particular topic" (p. 125).

National Call for Valid and Authentic Assessment of CLD Students

Current dissatisfaction with traditional school-based testing and recent views of literacy as social and cultural practices with an emphasis on making meaning has led to the push for alternative forms of assessment (Rueda & Garcia, 1994; Brown, 1994). This shift toward constructivism is reflected in the move toward performance-based assessments, portfolios, and student performance in authentic activities (Rueda & Garcia, 1996). The California State Department of Education (1992) suggests:

> Authentic assessment practices . . . are likely to differ from past ones at the elementary level in some surprising ways. They are likely to include integrated reading-writing assessments; the evaluation of student writings or of other work samples collected in portfolios; investigations conducted by small groups of students; and the staging of hands-on problem solving activities. They are likely to require both on-demand performance from students as well as performances completed over extended periods of time. Questions on authentic tests will not be jealously guarded secrets; they may be known well ahead of time. Speed of response will seldom be at a premium in the assessment instruments of the 1990s; students may demonstrate their scholastic achievement . . . over an entire term. And often, students who consult one another over their answers won't be "cheating"; they will be collaborating in much the same way that professionals in the world of business are expected to do. (p. 67)

Traditional methods of monitoring and measuring learning obviously do not correspond with this constructivist view of assessment.

Duran (1989) stresses the importance of test developers' and test users' sensitivity to professionally sound testing practices if significant progress in the valid assessment of CLD students is to be made. The Standards for Educational and Psychological Testing developed by the American Psychological Association, the American Educational Research Association, and the National Council on Measurement in Education (1985) explicitly refer to such sound testing practices in the assessment of CLD students:

> *Primary Standard 13.1*—For non-native English speakers or for speakers of some dialects of English, testing should be designed to minimize threats to test reliability and validity that may arise from language differences.
> *Primary Standard 13.2*—Linguistic modifications recommended by test publishers should be described in detail in the test manual.
> *Primary Standard 13.3*—When a test is recommended for use with linguistically diverse test takers, test developers and publishers should provide the information necessary for appropriate test use and interpretation.
> *Primary Standard 13.4*—When a test is translated from one language or dialect to another, its reliability and validity for the uses intended in the linguistic groups to be tested should be established.
> *Primary Standard 13.5*—In employment, licensing, and certification testing, the English language proficiency level of the test should not exceed that appropriate to the relevant occupation or profession.
> *Primary Standard 13.6*—When it is intended that the two versions of dual language tests be comparable, evidence of test comparability should be reported.
> *Primary Standard 13.7*—English language proficiency should not be determined solely with tests that demand only a single linguistic skill. (pp. 74–75)

The "Primary" designation attached to each standard means that it "should be met by all tests before their operational use and in all test uses, unless a sound professional reason is available to show why it is not necessary, or technically feasible, to do so in a particular case. Test developers and users and, where appropriate, sponsors, are expected to be able to explain why any primary standards have not been met" (pp. 2–3).

Equitable Assessment for CLD Students

Assessment tools, then, must be designed to help CLD students meet the educational goals set by and for them, as well as help educators monitor the effectiveness of educational programs in enabling all students to reach those goals (LaCelle-Peterson & Rivera, 1994). Useful, fair, and valid assessment is more than achievement testing. In order to understand student performance and to plan appropriate instructional activities, it is essential to know and understand the students' backgrounds and the strategies and processes that drive their classroom-based learning (Genesee & Hamayan, 1994). Assessment of CLD students should focus on the learning process and "value the unique characteristics of each individual and . . . respect individuals' cultural and linguistic differences" (Gonzalez, Brusca-Vega, & Yawkey, 1997, p. 83). Assessment should include information about the whole child and about instruction.

Cloud (1994) points out that in order to understand students' second-language development, it is useful to assess their literacy skills in the first language. Cummins (1984) adds that L1 cognitive/academic assessment can contribute to better interpretation of student performance. Thus, assessment in and through the home language is advisable to ensure an accurate and complete assessment of students' academic and language development (Genesee & Hamayan, 1994). When assessments heavily rely on L2 verbal interaction, it becomes difficult for second-language learners to participate fully and meaningfully in them. In these cases, the flexibility to use the first language will ensure that the assessment process and results are not distorted. In addition, assessment of CLD learners should include their ability to function in both cultural contexts (Brisk, 1998). Such information helps in understanding the whole student and his or her performance.

Authentic Classroom Assessment for CLD Students. A review of the literature calls for comprehensive authentic assessment that attempts to capture the approach and process CLD students use to accomplish tasks (Garcia, 1994; Garcia & Pearson, 1991). Rather than just assessing the end product, authentic assessment evaluates "how and what students know and can do in real-life performance situations" (Darling-Hammond, 1994, p. 6) and how readers construct meaning. Authentic assessment tasks are designed to elicit information about how CLD students approach, monitor, and process L1 and L2 text.

Authentic classroom assessment is found in the local classroom or school and it tends to be developed by teachers who believe in assessment that determines student growth and informs instruction. Authentic classroom activities include language-flexible running records or miscue analyses of students' oral reading, student-teacher conferences to discuss individual students' reading and writing development, dialogue or response journals, oral readings and retellings, reader logs, student think-alouds, anecdotal records of student literacy performance, and student portfolios of written work (Garcia, 1994; Garcia & Pearson, 1991).

Gonzalez and associates (1997) suggest taking an "ethnic researcher" approach to the assessment of CLD students because assessing a CLD student only using standardized measures will not provide a complete picture of the individual, and may even misdiagnose learning disabilities that do not exist (p. 82). This observation is consistent with Garcia's (1991) finding that oral open-ended comprehension questions tended to provide more information about Latino/Latina students' passage comprehension than did their actual performance on a standardized test. To have used the students' reading test scores to evaluate their reading ability would have "seriously underestimated their reading comprehension potential" (p. 388). Using mostly qualitative methods, then—such as developmental problem-solving tasks; unstructured observations of students in different environments; surveys and interviews with students, parents, and teachers; and teacher-made criterion-referenced measures—will assess skills mastered by individual students and will be useful for developing and planning educational and programs. A collection of pieces from the different academic disciplines, along with cultural and linguistic environments of the students, will provide a fair assessment of their abilities since "the diagnostic process demands deep knowledge of the constructs being evaluated as well as awareness of the influence of cultural and linguistic factors on the development of CLD students" (Gonzalez et al., 1997, p. 83).

Garcia and Pearson (1991) further call for a dramatically improved teacher knowledge base and a flexible approach to assessment in order to meet the assessment needs of CLD student populations. Educators must be aware of the extent to which assessment methods distort or reflect the literacy development of CLD students. When educators are knowledgeable about students' cultures, languages, and communities, authentic classroom assessment can benefit students whose styles of thinking do not fit the standardized testing model (Darling-Hammond & Goodwin, 1993). Authentic classroom assessment can further benefit bilingual students because knowledgeable teachers can document students' learning and capabilities in two languages (Garcia, 1994). The authors offer several recommendations on how to achieve these needed changes in assessment practices and policies. These include a reduction on the reliance on group testing as indices of individual, school, district, or state accountability; a preference for classroom- and school-based assessments; the education of teachers and administrators about issues of language and culture; new criteria for the evaluation of assessment tools that are "trustworthy, authentic, and instructionally valid" (p. 271); a change in conventional assessments; and a more realistic perspective on what different types of assessment tasks can do.

Toward Optimal Assessment for CLD Students

A review of the literature presents the difficulties inherent in the current and past assessment approach when testing CLD students. As Cummins (1986) and others have noted, "Assessment has played the role of legitimizing the disabling" of CLD students and "often . . . has been used to locate the 'problem' " within the student (p. 29). Yet, it still seems that our current assessment approach does not assess enough dimensions of language proficiency, does not take into consideration important sociocultural and motivational factors, and exhibits little discriminant validity (Damico, 1991). The host of confounding variables and problematic factors must be identified and resolved when assessing CLD students. Failure to do so may result in an invalid and potentially harmful set of evaluative conclusions and recommendations. It is crucial that all educators involved in the assessment of CLD students recognize the extent to which these variables operate to affect test results and the interpretation of those results.

Optimal assessment of CLD students for both instructional and accountability purposes need to be comprehensive, flexible, and responsive. Optimal assessment would consist of a comprehensive assessment system at the school level, in which a complete picture of each student's growth and development is collected, mostly through authentic tasks of performance (LaCelle-Peterson & Rivera, 1994). Assessment data of CLD students should include student background information, school background, language development and instruction histories, classroom-based learning processes, and proficiency in the students' first language as well as the second language. Authentic classroom assessment will most benefit CLD students when educators recognize the influence of their own cultural values and upbringing on their judgment and evaluation of student behavior and performance (Garcia, 1992).

Also, teachers and school personnel need to become informed about cultural and linguistic norms that prevail in students' communities and the types of learning activities and interaction patterns that are common in students' homes. The whole of students' learning should be kept in mind. For CLD students, this may mean combining formal and informal assessment strategies in order to gain a comprehensive picture of their abilities.

Furthermore, true bilingual assessment involves evaluating how a CLD student uses his or her two language systems to perform cognitive tasks (Ascher, 1990). It should consider issues of content and processing factors such as speed. Thus, a comprehensive bilingual assessment should be capable of comparing student performance on tasks across two languages. Clarizio (1982) recommends that a comprehensive bilingual assessment consider the maximum score attained in L1 and L2 tasks as the index of students' abilities or potential. We must ensure that educational excellence for all students includes all learners, especially "those who bring linguistic riches with them to school" (LaCelle-Peterson & Rivera, 1994, p. 73).

CASE REPORT: Reading and Writing in Two Languages

Background

Jeff, age 11 years and 6 months, was an intelligent and charming fifth-grade bilingual/biliterate student in a mainstream classroom. Jeff and his family immigrated to the United States from the Dominican Republic seven years ago. Although Jeff completed kindergarten in his home country, he was not allowed to continue on to first grade when he arrived in the United States because of age requirements. Jeff enrolled in a bilingual kindergarten class at age 5, and remained in the transitional bilingual education (TBE) program through the third grade. During these four years, Jeff achieved much academic success and acquired the necessary English language skills to exit the bilingual program and transition into the mainstream education program.

Although he did not receive direct L1 instruction in fourth grade, Jeff's teacher incorporated English-as-a-second-language (ESL) strategies into her daily classroom instruction in order to help foster his English language development. She also encouraged the maintenance of Jeff's L1 literacy skills by allowing him to practice reading and writing in his native language during Sustained Silent Reading (SSR) and/or free time in the library. In addition, Jeff maintained his Spanish skills by tutoring bilingual third-graders in an after-school literacy program. His first year in an all-English classroom was challenging for Jeff, but he was successful, nonetheless. The scaffolding strategies his fourth-grade teacher provided allowed Jeff to flourish under her caring guidance and support. His experience in the fifth grade has been quite different, though, as the use of his L1 has not been allowed during the school day. Although he continued to speak his native language at home, his exposure to L1 reading and writing has been significantly reduced in the past few months. As a response to Jeff's new academic environment, his parents also have decided to concentrate on L2 literacy at home, to the detriment of his native language.

Jeff's parents have greatly encouraged literacy in the home. They have modeled literate activities for the children by reading in front of them several times a week. They read regularly with Jeff twice a week and checked his homework on a daily basis. Jeff's older brother, age 13, has provided a good model of biliteracy for his younger siblings and has routinely helped Jeff with school assignments. Jeff indicated that he enjoyed reading during his free time and that he liked mystery books most of all. When asked about language choice for reading and writing, Jeff wrote that he preferred English because "I read more better in English then Espanish."

Like the majority of second-language learners, Jeff's first language supported his growing L2 literacy skills. Cummins (1991) states that at least four years are required before even socioeconomically advanced immigrant students can attain grade norms in English academic skills. He adds that better L1 readers/writers are better L2 reader/writers. In Jeff's case, he had not received first-language academic instruction for the past year and a half. Although he was succeeding in the classroom (he was recently selected Student of the Month), the gap in his L1 skills might be affecting his literacy and academic progress. In this study, I assessed Jeff's reading and writing skills in both his languages and analyzed the results. We met on four different occasions at the public library in Jeff's hometown in Massachusetts.

Reading Performance in First Language

As my student two years ago, Jeff had strong phonetic awareness in both L1 and L2 and he was a very meticulous reader. He was cautious upon encountering an unknown word and would silently sound it out before reading it out loud. For the current assessment, I looked at Jeff's oral reading and comprehension skills of unfamiliar text. Jeff and I selected a chapter book that we presumed would be challenging because of the vocabulary level. After thumbing through the pages, he guessed this would be a "little hard" yet a manageable text.

Oral Reading. Jeff read the first chapter of *Ningun Beso Para Mama,* a Spanish chapter book written by Tomy Ungerer. This was Jeff's first experience with this book. In order to explore his knowledge of print, integration of reading strategies, and reading fluency, I took a running record of Jeff's oral reading. He read with a 97 percent accuracy rate. Out of 109 words, he made 6 self-corrections and 3 errors. His self-correction rate was 1:1.5. Jeff's fluency was steady overall but was interrupted when he encountered an unknown word. His self-corrected and uncorrected errors were mostly unfamiliar polysyllabic words. Jeff used visual cues to decode but often inverted letters (one of them usually being *r*). For example, instead of reading *profundamente,* Jeff read *porfundamente.* These two words sound almost identical and may even be pronounced this way in certain Spanish dialects. This confused Jeff, though, because it did not make sense. He continued reading until the end of the line and later he said he was trying to find other clues in the sentence to help him find meaning. When he had finished the line, he went back and asked me about the word. He realized he still did not know the meaning of the word, so he probed further. He looked at context cues and guessed a synonymous word. When he was satisfied with the sentence's meaning, he continued reading. He repeated this pattern with all of his miscues that did not make sense.

On a separate occasion, I returned to the question of reading strategies. I asked Jeff what he did when he did not understand the meaning of words in the text. He said he used several different strategies, including "looking at pictures, sounding out words, using the dictionary, going back to the beginning of the sentence (or paragraph), reading until the end of sentence (or paragraph) and then going back to the beginning to see if it makes sense, and asking someone else for help." These strategies helped him cope with unknown vocabulary in both his languages, as he has learned to transfer his reading skills to English.

Reading Comprehension. In order to check comprehension, I asked Jeff to continue reading until the end of the first chapter and then retell what had happened in the story up to that point. Interestingly, Jeff chose to retell the story in English. (When given a choice, many bilinguals choose the language they feel most comfortable with to show comprehension, usually occurring with L2 text being retold in L1.) Jeff showed a clear understanding of story structure and chronology. He was able to name the characters, setting, major events, and problem in the chapter. I asked him several factual questions and he gave detailed answers to each. I also asked him inferential questions that he was able to explain by using facts from the text. That night, he chose to write a page-by-page English translation of the chapter to show he had text comprehension in both his languages. It was written in chronological order and included specific details and inferences he made about the reading.

Listening Comprehension.   Several tasks were presented to assess native-language listening comprehension. The Writing Conference, the Interest Inventory for Primary Grades, and the "retell" assignment were all presented in Spanish. Jeff said he understood all L1 directions and questions and did not ask for clarification or repetition. Jeff's answers were always appropriate to the task, but always in English, so I did not probe any further. He was able to show that he had clear receptive comprehension skills in his native language, but he did not produce answers or explications in L1.

Oral Skills.   Jeff did not provide many oral responses in L1. From the beginning of the study, I attempted to speak to him in Spanish but he claimed he was "forgetting" how to speak his native language. He said he did not talk to any of his friends in Spanish anymore because some of his new American friends only spoke English and they would be left out of the conversation. Jeff spoke Spanish with his parents and his little brother at home, but he said he gets "mad" when he can't think of words. The Interest Inventory for Primary Grades was intended to get oral responses from Jeff in Spanish, but he chose to respond in English. The few times he did attempt to speak Spanish, Jeff switched to English when he got stuck.

Reading Performance in Second Language

Jeff's L2 reading skills (oral reading, reading comprehension, and listening comprehension) were assessed using Silvaroli's (1997) Classroom Reading Inventory (CRI) (eighth edition). Here are the results:

Informal Reading Inventory Summary

Test: Classroom Reading Inventory (Silvaroli, 8th edition)
Child: Jeff   Age: 11.5   Grade: 5   Date: Nov. '97

Recognition Test   Informal Reading Inventory

Level	Oral Reading Task				Listening Comprehension (%)
	Flash (%)	Untimed (%)	Accuracy (%)	Comprehension (%)	
Preprimer (PP)	100	100			
Primer (P)	100	100			
First (1)	100	100			
Second (2)	100	100	99	100	
Third (3)	70	80	98	80	
Fourth (4)	50	75	97	80	
Fifth (5)			93	50	
Sixth (6)					60

Oral Reading. The preceding chart gives a summary of Jeff's performance on the CRI. Jeff achieved 100 percent accuracy on levels PP, P, 1, and 2 (timed) of the Graded Word Lists. He had 70 percent timed accuracy on level 3 (80 percent untimed) and 50 percent timed accuracy on level 4 (75 percent untimed.) Silvaroli suggests instructional reading level is determined at a 95 percent accuracy rate on the graded word lists. Below that score, the student is reading at his or her frustration level. Jeff's results showed that he was an independent L2 reader on second-grade material (and lower.) On a third-grade word list, he scored at a frustration level. Although he was able to self-correct (or sound out) many of the more challenging words with extra time, his fluency was affected as he perseverated on particular words (discussed later).

Reading Comprehension. The Graded Paragraphs assessed reading comprehension. I selected a passage that was at the highest level at which Jeff recognized 90 percent of the flashed words. Since Jeff only scored 70 percent accuracy on the level-3 list, I began with the level-2 graded passage. He made one significant word error on his oral reading and scored 100 percent accuracy on reading comprehension. Next, he read a level-3 passage and he scored on an independent level here, as well (98 percent reading accuracy, 80 percent comprehension.) He made more self-corrections on the next leveled passage, but he had a score of 97 percent reading accuracy and 80 percent comprehension accuracy (independent). Jeff had significant word recognition errors on the grade 5 and grade 6 passages, scoring at the frustration levels. On the level-5 passage, he made eight significant word recognition errors. He was not able to decode the words *advantages* and *disadvantages* and these caused him trouble each time they appeared in the passage. Even after I told him the words, Jeff was unable to pronounce them and he indicated he had never heard those words before. His comprehension score reflected the trouble he had with the vocabulary, as he answered 50 percent of the questions accurately. At this point, Jeff was becoming a little anxious, so I skipped ahead to the next leveled passage for a listening comprehension task.

On a separate occasion I asked Jeff to choose an easy book that he could read without difficulty. He chose *The Napping House* (by Audrey Wood). Before reading the text, Jeff used prior knowledge to summarize the story and to connect it to his own life. He said the story reminded him of visiting his grandmother in the Dominican Republic because all his cousins slept in one room there. Jeff read with fluency and rhythm. He self-corrected his miscues, sounded out longer words, and used text clues to figure out unknown vocabulary. It was interesting that although he could not tell me the exact definitions of *snoozing, slumbering,* and *dozing,* he knew they were all "sleeping" words. He was able to show he had built a schema on this topic. After reading the story, he completed a story web to show comprehension and knowledge of story structure. Jeff was able to give a detailed description of main characters, setting, problem, and solution.

Listening Comprehension. Jeff's L2 listening comprehension skills were assessed as part of the Classroom Reading Inventory. On a level-6 passage, Jeff was able to answer three out of five comprehension questions. He missed one factual question, but was able to give part of the answer for a second question of this nature. On the vocabulary question for this particular passage, the test asked what the word *secluded* meant. The choices were "hidden," "secret," and "hard to find." Jeff answered, "A mystery, something that is out of sight." Although his answer was not one of the choices from the test, I gave him credit since he was able to describe the concept using his own words. Also, he was able to recount the solution to the story's problem when prompted. His comprehension errors placed him at an instructional level in grade 5 and 6 materials (60 percent comprehension accuracy.)

Oral Skills.   Most of Jeff's oral responses throughout the assessment process were in English. Specifically, answers given during the Individual Characteristics Interview, the retell task (*Ningun Beso Para Mama*), and the Writing Conference were used to assess oral language. According to a holistic oral language scoring rubric (see Figure 8.1), Jeff predominantly achieved a rating of 4, with signs of transition into the next rating level. Specifically, Jeff spoke in social and classroom settings with sustained and connected discourse, and the errors he made did not usually interfere with meaning (a rating of 5). He spoke with occasional hesitation (a rating of 4), used some complex sentences and applied rules of grammar, but lacked control of irregular forms (a rating of 4). There were several examples of this in Jeff's responses in the Writing Conference, as he often inappropriately used the present tense in L2 speech. Some examples are "she *tell* me" and "something that *happen* to me when I was little." This may be a question of dialect, though, since he often left out past tense or plural endings while speaking and reading orally. Jeff also used adequate vocabulary but had some word usage irregularity (a rating of 4). Finally, he understood simple sentences in sustained conversation with occasional repetition (a rating of 5).

Writing Performance in First Language

Jeff declined to do a prewriting activity during the L1 writing task. The writing prompt asked him to describe a personal experience of his choice of an expressive/narrative nature. He wrote about a car accident that he was involved in several years ago. He titled the piece "El Acidente" ("The Accident") and proudly said he remembered this experience vividly and therefore had a lot of details to write about:

> *El acidente*
> Cuando yo estaba chiquito con mi hermano hibamos para la escuela, estaba nevando muchas nieve. Entonse miramos los dos lados y crusamos. Entonse me hermano me dijo que buscaba la sombrilla que el quedo en la casa. Despues yo la fui a buscar la sombrilla. Yo mire un lado y caundo yo hibia a mirar el otro lado el carro medio con el espejo de mirar. Yo me marie y cai a la nieve. El hombre que medio me trajo para los hospital. Me hermano grande fue corriendo a mi mama el le

FIGURE 8.1   Holistic Scoring Rubric for Oral Language

Rating	Description
6	• Communicates competently in social and classroom settings • Speaks fluently • Masters a variety of grammatical structures • Uses extensive vocabulary but may lag behind native-speaking peers • Understands classroom discussion without difficulty • Speaks in social and classroom settings with sustained and connected discourse; any errors do not interfere with meaning
5	• Speaks with near-native fluency; any hesitations do not interfere with communication • Uses a variety of structures with occasional grammatical errors • Uses varied vocabulary • Understands simple sentences in sustained conversation; requires repetition
4	• Initiates and sustains a conversation with descriptors and details; exhibits self-confidence in social situations; begins to communicate in classroom settings • Speaks with occasional hesitation • Uses some complex sentences; applies rules of grammar but lacks control of irregular forms (e.g., *runned, mans, not never, more higher*) • Uses adequate vocabulary; some word usage irregularities • Understands classroom discussions with repetition, rephrasing, and clarification
3	• Begins to initiate conversation; retells a story or experience; asks and responds to simple questions • Speaks hesitantly because of rephrasing and searching for words • Uses predominantly present tense verbs; demonstrates errors of omission (leaves words out, word endings off) • Uses limited vocabulary • Understands simple sentences in sustained conversation; requires repetition
2	• Begins to communicate personal and survival needs • Speaks in single-word utterances and short patterns • Uses functional vocabulary • Understands words and phrases; requires repetitions
1	• Begins to name concrete objects • Repeats words and phrases • Understands little or no English

Source: From O'Malley: *Authentic Assessment for English Language Learners* by J. Michael O'Malley & Lorraine Valdez Pierce. Copyright © 1996. Reprinted by permission of Addison Wesley Longman. Fairfax County, Virginia, Public Schools, *Suggestions for Assessment/Evaluation in the Integrated Language Arts Classroom,* 1989.

dijo que me paso. Mi mama se fui con el hombre que havio el acidente. Mi mama y mi hermano fueron al hospital con el hombre. Cuando yo desperte de el acidente yo tenia 3 puntos a entro y ocho a fuera.

Two scoring rubrics were used to assess his writing skills: a holistic scoring rubric (see Figure 8.2) and an analytic scoring rubric (see Figure 8.3). With the first rubric, Jeff's writing was assessed as level 4. Specifically, he clearly conveyed meaning, developed a logical and sequential paragraph by only including important details, wrote a variety of sentence structures with limited use of transitions (*Despues, Cuando, Entonces*), chose vocabulary that was adequate to his purpose, and wrote with some grammatical and mechanical errors that seldom diminished communication. On the second rubric, he achieved scores of 3s and 4s in the five different domains. For example, in the area of "Composition," Jeff's story had a central idea with some elaboration, but also some digressions (domain score of 3). The "Style"

FIGURE 8.2 Holistic Scoring Rubric for Writing Assessment

Level 6	• Conveys meaning clearly and effectively • Presents multi-paragraph organization, with clear introductions, development of ideas, and conclusion • Shows evidence of smooth transitions • Uses varied, vivid, precise vocabulary consistently • Writes with few grammatical/mechanical errors
Level 5	• Conveys meaning clearly • Presents multi-paragraph organization logically, though some parts may not be fully developed • Shows some evidence of effective transitions • Uses varied and vivid vocabulary appropriate for audience and purpose • Writes with some grammatical/mechanical errors without affecting meaning
Level 4	• Expresses ideas coherently most of the time • Develops a logical paragraph • Writes with a variety of sentence structures with a limited use of transitions • Chooses vocabulary that is (often) adequate to purpose • Writes with grammatical/mechanical errors that seldom diminish communication
Level 3	• Attempts to express ideas coherently • Begins to write a paragraph by organizing ideas • Writes primarily simple sentences • Uses high frequency vocabulary • Writes with grammatical/mechanical errors that sometimes diminish communication
Level 2	• Begins to convey meaning • Writes simple sentences/phrases • Uses limited or repetitious vocabulary • Spells inventively • Uses little or no mechanics, which often diminishes meaning
Level 1	• Draws pictures to convey meaning • Uses single words, phrases • Copies from a model

Source: From O'Malley: *Authentic Assessment for English Language Learners* by J. Michael O'Malley & Lorraine Valdez Pierce. Copyright © 1996. Reprinted by permission of Addison Wesley Longman. Developed by ESL teachers, Prince William County Public Schools, Virginia.

included purposefully chosen information, voice, vocabulary, and sentence variety (domain score of 4). "Sentence Formation" consisted of mostly standard word order with some enjambment (domain score of 3). Jeff used mostly standard inflections, agreement, and word meaning (domain score of 3). Finally, he had reasonable control of "Mechanics," as his errors did not usually detract from meaning (domain score of 3). It is interesting to note that Jeff's writing form of language was very similar to his oral form. He used highly dialectical language, sometimes dropping word endings in both forms, but usually conveying his meaning clearly.

As in his reading, Jeff used several strategies in his L1 and L2 writing. During the assessment process, he accessed prior knowledge and said, "I choose topics I know about and have a lot of details on." When he got stuck, he stopped to think, then continued writing. He also used the dictionary for words he was unsure of. In a postwriting conference, he said, "If I'm stuck with an idea, I have a friend read the paper and see if he can help me." He also edited for capitals, periods, commas, and accents. Finally, he said he checked that his main idea, solution to the problem, and spelling made sense. When he gave me his draft, he was able to talk about his process and clarified that it was not ready for publication yet, that it was only a "first try." Jeff indicated that he wanted to improve "his vocabulary and do the accents right." He also said, "Sometimes I forget the *h* because it's silent, and sometimes I mix Spanish and English words."

Writing Performance in Second Language

For this part of the assessment, Jeff decided to do two prewriting activities. As in the L1 task, Jeff was asked to write an expressive/narrative essay about a personal experience. First, Jeff wrote an outline of the events he remembered from his experience. Then he chose the six most relevant events and completed a "sequence" semantic map. He used complete sentences and organized his ideas logically. After he completed his semantic map, he began to write his story entitled "Going to a Football Game." As he wrote, he referred to his semantic map for story structure. Jeff was unsure of the spelling of three words: *humongous, touchdown,* and *entire.* He circled these words as he wrote them and then used a dictionary as an editing tool when he had finished. He also checked capitals and punctuation marks, adding an exclamation mark to one of his sentences:

Going to a Football Game

It all started when my teacher Miss Gort pick me up. On the car was Miss Gort friend his name is Bill, he is a cool guy. We stop to get gas and I put gas on Miss Gort car, it was fun. In the highway, my teacher and her friend we was going to Providence to see a football game. We got to the stadium, we talk then we buy the ticket to go inside, it was humagues (humongous.) The game started and I learned the difence of football. What is a safety, and how does they get points for each toughdown (touchdown). The stadium was crowed of a lot of people. On in back of me there was a guy explained the intager (entire) game step by step. One of my favorite part was when the player reach to get the ball.

Then out of nowhere the other team player knock him down. The guy got smoke so badly! The Brown won the Rhode Island score 23 to 15. When the game was over I went out to the field and I shock each hand to the three tall, and good players hand, it was cool. Then my teacher Miss Gort took me home and I was please that she take me to a football game in Rhode Island.

Again, both a holistic scoring rubric (Figure 8.2) and an analytic scoring rubric (Figure 8.3) were used to assess Jeff's L2 writing skills. His score reflected a level 4 when assessed holistically. He conveyed meaning clearly and expressed ideas coherently most of the time (a rating of 4–5); he developed a logical paragraph (a rating of 4); he wrote a variety of sentence structures with limited use of transitions (a rating of 4); he chose vocabulary that was appropriate to his purpose (a rating of 4); and he wrote with grammatical/mechanical errors that seldom diminished communication (a rating of 4). With respect to the individual domains, Jeff focused on his central ideas with organized and elaborated text ("Composing"—a score of 4); purposefully chose vocabulary, sentence variety, information, and voice to affect the reader ("Style"—a score of 4); used mostly standard word order with some enjambment or sentence fragments ("Sentence Formation"—a score of 3); made some errors with inflections and agreement ("Usage"—a score of 2); and made some errors with spelling and punctuation that did not detract from meaning ("Mechanics"—a score of 3). The data showed that Jeff's conceptual and emotional aspects of language were at the same level in L1 and L2, but the mechanical aspects were not. This was of no surprise since, as a second-language learner, Jeff was still in the process of acquiring the specific domains of the English language.

Jeff used several strategies during and after the writing task. He skipped unknown words and returned to them later, used drawings or pictures in the writing, checked to see if the writing followed the directions, reread to see if it made sense, and checked for spelling, punctuation, capitals, and grammar. Jeff said he hoped to improve several aspects of his L2 writing, including "to try to write full sentense or good words to discribe what I am writing about." In addition, Jeff wants to "work on spelling, . . . vocabulary and meaning . . . [and he wants] the story to make sense."

Current Abilities

Jeff, an 11-year-old fifth-grader, was an independent reader and writer in both his languages. He could read materials intended for third-graders (L2) or fourth-graders (L1) with fluency, adequate accuracy, and good comprehension. He generally had strong decoding skills and good sight vocabulary. Jeff used prior knowledge to make connections with the text. He predicted and corrected from meaning, but had a limited English vocabulary (for his age) as a second-language learner. Although he had several different strategies for dealing with difficult text, he could perseverate on words rather than blanking and looking at larger context. This affected his fluency and sometimes made his reading choppy.

FIGURE 8.3 Analytic Scoring Rubric for Writing

Domain Score*	Composing	Style	Sentence Formation	Usage	Mechanics
4	Focuses on central ideas with an organized and elaborated text	Purposefully chosen vocabulary, sentence variety, information, and voice to affect reader	Standard word order, no enjambment (run-on sentences), completeness (no sentence fragments), standard modifiers and coordinators, and effective transitions	Standard inflections (e.g., plurals, possessives, -ed, -ing with verbs, and -ly with adverbs), subject-verb agreement (we were vs. we was), standard word meaning	Effective use of capitalization, punctuation, spelling, and formatting (paragraphs noted by indenting)
3	Central idea, but not as evenly elaborated and some digressions	Vocabulary less precise and information chosen less purposeful	Mostly standard word order, some enjambment or sentence fragments	Mostly standard inflections, agreement, and word meaning	Mostly effective use of mechanics; errors do not detract from meaning
2	Not a focused idea or more than one idea, sketchy elaboration, and many digressions	Vocabulary basic and not purposefully selected; tone flat or inconsistent	Some non-standard word order, enjambment, and word omissions (e.g., verbs)	Some errors with inflections, agreement, and word meaning	Some errors with spelling and punctuation that detract from meaning
1	No clear idea, little or no elaboration, many digressions	Not controlled, tone flat, sentences halted or choppy	Frequent non-standard word order, enjambment, and word omissions	Shifts from one tense to another; errors in conventions (them/those, good/well, double negatives, etc.)	Misspells even simple words; little formatting evident

*4 = Consistent control
3 = Reasonable control
2 = Inconsistent control
1 = Little or no control

Source: From O'Malley: *Authentic Assessment for English Language Learners* by J. Michael O'Malley & Lorraine Valdez Pierce. Copyright © 1996. Reprinted by permission of Addison Wesley Longman. J. Self, *Virginia's Literacy Passport Test (LPT) for Writing: A Performance Assessment: A Resource Notebook for Teachers.* Radford, VA: Virginia Department of Education, Regional Field Services, Radford University, undated.

179

Jeff's biggest strengths were that he loved to read and he read for under-standing. He knew he could decode the words but was not satisfied with simply that. The text needed to make sense to him before he turned the page. He worked hard to develop his L2 literacy skills and had set clear goals for improvement. He had a very positive attitude toward learning and took pride in his achievements.

Jeff was able to write clear, detailed, and elaborate stories in both his lan-guages. He was a fairly good speller, but not afraid to use inventive spelling on a first draft. He showed confidence that he could correct his "inventive" words by using his editing strategy for spelling. He was able to focus on central ideas and use appropri-ate vocabulary, sentence variety, information, and voice to affect the reader. Although his dialect sometimes interfered, Jeff used mostly standard word order, inflections, agreement, and word meaning. Finally, his mechanical errors did not usually detract from meaning. His writing greatly benefited from the many strate-gies Jeff had developed and used on a daily basis. These included skipping unknown words and returning to them later, using drawings or pictures in the writing, check-ing to see if the writing follows the directions, rereading the story to ensure it makes sense, and checking for spelling, punctuation, capitals, and grammar.

Recommendations

Reading.   Although Jeff liked to be challenged, he would benefit from reading easy L1 and L2 materials from time to time. Although he focused on reading Eng-lish chapter books in school, Jeff should read primary-level stories to his 5-year-old brother in both Spanish and English. This would promote fluent reading habits and reinforce sight vocabulary. On more challenging text, building on prior knowledge and activating schema seemed to help Jeff with comprehension. Word webs or KWL charts might help him mentally prepare for the vocabulary that is to come, and hence make his reading more automatic. To further increase L2 vocab-ulary, Jeff would benefit from thematic instruction in which subject areas share a common theme. In this way, new vocabulary may be reinforced throughout the day in different situations. Also, associating new vocabulary with personal expe-riences or knowledge would help Jeff expand his developing L2 vocabulary. Finally, application, use, and practice of newly acquired vocabulary is essential for literacy development. Therefore, Jeff should use his new vocabulary words in oral language, storytelling, story reading, and writing.

Writing.   Jeff showed strong writing skills in both his languages. His own strate-gies already helped him greatly improve his writing. He would benefit from peer editing with a native English speaker who could help him with grammar and mechanics. Also, prewriting activities such as semantic maps, outlines, or discus-sion seemed to help him organize his ideas. He would then able to concentrate on vocabulary and the more difficult aspects of language while writing. Finally, Jeff flourished when he made personal connections with text or writing assignments. Allowing Jeff to write about things he is interested in or things he knows about would reinforce his existing writing skills and help him make the transition into higher writing performance levels.

9

Where Are They Now?

Andrew

Andrew is enjoying his sophomore year at a large university in the South, living in a suite of rooms in a high-rise dorm next to an in-ground pool. He has already told his sister to prepare his parents for a decline in his grades.

Andrew attended a small college in the Northeast during his freshman year because the school offered a degree in physical training. He fared much better academically than he had in high school, says Virginia, his mother. Unfortunately, Andrew felt left out of things socially.

Virginia says he liked to be in football and gymnastics in high school, but that the family had made the decision that he might overextend himself by trying to compete in sports in college. He tried wrestling but did not like it. Since he had been on the wrestling team, even for a short time, he was effectively isolated from the football players and gymnasts.

Andrew had followed my advice and sought tutoring his senior year in high school. Virginia chose a man she had worked with in a civic program for mentoring teenagers and shared my case report (see Chapter 1) with him. Andrew and the tutor worked on organizational skills, particularly deciding how much time Andrew actually needed to allocate for homework reading, given his slow reading speed. They also worked on exam study techniques and SAT preparation. Andrew retook the SAT 1 with extended time and improved his score.

Reading, however, continues to trouble Andrew. "He missed learning to love to read," Virginia says regretfully. "He's not a real student." Virginia understands because she, too, had a reading problem in school. She often found herself cheating to avoid embarrassment in class. "I love to read now," she says, although she reads slowly.

This brings me to novels and bon-bons. My sister, Shirley, who has always been older and wiser than I, says that vacations are for reading novels and eating bon-bons. During graduate school, I was assigned between 500 and 1,000 pages per week of textbook reading, leaving little time for novels and bon-bons, despite the poet Mekeel McBride's advice that "Even a camel needs an oasis in the desert." Andrew's undergraduate reading load may be smaller, but with his reading speed it probably feels like graduate school to him. During his freshman year, as I did in graduate school, Andrew bypassed the oasis and brought home exemplary grades. This year, the pool is right outside his dorm.

Without time for novels and bon-bons—that is, easy reading done at his own pace—Andrew is unlikely to develop the reading habit his mother has found. Luckily for me, graduate school lasted only three years. Andrew has two more to go.

Jason

Jason currently attends seventh grade in a residential school for dyslexic boys. "All 30 boys have the same problem," says his mother, Donna. Jason has individual language instruction and he studies composition in a class of three boys and the teacher. Unlike his work in public school, the entire day is taught through Orton-Gillingham methods.

During Jason's sixth-grade year, he was pulled out of regular classes for both Reading Recovery and Orton-Gillingham tutoring. The Reading Recovery teacher was hired as a result of my report. In January, she wrote that Jason had had 40 lessons and had met many of the goals set in September. Using an L-shaped marker, he had developed one-to-one correspondence to print with his oral reading. He had also begun self-monitoring and cross-checking information and had developed a sight vocabulary including *the, then, them, they,* and *there.* He had begun reading readiness and preprimer books (levels 2 and 3) but had moved to level 12 by January. His teacher hoped he would be able to read levels 16 to 18 books (mid-grade 2) by the end of the year.

A learning disabilities specialist reviewed Jason's case for the school district, labeled him dyslexic, and discounted the Reading Recovery tutoring as not designed for dyslexics. She suggested Orton-Gillingham tutoring, and the district provided both pull-out teachers for Jason. In May of that year, his Orton-Gillingham teacher reported that he had been instructed in all the consonants, five vowels, five digraphs, and the vowel-consonant-silent *e* (VCe) pattern. He had used keywords, phonograms, and finger-typing (a tactile-kinesthetic support for decoding). She read aloud to him, helped him with computer skills and cursive handwriting, and assisted him in editing his writing. She also noticed that he lacked motivation and appeared tired most of the time.

The month before he entered fifth grade, Jason wrote, "Pat ITS ham," and read it as "It's Pat's ham." In November of his seventh-grade year, he wrote the letter shown in Figure 9.1. Donna tells me the boys must write one letter a week, with help in editing, but that the letters are not dictated and recopied. Jason has clearly learned to encode English words well enough to write a letter typical of many elementary-aged children.

During his most recent visit home, Jason read a "Step into Reading" book, *Wake Up, Sun!* (Harrison), a book intended for beginning first-grade readers. "He read a little bit to me every night," Donna said. "He tries to sound out the words himself, and if he can't, he will say, 'What is it?' but he doesn't refuse to read." Again, Jason has clearly progressed from the boy who could only read linguistic

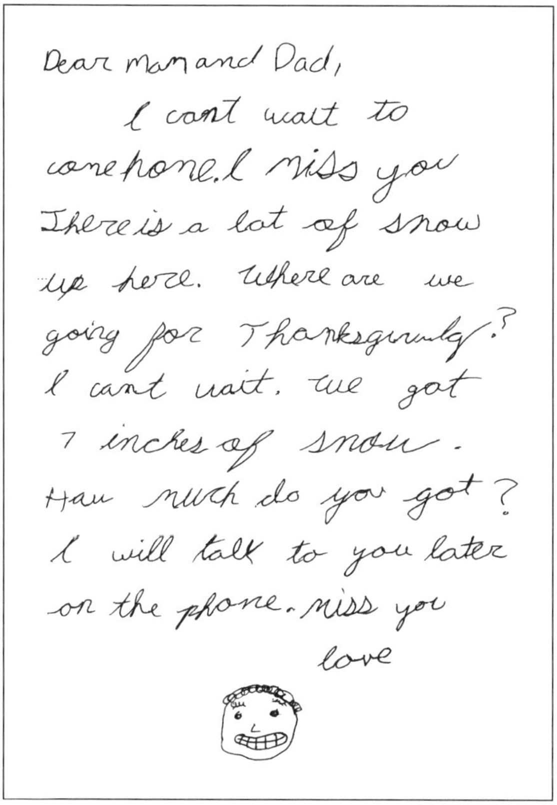

Dear Mom and Dad,
    I cant wait to come home. I miss you There is a lot of snow up here. Where are we going for Thanksgiving? I cant wait. We got 7 inches of snow. How much do you got? I will talk to you later on the phone. miss you
                love

FIGURE 9.1   Jason's Letter

readers that he had read repeatedly in class, allowing memory of the text to override the visual information in the text.

Donna says the residential school is intended to be a two- or three-year program. Jason is in his second year. "Last year he was trying to get kicked out in any way he could. But we were firm and told him, 'This won't get you home.' He finally grasped it," she says. "It was horrible and heartbreaking. There were days we hung up and thought we should go and get him, but we didn't do it."

Donna and Russell, Jason's father, have been firm because they saw that the public school was not working and that Jason was seriously depressed. "The last year in public school, he didn't have to do anything as long as he behaved," Donna says. The new school understands that the first year is basically an academic loss, as the boys accept their placement, she explains. "Jason would like to go to public high school," she says, "but no one has said how long the residential placement will last."

To its credit, Jason's school district has provided every intervention suggested for his learning difficulties. To the ongoing shame of our profession, whole-language and Orton-Gillingham specialists have continued to fight over the name of programs provided for labeled students, rather than examine the behavior and learning of the students. A whole-language expert reviewed a draft of this book and castigated me for suggesting Orton-Gillingham tutoring for Sadie. Jason's learning disabilities specialist dismissed Reading Recovery as not a derivative of Orton-Gillingham and therefore not appropriate for him. Later in the chapter you will see what two years of Orton-Gillingham training have done for Sadie.

In January of his fifth-grade year, after four months of Reading Recovery lessons, Jason was able to read first-grade books with self-monitoring and cross-checking behaviors. In November of his seventh-grade year, he is able to read first-grade texts to his mother, self-monitor and cross-check, and ask for help if he cannot figure out the word. His letter home is a marked improvement over his inability to write more than individual words independently in August before he began fifth grade, but as a reader he is exactly the same. If Jason is to have any hope of succeeding in public high school, the next year and a half of his residential schooling will have to provide him with at least six years of reading growth.

Kristen

In the spring of her second-grade year, Kristen wrote for me (her reading of the text is in parentheses):

> Caring adout horse (Caring about horses)
> You havd to hus them (You have to breed them)
> You haf to hid them (You have to feed them)
> word them give them a home (You have to water them. You have to give them a good home)
> Do all difint tings. (You have to do all those good things.)

In the fall of her fourth-grade year, she went on a field trip to a local historic house and was asked to write a sentence about the history of Thanksgiving, beginning with the letter *O*. She wrote:

> Over the year their
> has been changes.
> Since when the
> first feast
> happened

In the spring of grade 2, Kristen misspelled 9 of 23 words, including basic sight words such as *about, have,* and *things.* She wrote all simple sentences with punctuation only at the end. She omitted words and began each sentence with *You have to . . . .* Now, in fourth grade, she misspelled only 2 of 13 words. She wrote a complex sentence, beginning with a prepositional phrase of time and ending with a dependent clause. Every word she wrote was a real word, although she left off one inflection and chose the wrong homophone for *there*. She used the word *feast* and spelled it correctly.

Kristen's mother, Beth, was worried that Kristen did not punctuate the sentence correctly and that her teacher had not mentioned the fact nor made Kristen correct it. I pointed out the marks of growth and explained that as children develop more complex sentence structures, they often fail to punctuate them correctly. "In effect, her reach exceeds her grasp," I said. Kristen's father, Victor, was impressed by the evidence of learning, but he remained concerned about the lack of attention to detail. "I'm the poster boy for winging it," he said, referring to his own history of learning difficulties, "and I know Kristen can wing it."

Both he and Beth felt that Kristen's third-grade teacher, Mr. Randolph, would have pointed out irregularities and challenged Kristen to go back, find them, and fix them. In grade 3, Kristen had also kept a learning log, a self-reflective journal that she reread occasionally, in the manner of Calkins (1991), to extend her learning and her use of language, and to share her growth with others. Beth and Victor had been invited to read her log prior to teacher conferences and to respond in writing to Kristen's work.

Mr. Randolph had therefore incorporated some of the recommendations in my report, making Kristen's writing meaningful and directed toward actual readers who would comment on it. He made editing her responsibility and showed her how to do it after writing. But he went further. "He translated the Benchmark language," Beth said, for use in the classroom. "The Benchmark strategies were posted in the classroom," she added. Notice that Kristen spelled *feast* correctly (as just discussed), a vowel digraph she missed on the Names Test 18 months earlier. As Victor said, "It was chartable. She was catching up." In fact, testing done in the late winter of her third-grade year did show growth:

Durrell Analysis of Reading Difficulty

Subtest	Grade 2	Grade 3
Oral Reading	1H-2L	2M-2H
Silent Reading	N/A	2H-3L
Listening Comprehension	4M	5M
Listening Vocabulary	3M	5L
Word Recognition	1H	1H-2L
Word Analysis	1H	1H-2L
Spelling	2L-2M	3M
Visual Memory for Words	2M	2L-2M*
Sounds in Words	3M	3M**
Sounds in Isolation		
Blends and Digraphs	3M	2M-3L*
Phonograms	Below norms	2M***

*Scores actually show a decline.
**Ability to hear and segment sounds remains grade appropriate.
***Phonograms show largest increase and are the focus of Benchmark instruction.

These scores show Kristen reading silently slightly better than orally, which is to be expected since she is released from the need to pronounce each word correctly. Although the scores show her six months to a year below grade level, the special education team deemed her two years behind in reading. They did notice her gains in phonogram knowledge, presumably from the Benchmark instruction and Mr. Randolph's in-class carryover. Her oral language abilities, measured by the listening tasks, continue to grow ahead of grade-level expectations. Woodcock-Johnson scores tell a similar tale:

Woodcock-Johnson Psychoeducational Battery–Revised

Subtest	Grade 1 Percentile	Grade 3 Percentile
Writing Samples	43rd	24th*
Dictation	17th	16th**
Letter/Word Identification	15th	19th**
Reading Vocabulary	30th	31st**
Passage Comprehension	8th	25th***
Word Attack	12th	26th***

*Decline
**No change
***Improvement

I note here that Kristen has shown no gain or actually a loss in accuracy of performance in the subtests that require strong visual memory of word forms or extemporaneous writing. She improved in the areas in which she had been instructed: blending sounds to make words and understanding grade-level text. Even the WJ–R grade-level score in reading gave her a 2.5 (fifth month of second grade) during her sixth month of third grade. Surprisingly, the district team that labeled Kristen called her two years below grade level in reading. To the district's credit, the speech and language specialist discounted low performance on the Clinical Evaluation of Language Fundamentals–Revised in light of Kristen's demonstrated oral language proficiency in class and in the testing session.

Beth and Victor are concerned that Kristen's fourth-grade teacher, much less experienced than Mr. Randolph, is not providing enough code instruction. They have seen the disparity between Kristen's work and that of her peers grow. Kristen also hates the Benchmark training this year. Twelve students from Kristen's class leave for Benchmark four times a week for 30 minutes; the eight who remain do "enrichment" activities in the content areas the class is studying. For instance, they have done research about Thomas Edison and prepared a written report. Beth objected to the term *enrichment* because "Kristen had feelings about that," and so the teacher has renamed the work. Still, such extended, content-integrated reading and writing does not exist in the rest of Kristen's day. The whole class writes 15 or 20 minutes in journals during bus arrivals at the beginning of the day. They do not reread their journals for writing ideas. For the "writing process," they write stories.

Consequently, Kristen is lobbying to get out of Benchmark, saying she is bored because there so many more students in the special class now. Only five or six students attended Benchmark last year. She also misses the things the other kids are doing. "She knows she's labeled," Beth says. "She sees the kids who are not going out the door with her." Victor says that when he and Beth met with the principal and the Benchmark teacher, the principal seemed to be reacting to "external pressure to support Benchmark" because the school's scores were the lowest in the district on recent statewide assessments.

Beth and Victor have arranged for a tutor from the local university to meet with Kristen twice a week. Molly, the tutor, is spending the first few sessions getting to know Kristen as a reader. She and Kristen are partner reading *The Twits* (Dahl, 1980), which the publisher rates as a third-grade book. After the first session, according to Beth, Kristen came running downstairs shouting, "Molly makes reading *fun!*"

The special education team decided to code Kristen as learning disabled due to visual memory deficits, and they developed an individual educational plan that included many elements of the case report in Chapter 5:

- Kristen will use structural analysis, context clues, and phonograms to decode words with 90 percent accuracy.
- Kristen will practice reading the sight words and be able to recognize their spelling patterns with 100 percent accuracy.
- Kristen will be able to recognize vowel diphthongs such as *ea, oo, ou, ur,* and *ir* and the sounds that they make in words with 80 percent accuracy.
- Kristen will choose her spelling words weekly and be responsible for learning them with 95 percent accuracy.
- Kristen will identify the purpose and the audience that she is writing for 100 percent of the time.
- Kristen will edit her writing for correct punctuation, capitalization, and spelling. She will be able to use resources in the class and peer conferences to do this with 100 percent accuracy.
- Kristen will revise her writing for meaning and focus using peer response and teacher conference feedback.

Of course, I worry that the goals also include oral reading at least three times a week and the sight word practice does seem to imply reading of flash cards or lists. The spelling words do come from the Benchmark lists. But this IEP, although maintaining the behavioristic language of "90 percent accuracy," does focus on whole acts of writing (and sometimes reading) among a community of learners. No wonder Kristen has made gains!

Mike

Mike finished sixth grade at his Montessori school and he and his family decided he would go public school "where everyone else in town goes," an important consideration for Mike, who desperately wanted to read what everyone else was reading in fifth grade. He has done well in language arts, receiving a 90 for the first marking period of his seventh-grade year. He is allowed to choose his own books and is currently reading his way through Gary Paulsen's work and writing the required book reports. His mother, Elizabeth, observes that Mike selects "the skinniest books he can find, not for interest at all," so Mike is still counting the pages.

Mike worked with a tutor outside of school during grade 6, doing articulation games, but refusing to do the homework, including assigned reading. He did write poems, however, and learned how to edit them on his own after composing. Elizabeth says he can now edit his written work to 90 percent accuracy before he hands it in. There is no evidence, however, that Mike has received any syntactical, text structure, or story grammar instruction suggested in the report. He does, occasionally, write crime stories on his own, Elizabeth says, just as he did in fifth grade. When she edited one before he asked her to, Mike abandoned the project.

Mike's case makes clear, however, that improvement in reading and writing does not solve all of life's problems. Elizabeth and Daniel (Mike's father) call Mike's seventh-grade year "horrible" because of the academic and social problems he has encountered entering the public system from the Montessori school. Although Mike scored two 90s, two 80s, and two 70s on his report card, he had never had homework, note taking, or tests in his Montessori experience. His current teachers do not want Elizabeth working with him, but she says, "If a kid doesn't know how to take notes or how to study for tests, and no one's going to teach him, I have to help him." In fact, Mike missed the first six days of school with medical problems, yet he was expected to take the first tests, with no chance for make up, she says.

Socially, things have been better. Because Mike has had difficulty in language arts, he has been placed in a lower-level math class, despite demonstrated strength in that area, and the students in this class have been beating him up. Mike has had his head smashed into the wall, has had his shirt ripped when he refused to vacate a seat on the bus, has been choked in the hallway for allegedly insulting another boy's girlfriend, and has been "assaulted" (his father's term) by a boy with a plastic knife, suffering a cut hand. Elizabeth says that the boys admitted attacking Mike but that the principal had meted out no discipline until Daniel and Elizabeth complained. "Probably five kids have been suspended because of Mike," she says. Other students have learned to take this intimidation, according to Elizabeth, but she refuses to let Mike accept it. She and her husband are searching for another school.

Tara

Tara is now in seventh grade in the same parochial school she previously attended, and her fifth-grade teacher is no longer employed there. Tara's mother says that they considered the local public school but that most of Tara's friends would not have been in the same building. Instead, Tara continued at Assumption, and the family shared my report with her sixth- and seventh-grade teachers who work in three-member grade-level teams.

Tara is given more time to finish her writing, often composing on the computer, which helps with her spelling, as first-draft spelling continues to be poor. According to her mother, Tara does not make brainstorm lists prior to writing, but appears to memorize information, then write. Her grades have been much better over the last two years.

Tara has continued to read easier books to her little sister, and there has been a noticed improvement in Tara's reading speed. "She's a lot happier, and things are starting to click for her in school," Tara's mom says.

Sadie after Fourth Grade

Sadie Is Sick

Virginia walks over and around the bouncing puppy on her way from the garden to the house. At the end of the lane, intermittent July sun frosts the ocean.

"Don't mind Clover," she says. "She's just begun to nip and chew and be noisy." We go into the kitchen, now sporting a child gate and a large stainless cage. Clover whines outside the screened slider.

"Sadie's lying down. I picked her up from camp with an ear infection today. I told the doctor last week that's what it was, but he wouldn't listen." Where have I heard that before? I think to myself. "Sadie, come on out. Jay's here."

Sadie unwraps herself from a quilt on the couch, reddish blonde hair limp around her freckles.

"How are you feeling?" I ask.

"I don't feel like reading," Sadie tells Virginia, as she slides in behind the kitchen table. Two parakeets chatter to each other in a cage on a shelf nearby.

Sadie agrees to try anyway, since I have come so far, much as she did last year at school, although she had been nervous all day.

Virginia has collected a stack of Sadie's writing, some test reports, and a few books. She begins to tell me that she had some trouble finding examples of Sadie's writing this year. "These are what came home, but I'm not sure they're all from writing. There's writing in everything these days."

"We didn't use the book," Sadie cuts in.

"You mean the handwriting book," Virginia adds.

"We could choose to print or use cursive," Sadie says.

"Which do you like better?" I ask.

"*I* think I can print faster," Sadie says, sliding a look at Virginia, who explains that Sadie went to Orton-Gillingham tutoring three times a week during handwriting time. Otherwise, she used the fourth-grade literature-based basal with her special education teacher, Ms. Billings, or a teacher's aide, or her "cool" (Sadie's word) teacher, Mr. Davis. They completed comprehension worksheets on predictions and characters' motives.

Mr. Davis, Virginia told me, was very good about finding easy supplemental reading for Sadie. The fourth-grade literature-based package included no more

E. B. White
Famous Story Writer

What was E. B. White's job? White was a very famous story writer. He wrote kids' books. He also wrote grown up books, too.

E. B. White was born in Mount Vernon, New York on July 11, 1899. He had three brothers, Marian, Albert, and Stanley. He also had three sisters, Clara and Lillian. He grew up in a comfortable home with his family. In 1904 he entered kindergarten. He was terrified of school. When he was fourteen years old he went to Mount Vernon High School and became a very good student.

He graduated from high school in 1917. He began writing when he was a junior at Cornell University. He wrote for the college newspaper. After he graduated from college in 1921, he got a job in New York at the United Press. He soon left the United Press and went to the American Legion News Service where he learned about publicity. Between 1922 and 1923 he worked for the Seattle Times and traveled to Alaska on the ship S.S. Buford. He worked on the ship and returned to New York in 1925 at age twenty six to work in advertising. He then found a job at the New Yorker Magazine. Eventually he married Katharine Angell in 1929. The same year he published his first two books. His son was born in 1930.

In 1938 he moved from Maine and in 1945 he wrote Stewart Little. In 1952 Charlotte's Web was published. E. B. White wrote these books by observing the animals on his farm. In 1958 the book received the Lewis Carroll Shelf Award. E. B. White was also awarded the gold medal for essays by the National Institute of Arts and Letters for his work.

Charlotte's Web was considered not only White's best book for children, but also the crowning achievement of his career. In 1963 E. B. White received the Presidential Medal of Freedom.

In 1969 he wrote the Trumpeter of the Swans. His books received many awards. His wife Katherine died in 1977 from a heart attack. Many years later E. B. White died of an illness but his friends say he died of a broken heart.

sad but very interesting!

FIGURE 9.2   Sadie's E. B. White Piece

below grade-level supplemental books than had the third-grade package, but after last year's assessment, Virginia knew what to ask for this year. "Of course, the class never had time to do choice reading," Virginia explains. No surprise there.

Sadie Does Not Want to Be a Girl

Sadie has a research paper on E. B. White and a story about a class fishing trip to share. She picks the E. B. White piece (see Figure 9.2) as her best. "I'd say the best project we did was the wax museum. We pretended to be our person and we had to sit still for about two hours but we just ended up wandering around," Sadie explains. She still chooses her best piece based on the subject, but she has also added the dimension of her experience writing or sharing it, as do many younger writers (Simmons, 1992). This is hardly surprising, since the students did not get to choose their subjects, either.

"He gives us a piece of paper and it has who we are on it," Sadie explains. "First, I was a girl and I didn't want to be a girl because then you have to wear a dress. We didn't have to wear it for the day, but then you have to wear tights." Virginia adds that dresses make it hard to hang upside down on the playground.

"So I went up to him," Sadie continues, "and he said, 'Any girls don't want to be girls?' Me and another one raised our hands and he said, 'O.K. We'll be going down to the library to pick out people.' But there was nobody we wanted there, but the other girls picked out who they wanted to be but I didn't and he just came up to me and said, 'How would you like to be E. B. White?' "

The process was also teacher directed. "He gave us books, and we just looked through the books. He gave us two or three cards to start off with, and we wrote down the important things," Sadie explained. They used the cards to make an outline, wrote from the outline, then got their costumes together.

I ask Sadie if the writing is good for any other reasons. "I'd say I got all the important facts—you know, when he was born, and how he felt when he became what he wanted to be, and how his family felt when he died," Sadie says. These reasons are new—Sadie values including people's feelings in her writing, which is a possible intertextual link to her literature-based basal worksheets. However, looking at her writing (Figure 9.2), I do not see references to feelings, except the comment that White may have died from a broken heart. Sadie, therefore, seems to understand intuitively what makes good writing, but she has had little practice writing and revising to achieve these ends.

Easy Reading: Her Own Work

I ask Sadie to read the beginning of the piece aloud to me to see how she reads her own work. She reads the first 92 words with 10 miscues and 3 self-corrections, uncorrected accuracy of 89 percent, corrected accuracy 96 percent, a self-correction rate of 30 percent, and a comprehending score (Weaver, 1988) of 50 percent (self-corrected or meaning-preserving miscue percentage). Her miscues are summarized as follows:

Sadie	Text	Matches Preceding Context	Matches Following Context	Self-Corrects	Preserves Meaning	Corrected or Preserves Meaning
Virgin	Vernon	yes	yes	yes	no	yes
birthday	brothers	no	no	yes*	no	yes
main	Marian	no	no	no	no	no
marina	Marian	no	no	no	no	no
Carl	Clara	yes	yes	no	no	no
Linden	Lillian	yes	yes	no	yes	yes
Lydia	Lillian	yes	yes	no	yes	yes
the	a	yes	yes	yes	yes	yes
trifted	terrified**	no	no	no	no	no
traded	terrified***	yes	no	no	no	no
		60%	50%	30%	20%	50%

*Sadie corrected *brothers* when I showed her *birthday* and *brothers* together.
**Sadie was unable to read the blend when I showed her *terrified* and *trifted* together.
***Sadie could not read the syllables when I progressively uncovered them for her.

Sadie's corrected accuracy of 96 percent technically qualifies this piece as independent-level reading, as her own writing should be, but the uncorrected rate of 89 percent makes it closer to frustration level. Six of her nine miscues occur on proper nouns, those "facts" she had to include in her report, so we can argue that she did not lose much meaning here. But I note that for *Marian* Sadie guesses *main* and *marina*, which are not even names but do resemble the target word in print. Sadie also guesses *Carl* for *Clara* and *Linden* for *Lillian*, using names this time but not necessarily *sisters'* names. Again, she attends to print features. Sadie finally guesses *Lydia* for *Lillian*, using some print features but trying a sister's name. Overall, in this easy-level text, Sadie matches print or sound with her substitutions as follows:

Sadie	Text	Matches Preceding Context	Matches Sound/ Print	Initial Sound Sampled	Medial Sound Sampled	Final Sound Sampled
Virgin	Vernon	yes	yes	yes	yes	yes
birthday	brothers	no	yes	yes	yes	no
main	Marian	no	yes	yes	no	yes
marina	Marian	no	yes	yes	yes	no
Carl	Clara	yes	yes	yes	yes	no
Linden	Lillian	yes	yes	yes	no	yes
Lydia	Lillian	yes	yes	yes	yes	no
the	a	yes	yes	no	yes	yes
trifted	terrified	no	yes	yes	yes	yes
traded	terrified	yes	yes	yes	no	yes
		60%	100%	90%	70%	60%

Last year, Sadie used print and meaning to guess at words, too. In her easy-level reading, she makes the following miscues:

Sadie	Text	Matches Preceding Context	Matches Sound/ Print	Initial Sound Sampled	Medial Sound Sampled	Final Sound Sampled
my	maybe	yes	yes	yes	no	no
my	maybe	yes	yes	yes	no	no
my	maybe	yes	yes	yes	no	no
desturb	desert	no	yes	yes	no	no
my	maybe	yes	yes	yes	no	no
take	talk	yes	yes	yes	no	yes
		83%	100%	100%	0%	17%

Sadie has changed dramatically the way she samples print in comfortable reading. In both years she predicted acceptably from context (83 percent last year, 60 percent this year). In both readings Sadie attended to print or sound 100 percent of the time, focusing on the initial sound or letters all the time last year and 90 percent of the time this year. Most noticeably, Sadie now attends to the internal structure of words (Adams, 1990), 70 percent of the time for medial sounds and 60 percent for final sounds. Last year in easy reading, she used none of the medial sounds and only 17 percent of the final ones.

Just-Right Reading: Lots of Miscues and Little Automaticity

Sadie chooses *Amelia Bedelia* (Parrish, 1963) to read as her easy book. She reads the first 232 words with 37 miscues and 24 self-corrections, for a 65 percent self-correction rate and 94 percent corrected accuracy, but only 84 percent uncorrected accuracy, indicating that most books are not easy, but "just right," or instructional, for Sadie.

Since she has not had much chance to read easy books, in the form of supplemental "choice" reading, Sadie has not developed a wider or more stable sight vocabulary. Virginia tells me that sight word practice (on the words for which phonics do not work) is included in Sadie's Orton-Gillingham training, specifically such words as *could, would,* and *was.* Last year, in fact, Sadie miscued on these words, as well as *the, my, didn't, that's, they, he,* and *him.* Although Sadie recognized these words perfectly this year, she missed other basic sight words: *own, a, here, said, I, there, into, she, has, let's, what, this, those, off, your, you,* and *up.*

I note that Sadie has learned what she has been taught, but that direct instruction cannot account for all sight word learning. Despite the claims of Carver and Leibert (1995) that easy reading does not improve the rate or vocabulary of less able readers, I have found that frequent, recreational reading used as part of a diverse and language-rich reading and writing program does produce better readers. Carver and Leibert did not match the students to the books, nor did they determine that the readers in their study needed fluency or sight word development. Moreover, the authors used computer-driven reading of brief passages as output measures, not exactly rates and miscues observed in comfortable reading settings.

More than 20 years ago (Simmons 1977), I tested hundreds of seventh- and eighth-graders in Portsmouth, New Hampshire, and found that about 20 percent demonstrated multiyear gaps between their instructional and frustration levels, as measured by informal reading inventories. Theoretically, in a year of perfect learning, a student can close that gap. I saw large numbers of undeveloped readers and wanted to do something about it.

In an eight-week period, the seventh-grade interdisciplinary team asked their students to read in English, social studies, and science classes from self-selected materials and assigned books; to keep track of new words they encountered and learn their meanings and uses; and to write about what they had read. No changes were made in the eighth-grade curriculum, but frequent, self-selected easy reading was not normally used in these classes. At the end of two months, I retested the same 20 percent of each grade and found that the seventh-graders averaged 1.25 years of growth in their instructional levels, whereas the eighth-graders had not changed at all. Unobtrusive measures of attitudes of both teachers and students as well as home behavior of the students showed no significant differences between the groups. In other words, students who read, wrote, and paid attention to words, as part of their regular classwork, became better readers.

For 13 years at Oyster River High School in Durham, New Hampshire, I offered reading classes in which students selected their own books, magazines, newspapers, comic books, or assigned readings from other classes. They did what the seventh-graders in Portsmouth had done: read, wrote, and paid attention to words. In addition, I asked them to read each other's writing, to share their books and words, and eventually to keep portfolios of their work, in order to set and fulfill personal reading and writing goals. Two hours of personally selected reading each week was required to pass, four hours for a grade of A.

We kept track of their times and calculated their reading speeds. Many students entered class reading 50 to 75 words per minute—about where Sadie is at the end of fourth grade. Most of them doubled their reading speeds, still leaving them far behind their average high school peers (252 words per minute; Gilmore and Gilmore, 1968). More significantly, most finished their first book *ever*; all left with plans to read more. Sadie needs the same chance. Choice reading is not a luxury to be cut for lack of time but a staple of all good reading instruction.

Just-Right Reading: Capable Decoding

Sadie continues to need to decode but does so capably. Her miscues in *Amelia Bedelia* are as follows:

Sadie	Text	Matches Preceding Context	Matches Following Context	Self-Corrects	Preserves Meaning	Corrected or Preserves Meaning
—	your	yes	yes	no	yes	yes
her	here	yes	yes	no	no	no
and	said	yes	no	yes	no	yes
Rose	Rogers	yes	yes	no	no	no
gate	got	no	no	yes	no	yes
a	—	yes	yes	yes	no	yes
flowers	folks	yes	yes	no	no	no
and	said	yes	no	yes	no	yes
garden	grand	yes	yes	no	no	no
hose	house	yes	yes	no	no	no
and	—	yes	yes	no	yes	yes
rice	rich	yes	no	yes	no	yes
guest	get	no	no	yes	no	yes
flowers	folks	yes	yes	no	no	no
her	here	yes	yes	no	no	no
eyes	I	yes	yes	yes	no	yes
her	there	yes	no	yes	no	yes
and	a	yes	no	yes	no	yes
gave	—	yes	no	yes	no	yes
admitting	a minute	yes	no	no	no	no
thank	think	no	no	yes	no	yes
MP	meringue	no	no	no	no	no
to	into	yes	yes	yes	yes	yes
the	she	yes	no	yes	no	yes
she	said	yes	no	yes	no	yes
lest	let's	yes	no	yes	no	yes
the	what	yes	no	yes	yes	yes
thing	this	yes	no	yes	yes	yes
towel	towels	yes	yes	no	yes	yes
Amelia	she	yes	yes	yes	yes	yes
—	had	yes	yes	yes	yes	yes
the	she	yes	no	yes	no	yes
and	said	yes	yes	yes	yes	yes
and	—	yes	yes	no	yes	yes
her	here	no	no	yes	no	yes
here	there	yes	yes	yes	no	yes
the	those	yes	yes	yes	yes	yes
		87%	51%	65%	30%	76%

In this year's instructional-level text, Sadie continues to predict over 80 percent of the time from preceding context, but her predictions match following context much better (51 vs. 0 percent) than last year. She also shows more flexibility in self-correction, dropping from 100 to 65 percent, but continuing to comprehend at the sentence level 76 percent of the time. As Johnston (1997) points out, not all miscues require correction, nor are all corrected orally.

Silent Reading: Slow but Steady

Sadie continues to understand her reading material well. From scanning the pictures in the book, she predicts that Amelia will make a mess in the house where she works and will probably be fired but will be rehired. Sadie also predicts Amelia's mess will be a result of her clumsiness. After reading, Sadie corrects her predictions, saying Amelia had not been clumsy, she had just misunderstood what the note had meant her to do. Also, Amelia had not been fired, at least as far as Sadie had read.

Last year, after reading several hundred words, Sadie was exhausted and began to have trouble with books she had read with ease earlier in the session. I am interested to see if she can continue reading *Amelia Bedelia* silently and, if so, at what rate. I notice that Sadie is pointing at words with her finger this year, perhaps another indication that she is sampling print more carefully, but also a likely sign of slow reading speed.

Sadie reads the next several pages silently for two minutes, finishing 140 words for a rate of 70 words per minute, well below the 86 words per minute expected from second-graders (Gilmore & Gilmore, 1968). These authors report oral reading rates of 66 to 104 words per minute for the 2.8 grade level, about where I would put *Amelia Bedelia*. I suspect Sadie reads silently just as she does orally, stopping for each word. Since she has had "no time" for those repeated readings of easy material, Sadie has developed neither a larger store of sight words nor the eye movement patterns typical of silent reading.

Sadie does understand what she reads silently, however, as she is able to summarize Amelia's continuing confusions with requests to "dust the furniture" and "draw the drapes" as more proof that she is not clumsy, but rather just misread what Mrs. Rogers wanted her to do.

Continued Attention to Print

Sadie has continued sampling more fully from the middles and ends of words than she did last year in just-right, or instructional, text. After a year of Orton-Gillingham single-letter phonics, Sadie still makes 31 substitution miscues in 232 words of instructional text, as summarized here:

Sadie	Text	Matches Preceding Context	Matches Sound/Print	Initial Sound Sampled	Medial Sound Sampled	Final Sound Sampled
her	here	yes	yes	yes	yes	yes
and	said	yes	yes	no	yes	yes
Rose	Rogers	yes	yes	yes	yes	yes
gate	got	no	yes	yes	no	yes
flowers	folks	yes	yes	yes	yes	yes
and	said	yes	yes	no	yes	yes
garden	grand	yes	yes	yes	yes	no
hose	house	yes	yes	yes	yes	yes
rice	rich	yes	yes	yes	yes	yes
guest	get	no	yes	yes	yes	yes
flowers	folks	yes	yes	yes	yes	yes
her	here	yes	yes	yes	yes	yes
Eyes	I	yes	yes	yes	yes	no
her	there	yes	yes	no	yes	yes
and	a	yes	yes	yes	no	no
admitting	a minute	yes	yes	yes	yes	no
thank	think	no	yes	yes	no	yes
m-	meringue	no	yes	yes	no	no
to	into	yes	yes	no	yes	yes
the	she	yes	yes	no	yes	yes
lest	let's	yes	yes	yes	yes	no
the	what	yes	yes	no	yes	no
thing	this	yes	yes	yes	yes	no
towel	towels	yes	yes	yes	yes	no
Amelia	she	yes	yes	no	yes	no
the	she	yes	yes	no	yes	yes
and	said	yes	yes	no	yes	yes
her	here	yes	yes	yes	yes	yes
here	there	no	yes	no	no	yes
the	those	yes	yes	yes	no	no
		84%	100%	68%	80%	61%

Last year, in an instructional passage from *Junie B. Jones and Her Big Fat Mouth*, Sadie made 10 substitution errors as follows:

Sadie	Text	Matches Preceding Context	Matches Sound/Print	Initial Sound Sampled	Medial Sound Sampled	Final Sound Sampled
girl	giggle	no	yes	yes	no	yes
beautiful	bullfighter	yes	yes	yes	yes	no
butterfly	bullfighter	yes	yes	yes	yes	no
then	the	yes	yes	yes	yes	no
bumped	butted	yes	yes	yes	yes	yes
face	stomach	yes	no	no	no	no
the	my	yes	no	no	no	no
did	didn't	yes	yes	yes	yes	no
it	that's	yes	yes	no	no	no
it's	that's	yes	yes	no	no	yes
		90%	80%	60%	50%	30%

Again, Sadie continues to predict well from context (90 and 84 percent) and has improved her sampling of print (100 vs. 80 percent). She continues to rely on the first letter or sound (60 percent last year, 68 percent this year), but she much more frequently reads through a word to see the middle (80 vs. 50 percent) and the end (61 vs. 30 percent).

Harder Reading: Less Variability

Sadie has chosen Paula Danzinger's *You Can't Eat Your Chicken Pox, Amber Brown* as her just-right book, but she complains, "I hate reading this!" because "it's not exciting." Virginia has been trying to get her to read this book because Sadie's family is going to Europe in a few weeks, which is the theme of this book. Sadie shows trouble remembering just where she is in the book, but eventually reads 120 words on pages 11 through 13 with 13 miscues and 2 self-corrections, for a corrected accuracy rate of 91 percent, bordering frustration. Her miscues are summarized as follows:

Sadie	Text	Matches Preceding Context	Matches Following Context	Self-Corrects	Preserves Meaning	Corrected or Preserves Meaning
of	off	yes	no	no	no	no
mirrors	mirror	yes	yes	no	yes	yes
—	absolutely	no	no	no	no	no
—	absolutely	no	no	no	no	no
there	three	yes	no	yes	no	yes

Sadie	Text	Matches Preceding Context	Matches Following Context	Self-Corrects	Preserves Meaning	Corrected or Preserves Meaning
you	your	yes	no	no	no	no
to	you	yes	no	no	no	no
you	up	yes	yes	no	yes	yes
sink	sneak	yes	yes	yes	no	yes
and	your	yes	yes	no	yes	yes
trains	Tarzan	yes	no	no	no	no
one	own	yes	yes	no	yes	yes
and	has	yes	no	no	no	no
		85%	39%	15%	31%	46%

Following her reading, Sadie exclaims, "I didn't understand that at all!"

"You didn't understand what she was doing?" I ask. Amber has been packing, unpacking, and repacking, getting ready for a trip to France. Every time she thinks she's finished, she finds something else she wants to take, and her mother has to make her repack to keep her bags light enough for the airplane. Sadie can explain all of this.

"I just didn't understand why she kept saying, 'Pack. Unpack. Repack.'" Sadie's comprehending score of 46 percent in the last column reflects her confusion at the sentence level, despite her strong understanding of the passage overall.

Sadie's attention to print in substitution miscues also reveals another interesting pattern compared to last year:

Sadie	Text	Matches Preceding Context	Matches Sound/Print	Initial Sound Sampled	Medial Sound Sampled	Final Sound Sampled
of	off	yes	yes	yes	yes	yes
mirrors	mirror	yes	yes	yes	yes	no
there	three	yes	yes	yes	no	yes
you	your	yes	yes	yes	yes	no
to	you	yes	yes	no	yes	yes
you	up	yes	no	no	no	no
sink	sneak	yes	yes	yes	no	yes
and	your	yes	no	no	no	no
trains	Tarzan yes	yes	yes	yes	no	
one	own	yes	yes	yes	no	yes
and	has	yes	yes	no	yes	no
		100%	82%	64%	55%	45%

In her harder reading last year, Sadie balanced print and meaning as follows:

Sadie	Text	Matches Preceding Context	Matches Sound/Print	Initial Sound Sampled	Medial Sound Sampled	Final Sound Sampled
little	ladder	yes	yes	yes	no	no
lander	ladder	yes	yes	yes	yes	yes
camels	climbing	yes	yes	yes	no	no
soft	lot	yes	yes	no	yes	yes
lots	lot	yes	yes	yes	yes	no
the	there	yes	yes	yes	yes	no
world	would	yes	yes	yes	yes	yes
quickly	loudly	no	yes	no	no	yes
quietly	loudly	no	yes	no	no	yes
in	on	yes	yes	no	no	yes
lots	lot	yes	yes	yes	yes	no
it	him	yes	yes	no	yes	no
		83%	100%	58%	58%	50%

The percentages of initial, medial, and final sound/print sampling remain the same from last year to this year in harder reading, showing that Sadie has always read through words at least half the time when reading is difficult for her. This year, following training in Orton-Gillingham word recognition techniques, she samples all parts of words at least 60 percent of the time, even when reading is easy or just right (see Table 9.1).

TABLE 9.1   Sadie's Attention to Print

Text and Grade	Matches Preceding Context	Matches Sound or Print	Samples Initial Sound	Samples Medial Sounds	Samples Final Sound
Easy					
Grade 3	83%	100%	100%	0%	17%
Grade 4	60	100	90	70	60
Just Right					
Grade 3	90	80	60	50	30
Grade 4	84	100	68	80	61
Hard					
Grade 3	83	100	58	58	50
Grade 4	100	82	64	55	45

It might seem that Sadie is working harder to read than she was even last year, having been trained to decode even in easy text, but I do not think so. I am dismayed to see that Sadie needs to be reminded to break words into syllables or to ask what might be sensible, or to blank or rerun sentences—strategies she employed automatically last year. I encourage her parents to insist that more attention to meaning and cross-checking be included in her instruction in fifth grade. Of course, Sadie also needs time for independent practice in silent reading to build her reading speed.

Despite the fact that Sadie continues, in the summer following her fourth-grade year, to read slowly and with difficulty in materials intended for third-graders, I sense that she is reading better. Last year, I watched her attention and capacity drain away, so that at the end of the session, she could not read the same book she had earlier read with ease. When she read at home with Virginia, the same thing happened. This year, however, Sadie has read even long passages with consistent levels of comfort throughout. Moreover, her comprehension remains strong in whole texts, and *she has chapter books at home that she can read.* Last year, no book would have been easy, except controlled vocabulary readers from the school reading room.

Other Measures of Growth

Sadie took the Wechsler Individual Achievement Test (WIAT) again in the spring of her fourth-grade year, and the school reported large gains for her in most areas:

WIAT		*Grade 3*			*Grade 4*	
Subtest	*Score*	*Grade Level*	*Percentile*	*Score*	*Grade Level*	*Percentile*
Basic Reading		2:0			4:0	
Math Reasoning		2:5			3:8	
Spelling	72	1:3	3	76	2:1	5
Reading Comp.		2:9			3:1	
Computation		2:5			3:6	
Listening Comp.		4:9		115	7:9	84
Oral Expression		7:4		135	>12:9	99
Written Expression	89	1:2	23	113	7:9	81
Area						
Reading	85	2:3	16	92	3:6	30
Math	87	2:7	19	91	3:8	27
Language	120	7:1	91		>12:9	
Writing		K:3			3:2	
Total		2:4			4:4	

Notice that few percentile ranks are provided in the report, leaving us to rely on suspect grade-level scores. Still, these results indicate that Sadie has learned a great deal this past year. Specifically, she has improved in basic reading, such that her overall reading score has moved from the low-average range (16th percentile) last year, to the average range (30th percentile) this year.

Sadie did better decoding printed words (Basic Reading) than answering questions from written paragraphs (Reading Comprehension). The miscue analyses and retells flesh out these results. Sadie's comprehending scores (percentage of miscues that preserve meaning or are self-corrected) consistently fall below her able retellings, predicting that she will have trouble with comprehension tasks that focus on snippets of text, essentially comprehension at the sentence level. Tests such as the WIAT do not portray her strength with whole texts.

I am more concerned, however, with the glowing report of two years' growth in decoding ability reflected in the Basic Reading score. We have seen Sadie struggle with word recognition in text intended for second and third graders. She was unable, for instance, to sound out *terrified* or *absolutely* in connected reading. I decide to ask Sadie to try the Names Test (Dufflemeyer et al. 1994) that she attempted last year.

Sadie is able to read 27 of the 70 names, up from 18 last year, an improvement, but hardly successful completion of a task normally used with second- through fifth-graders. The analysis of her knowledge below is more illuminating:

Names Test

Phonics Category	Grade 3 (percent)	Grade 4 (percent)
Initial consonants	92	87
Consonant blends	64	58
Consonant digraphs	73	53
Short vowels	50	75
Long vowels	43	52
Vowel digraphs	60	60
Controlled vowels	56	48
Schwa	20	73

Sadie's attempts to recognize English names reveal once again that she has learned what she has been taught. Her Orton-Gillingham program ran only a portion of the year, starting in October and interrupted frequently by school cancellations in November and December. Therefore, by April she had really only concentrated on words with short vowels. Her growth with short vowels and schwa probably reflects this work. Combined with our observation of Sadie's attention to beginnings, middles, and ends of words in connected, comfortable reading, these results testify to the usefulness of code instruction for Sadie. Moreover, her ability to read longer without tiring supports Ehri's (1987) argument for speeded automaticity and the Coltheart (Coltheart et al., 1988) model of phonological recoding as key to efficient, mature word recognition.

Observing Sadie's "Learning Style"

Sadie's special education teacher, Ms. Billings, who gave the WIAT, reported her to be active, talkative, and distractible. In contrast, Sadie was sick the day I saw her and was giving up some of her summer vacation, but still she worked well for more than two hours. In fact, I had to stop her during our writing time because she had more ideas than we had time to finish before I had to leave.

Ms. Billings also says Sadie is more of an auditory than visual learner, but there has long been debate as to whether sufficient evidence exists to classify and instruct students on such a basis, especially in reading (Stahl, 1988). I suggest that at a minimum the processing of print be separated from the processing of numerals and from some of Sadie's favorite activities—painting and drawing. Ron, her father, tells me Sadie has a painting on display in town and he shows me a giraffe she painted in acrylics and a watercolor of green pears and a red strawberry that takes my breath away. I am struck by the lighting and the use of shadow. Clearly, someone has taught Sadie to use this symbolic medium, and she has had little trouble "processing" this visual information.

Virginia shows me two series of cartoons Sadie drew in class.

"I give her a block of paper every so often so that she can draw in school. She seems to concentrate better that way," Virginia says. "But I just can't bear to throw these things away—they're really animations, you know?" She shows me the first, a brachyosaurus (Sadie points this fact out to me), saying, "We love mund" (mud). In the next drawing, the brachyosaurus has turned sideways, its tail lifted and dripping, and it is saying, "We alsow love sholow woter." The water has deepened on page three, and the tail is curled under the dinosaur, who is looking into the water, spying fish, and says, "We eat fis."

Next, the brachyosaurus is underwater, its tail curled behind it, saying, "We love water and mud." In the final scene, the long-necked dinosaur flips its flippers in mud, so indicated by it saying, "I am a mud monster." Eighty percent of her words are conventionally spelled, I note, and her accuracy improves as she continues drawing. In contrast, she misspells 56 percent of her extemporaneous writing with me (which I will discuss later). Better concentration, indeed.

In the second sequence of six pages, the brachyosaurus is paddling along in water up to its neck and seems unaware of four fish approaching it. One of them, though, has spotted it. In picture two, the head has dipped toward the water and the fish, now 9 of them, are in various stages of turning around. On page three, the long neck has submerged, and the brachyosaurus, mouth open, lunges at fleeing fish, now 22 strong, 2 of which are splashing on the surface. A turtle lumbers along the bottom. In frame four, the last 4 fish scurry offstage, while a flipping tail disappears into the dainty mouth of our resurfaced brachyosaurus. Next, a dinosaur tail flips happily, with the bulk of the beast offstage to the left, having apparently finished its meal and heading home. Only quiet waves appear in the last panel.

In her WIAT testing, Ms. Billings noted, "As the tasks increased in length and difficulty, Sadie became more active and her responses became quieter and more hesitant." With print, when she is expected to use accurate conventions, as in a test, Sadie may be "quieter and more hesitant." Sadie's cartoons and paintings demonstrate she can orchestrate lengthy, difficult tasks that involve visual information and can integrate what she knows about the world with humor and economy of expression. The tests seem to have missed these abilities.

Sadie Loves to Write

As Sadie and Virginia have noted, Sadie has been asked to write in order to report on her learning in other subject areas, in order to demonstrate the ability to do library research, and in order to demonstrate good spelling and mechanics. She has not, however, been asked to keep a folder or portfolio of her work, to share it with peers, or to edit pieces for publication. "We could show them to other people if we wanted," Sadie tells me.

Sadie seems to have developed the idea that writing about people should include their feelings, since she focuses on inclusion of feelings as her reason for choosing her E. B. White piece as her best. She also mentions feelings in her unedited journal about a class fishing trip (see Figure 9.3). She likes it because it tells how she feels about the trip, but she is not sure if the story was passed around in class, so likely no one ever read her feelings or told her if they understood them from her writing. Moreover, beyond mentioning that the class and Mr. Davis were having fun, she really does not say how she felt about the trip.

As with her E. B. White piece, what Sadie intended to do and what she has done seem different, and Sadie has not developed a writer's "sense" nor the use of reader feedback to evaluate the effect of her own writing. I wonder what she can do with some modeling of writers' behaviors.

At the end of nearly 90 minutes of reading, I ask Sadie if she has energy left to write. "I love to write," she tells me, and agrees to write with me. I tell her we will brainstorm lists of people, places, and things we know about and care about, pick a group to write about, invent some titles, then begin to write about one title.

Sadie immediately begins her list of things (see Figure 9.4). She lists names in two columns, then adds titles to the columns, including "Peple," "Pets," "Things," and "Plases." Altogether, her 30 items surpass any of the other writers in this book, and I have to stop Sadie, who is still busily adding ideas. I ask her to think of a category she wants to write about, and Sadie looks back at her columns. "I have two," she says after a pause. "I have 'People' and 'Pets.'"

"You could put 'People' and 'Pets' together if you want, but I want you to think of titles you might use. See, I'm thinking of titles for a new book I want to write, so I'm listing some here, then I will pick one. I'm going to ask you to pick one of the titles that you might write about."

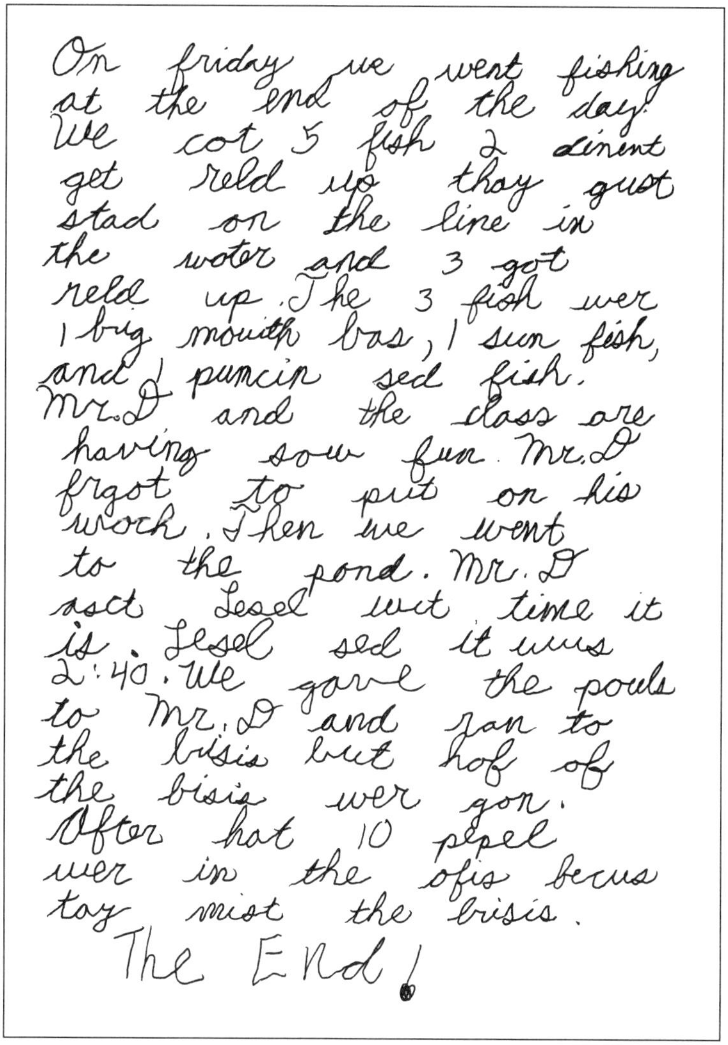

On friday we went fishing at the end of the day. We cot 5 fish 2 dinent get reld up thay gust stad on the line in the woter and 3 got reld up. The 3 fish wer 1 big mouth bas, 1 sun fish, and 1 puncin sed fish. Mr. D and the class are having sow fun. Mr. D frgot to put on his wroch. Then we went to the pond. Mr. D asct Lesel wit time it is. Lesel sed it wus 2:40. We gave the pouls to Mr. D and Jan to the bisis but hof of the bisis wer gon. Ofter hat 10 pepel wer in the ofis becus tay mist the bisis. The END!

FIGURE 9.3   Sadie's Fishing Journal

She moves quickly to writing titles and generates 4. I show her my list of 15, explaining what each means to me. Sadie picks, "My Teacher Never Writes" as her favorite.

"I could do a chapter on that—follow a teacher who doesn't write and see how he teaches," I say. "Which of your titles do you think you'll pick?"

"I have two that sound exciting. One of them is 'David and the Mystery of the Missing Fish' and the next one is 'Montey Attacks Daniel.' "

FIGURE 9.4   Sadie's Writing Sample

"Who's Montey?"

"A snake, a python I have."

"And who's Daniel?"

"My cousin."

"Oh, your cousin was attacked by your python?" I laugh.

"It's my favorite title," Sadie says, explaining that she's making it up. She decides to write about David and the missing fish, however.

After two minutes, she has written the title and two sentences (see Figure 9.5). "When we start a paragraph, do we go to the next line?" Sadie asks. "Or do we just stay on that?"

"When I'm typing letters," I explain, "I skip a line and don't start out here, but when I'm writing, I don't skip a line and just move over a little," I say, show-

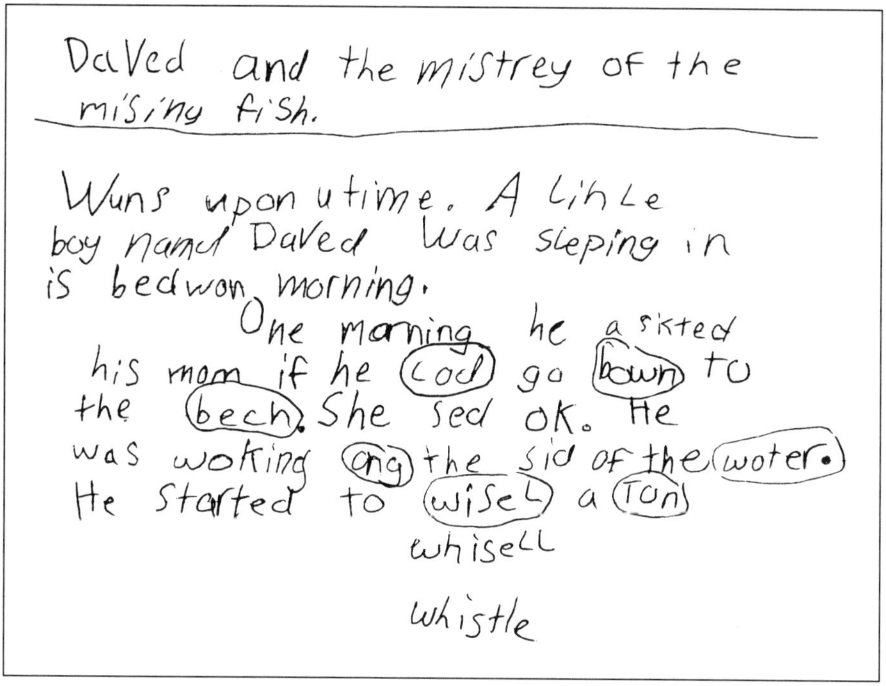

DaVed and the mistrey of the missing fish.

Wuns upon u time. A Lihle boy named DaVed was sleping in is bed won morning.
One morning he a skted his mom if he (cod) go (bown) to the (bech) She sed ok. He was woking (ong) the sid of the (woter.) He started to (wisel) a (Ton)

whisell

whistle

FIGURE 9.5 Sadie's Story

ing her my beginning piece. Sadie goes back to work. After another two minutes, she has written three more sentences. I stop her.

"A writer I know says never be afraid to stop in the middle of something," I tell her, "because it makes it easier to start again. So, what did you write about?"

Sadie reads aloud to me, then explains, "A fish is going to copy him. A fish is going to start whistling a tune."

"I knew the whistling was going to be important. Do you like that so far?"

"Yeah, it's about my cousin and it's about an animal. Fish are interesting and a whistling fish is kind of unusual," Sadie says, showing me she has focused on her favorite subject, marine animals, and knows to create a problem that needs explanation.

"That would be a good children's book," I tell her. When I read my beginning to her, she asks what will happen next, showing me that she expects writers to have plans, to do what my son Zack calls "thinking about page 4 when I'm writing page 2."

Sadie has demonstrated that she knows how to generate ideas for writing, how to focus on a topic, and how to develop a story from an initial problem. I notice that she has moved into writing about other people than herself. Last year's choices either included her as a character or were written from the first-person point of view. Here, Sadie has used third-person narration. Sadie also knows when to ask for help, as she showed when she asked me about paragraphing.

Sadie Can Edit

I decide to find out if Sadie can benefit from instruction in how to edit her own writing. I ask her to start at the bottom of her page and skim backward over the lines, looking for any word that might be misspelled. I tell her to circle or put a mark next to any one that might be misspelled. She looks up at Virginia as if to ask, "Aren't they all?" but she humors me and circles the words as shown on Figure 9.5. I stop her before she can finish the whole paragraph, and she has marked 8 words of a possible 11 mistakes, circling *started,* which is correct, but missing *sed, woking,* and *sid.*

"Now pick one of the words," I tell her, "any one." She points to *started.*

"What's that word?" I ask.

"Started?"

"What parts of the word are you not sure of?"

"I think there's an extra *t* in there."

"Do you hear it?"

"Star - ted. Yeah."

"Well, that one's O.K."

"Cool!" She is truly surprised.

I ask her to find another and she picks *wisel.* "Right underneath it, write it another way." I wait as she writes *whisel.* "What did you change?"

"The *h.*"

"That's a real good guess. If I told you it was right right up to the *s,* what would you change at the end?" Sadie adds an *l.*

"That's a good guess, too. What I want to show you is that when you went back over the lines and you just looked at the words, you could pretty much pick out the ones you had trouble with. That's a good plan, because when you're writing you're trying to remember what you're saying, so you can't concentrate on what the words look like. When you finish getting your ideas down, you can go back and ask, 'Does it look right?'"

"So, is the *whisell* right?"

"The *whisell* is close, and there's no way that you would necessarily know," I explain, writing *whistle* under her spelling.

She laughs as I continue, "You don't hear the *t,* do you? What I wanted to show you was that you go backwards and circle it and then you guess. You can also look it up and ask for help. When you checked it, I asked you to pick the ones that didn't look right. Then I asked you to check it out against the sound, and you could hear the *t* in *started.* So you took the way it looked and then the way it sounded. Trying to remember the way it looks is the hardest thing for you, right?"

Sadie nods.

"Then you can sound it out, as you do in Orton-Gillingham. It's hard work, so I understand if you don't like it, but it's useful. The trick is not to rely on just one or just the other way, but both. See, *whisell* makes more sense than *whistle* because that's the way it sounds, so you can sound words out. But look, you changed that *h* because you remembered how it looked; there's no reason for that *h* to be there; you don't hear it. So you can rely on how it sounds and how it looks, and correct more than half of your own misspellings.

"Do you have your own spelling book?" Sadie shakes her head, indicating no. "I'll show you how to make one. Get a steno book or small notebook." Virginia shakes her head in agreement. "And divide it into sections for each letter of the alphabet. Every time you misspell a word, put it correctly in the book under its first letter."

"So," Virginia says, "you know that *was* is *w-a-s* but you keep writing it *w-u-z* because it sounds that way. You could put *was* in the book and check yourself. That's more comfortable."

"In your own spelling book, you don't have to look through words you don't use," I add, wrapping up our session. Sadie runs off to find Clover.

What Sadie Can Do

Sadie has shown us that she can benefit from instruction in materials intended for second- and third-graders but that she will read silently quite slowly even with these books. She has begun attending more closely to the internal structure of words, and continues to read with strong overall comprehension, although sentence-level comprehension can be a problem. Sadie decodes short vowel and initial consonant sounds effectively.

Sadie has widened her reasons for writing, now focusing on people's feelings and fictional stories, possibly through intertextual connections from her basal reader instruction. She can generate ideas for writing on her own, can focus on a particular purpose for writing, and can plan her next moves as she writes. She continues to spell most words incorrectly in extemporaneous composition, but she attends to capitalization and punctuation of sentences as well as indentation of paragraphs capably.

Instructional Needs

Since she has clearly benefited from organized code instruction, Sadie should continue with Orton-Gillingham tutoring next year. She particularly needs to work on consonant clusters, vowel digraphs, and syllabication. However, Sadie should be encouraged to use her knowledge of context, as well as onsets and rimes, to reduce the frequency with which she needs to resort to letter-by-letter decoding.

Sadie also needs to read silently more frequently from easier materials of her own choice. I would suggest nature magazines such as *National Geographic World* as sources of brief articles on topics of interest to her. She must develop a wider store of automatically recognized words.

Let Writing Lead Her to Reading

Virginia tells me that the school continues to be worried about Sadie's lack of attention, a phenomenon I have never observed. When they return from Europe, Virginia tells me that Sadie took a sketchbook with her. She and Ron often marveled as Sadie sat at a sidewalk cafe in Paris, happily drawing for up to 40 minutes at a time.

"Her art is story art," Virginia says. "Each picture is there because she is thinking of the whole story." That's how she reads, too, I notice; she reads the story just fine, despite the words.

And that's how Sadie writes. Last year, when she responded to the *Titanic* assignment, Sadie told the story of herself as a passenger on the ship, including information she had learned, some she invented, and some from her favorite subject, marine mammals. Even this year, pretending to write a letter for the WIAT testing, Sadie created a story of what she would see if she went to Colorado (naturally including dolphins because she likes them).

Despite constrained writing tasks, such as the research on E. B. White, and "audienceless" personal writing, such as the class fishing trip, Sadie continues to write stories with information, voice, and flair, when she is given the chance. She needs to become part of a writing community in which she can try her stories out on other people, see how they respond, and then change her work to meet her ends.

Sadie also needs to write with the responsibility to edit her own work. Stahl (1992) points out that students who use invented spelling and write frequently develop wider writing vocabularies and can improve their phonics knowledge. Sadie has shown us that she can edit her own work and that she can cross-check her spelling inventions for sound and print. She needs to be given the chance.

This chapter concludes with a final case report on Sadie's learning after her fifth-grade year. We can see that some of the instructional recommendations have been followed, especially in her Orton-Gillingham tutoring and her resource room editing sessions. These modifications to tutoring have paid off; Sadie can read grade-appropriate material independently with good comprehension at the end of grade 5. She has increased her silent reading speed 57 percent, from 70 to 110 words per minute. She can edit her own writing to be almost error free and can extemporaneously spell 80 percent of her words correctly, compared to 44 percent last year. But the practices of pull-out tutoring have always been the easiest parts of schooling to change. We will see in Sadie's final case report that there is no evidence that she has become part of a writing community, either because she has been pulled out of the community (regular classroom reading and writing time) or because no such community exists.

Sadie's disabilities have been treated with special programs, but her abilities as a storyteller and artist have not been engaged by an ongoing cycle of inquiry and response found in the classrooms described by Short and colleagues (1996) and by Cunningham and Allington (1994). She has been taught story grammar and has practiced plurals, commas, and grammar in a workbook. She has learned a great deal despite a frustratingly fragmented and boring approach. How much more would Sadie, Andrew, Tara, Kristen, Mike, or Jason have learned if their schools were communities of learners—teachers, students, and administrators— who regularly engage in the reading and writing people use outside of school, and do so together, so that they understand the whole fabric of literacy, not just some of its threads?

The forms of assessment we have practiced in this book show what readers and writers who have had trouble learning can do when they are asked to read and write. Such assessment can suggest productive instruction and begin the remarkable changes we have seen in Sadie. But most promising (or terrifying) of all, assessments that are built from the reading and writing people actually do will show us where our schools need to change. That change will require us to open our bookshelves to whole books written by published authors and our students; open our classrooms to discussion among students and teachers as readers and writers who carry their thinking home with them and back; and open our minds to a deeper understanding of how individual readers and writers process print, as well as how communities of learners read and write together.

C A S E   R E P O R T :   What Has Sadie Learned?

Summary of School-Based Testing

Gray Oral Reading Paragraphs Test

	Grade 3	Grade 4	Grade 5
Raw score	5	15	20
Grade equivalent	2.1	3.7	4.5

Woodcock Reading Mastery Tests–Revised, Form H

	Word Identification	Word Attack	Word Comprehension	Passage Comprehension
Percentile range	6–12	10–25	14–28	36–61

Kottmeyer Diagnostic Spelling Test

	Grade 3	Grade 4	Grade 5
List	List 1	List 1	List 2
Score	15/32	24/32	20/32
Grade level	below 2nd	3rd grade	4th grade

These scores show steady growth in Sadie's reading and spelling abilities, although she continues to be rated below grade level in oral reading (Gray test) and spelling of dictated lists (Kottmeyer) and considerably below average nationally in recognition of sight words (Woodcock Word Identification), blending of isolated sounds (Woodcock Word Attack), and analogies (Woodcock Word Comprehension). Sadie's Woodcock Passage Comprehension score falls into the average range, indicating that she can fill in a missing word about as well as her chronological peers when reading brief passages silently.

Although Sadie's oral reading scores have fallen further and further below grade level (2.1 in year 3.0; 3.7 in year 4.8; and 4.5 in year 5.9; for differences of 0.9, 1.1, and 1.4), the rate at which she has fallen below grade level has declined (0.45 for each of the first two years; 0.2 in grade 3; 0.3 in grade 4). These numbers are encouraging, since students who lack knowledge of the alphabetic code tend to fall behind faster as the years progress (Stanovich, 1986; Freebody & Byrne, 1988). Therefore, although her scores on isolated word recognition subtests continue to be extremely poor, Sadie has apparently learned a good deal about English phonics through her Orton-Gillingham tutoring (the largest instructional change in the last two years); moreover, she applies that knowledge in connected, silent reading.

Sadie actually read more slowly, although more accurately, on the Gray Oral Reading Paragraphs Test in 1997 than she did in 1996:

Gray Oral Reading Paragraphs

	Paragraph 3		Paragraph 4		Paragraph 5		Paragraph 6	
	Grade 4	Grade 5	Grade 4	Grade 5	Grade 4	Grade 5	Grade 4	Grade 5
Time	36.75	28.02	40.03	1:28.62	1:07.44	2:38.49	1:15.19	3:37.99
Errors	2	3	0	1	7	3	7	1

In addition, Sadie self-corrected herself four times during the last two paragraphs noted above in grade 5, and went on to read two more paragraphs that she had not even attempted the year before. These results confirm Adams's (1990) contention that students with more knowledge of sound-letter relationships have more access to the internal structure of words, since it takes longer to read through a word than to guess it from the first letter. Self-corrections also take more time. These results also confirm my findings last year that Sadie now *automatically* uses sounds from the middle and end of words, whereas she previously read those parts in only extremely difficult material.

In other words, Sadie has learned what she has been taught: to recognize the sound-letter relationships in words. The Kottmeyer spelling results offer more proof that she has learned what she has been taught. When in grades 3 and 4, Sadie was asked to spell the same words (List 1):

Kottmeyer Lists

Word	Grade 3	Grade 4
but	bot	√ (correct)
man	main	√
boat	bot	bot
train	√	trane
down	√	doune
soon	sone	√
good	god	√
very	varey	√
kept	cept	cept
come	com	cum
what	whut	√
those	thows	√
will	whil	√
doll	bol	√
toy	tow	√
little	litel	litel
one	wun	√
would	wod	wod
pretty	pritey	pritey

We can see that Sadie has learned 11 of the words missed the year before, while only missing 2 she spelled correctly the year before. She continued to have difficulty with vowel digraphs (*ow, ai*), the variable consonant *c,* and sight words (*would*).

In grade 5, Sadie took List 2 and made 12 errors. However, 8 of the 12 errors were phonetically irregular or sight words (*whiel/while, therd/third, duesn't/doesn't, broght/brought, agen/again, lagf/laugh, becouse/because,* and *throu/through*). We should expect Sadie to have the most difficulty with words requiring accurate retrieval of words by sight or visual memory. She has learned the spelling patterns she has been taught: compound words (*afternoon, grandmother*), silent *e* + ending (*biting*), VCC + ending (*jumped, darkest*), and some vowel digraphs (*shoot, flower*).

These gains are not borne out in her extemporaneous writing but do appear in her editing. In one daily journal entry, she wrote:

> We had a show cald BamuDelay. It was pritey net But I got so tierd of claping my hands and sining. But other then that it was cool. The two Dansers and two Dromers were verey good.
>
> My mom thot of it and put it in the cratov arts. And thay porormed.

Under the demands of composing, then, Sadie continues to have trouble with inflectional endings (*cald/called, tierd/tired*), sight words (*verey/very, then/than*), variable consonants (*Dansers/dancers*), double letters (*claping/clapping, Dromers/ drummers*), and vowel digraphs (*net/neat*).

When asked to edit, after composing is over, however, Sadie applies her new knowledge more effectively. In May, Sadie was asked to write a story in her resource room class of six students. She wrote the first draft of "The Gost Cat" (see Figure 9.6), then typed it on the computer, changing some things as she typed. For instance, Sadie changed the first sentence from *One night wen I was sleping I herd the door open in my room* to *One night when I was sleping in my bed. I heard a noise. It was the door opening* (see Figure 9.7). After typing her story and printing it out, Sadie was asked to self-edit, which she did, as reflected in the handwritten marks in Figure 9.7. Notice that while typing (without the charge of editing), Sadie changed both the spelling (*when/wen, heard/herd*) and the content of the sentence (instead of hearing the door open, she heard a noise and realized it was the door opening). When asked to edit, Sadie did just that—fixed spelling and punctuation but not content.

She edited the next draft with her resource room aide, and they found four spelling errors that Sadie had not found herself (*GOST/Ghost, oprning/opening, throw/through, Starpy/Starpie*). Her resource room teacher edited the last draft and found only two spelling errors (*cowld/could, Starpy/Starpie*). This is pretty impressive evidence of Sadie's ability to apply her word knowledge when attention is not consumed by the demands of composing. Unfortunately, except for punctuation, usage, and spelling, her teachers gave her no feedback on the content or story structure of the piece, and no peers ever read or responded to the story as part of a class activity.

Grade 5 Instruction

Sadie was taught reading and writing in three settings during grade 5: in her regular classroom, in the resource room class of six students, and during weekly sessions of Orton-Gillingham tutoring. Sadie left the regular classroom during reading and writing instruction, so she only read in class during sustained silent reading time. On the day I spoke with her in June, she had just read the first chapter of *Where the Red Fern Grows* (Rawls, 1961) independently in class. For the first few months of school, Sadie wrote in a daily journal in her regular class. She left class during language instruction time for Orton-Gillingham training.

Sadie received her reading and writing instruction in the resource room, where she met with the teacher and an aide in a group of six students. During the fall semester, they read aloud *The Mouse and the Motorcycle* by Beverly Cleary (1965) a chapter at a time, round-robin style. If a student had trouble with a word, the teacher waited for the student to decode it and then gave the student the word, Sadie said. After reading, students responded to questions about the chapter in writing. During the spring, they were reading *Takao and Grandfather's Sword* by Yoshiko Uchida (1993).

Sadie said they kept a writing portfolio in the resource room, but no one could find hers. She remembered being asked to write a friendly letter, a letter of

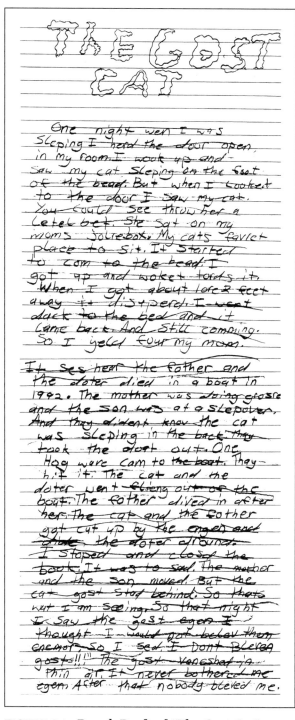

FIGURE 9.6 Rough Draft of "The Gost Cat"

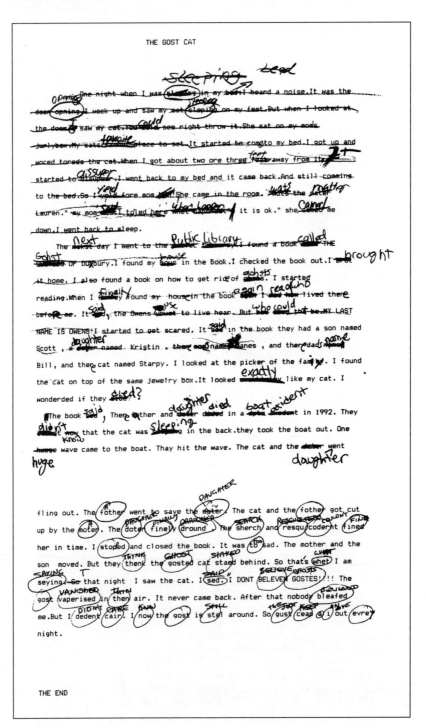

FIGURE 9.7 First Typed Draft of "The Gost Cat"

complaint, something about her summer vacation, and "The Gost Cat" (see Figures 9.6 and 9.7).

During her Orton-Gillingham sessions, Sadie drilled on phonemes, spelling, syllable rules, dictation, and sight word recognition. She read controlled vocabulary readers and used the Lexia Learning Systems computer-assisted phonics drill system. Her mother reports that the resource room teacher coordinated with the Orton-Gillingham program by using the same words on spelling tests. Sadie could not recall being asked to finger spell or to use the phonics patterns studied in tutoring to decode unknown words in round robin oral reading.

Reading and Writing on Her Own

At home, Sadie's mother reads to her from the *Animorphs* series, which Sadie calls "very exciting." In response, she began to write her own book in September in school, "The Rapter of Dome '!!' " (see Figure 9.8) modeled after *Jurassic Park* and the *Animorphs* series. A friend started writing with her but stopped, so Sadie has finished three chapters on her own. She told me she "had a thought and couldn't get it out." Her solution was to talk about it with her friend, and then express the thought on paper, a page or two at a time, during reading or free time at school. Her mother got Sadie to commit to finishing the book by the end of fifth grade (only two weeks away), so Sadie plans to write one more chapter. Last year, Sadie doodled during class to focus her attention, but her current classroom teacher banned doodling during class time. "The Year of No Doodling," her mother called it. Sadie was even "marked off on a report" for doodling. Her resource room teacher allows her to doodle when she is not engaged in writing or taking notes.

Sadie has been keeping "The Rapter" in a binder at school, but has received no help or response from peers. Her resource teacher noticed her activity one day and asked her what she was writing, but she told him, "Nothing." He later read it and told her it was creative. The aide read it and called it "interesting." Sadie believes it is good "because I'm writing it!" She thinks the story is "fun and interesting, even with my terrible spelling."

Sadie continues writing about her favorite territories: dinosaurs, friends, and mystery. She is also continuing to make intertextual links—in this case, consciously adopting the cliffhanger effect of each chapter of the *Animorphs* series by having some exciting but unresolved event occur at the end of each chapter. More important, on her own, Sadie knows what writing is for (to express an idea you can't "get out" any other way) and is planning the structure of her story (thinking like a writer) based on her reading of the *Animorphs* series (reading like a writer). By contrast, her instruction has been limited to a skeletal "writing process": rough draft, type it on a computer, self-edit, teacher edit, retype.

Since "The Rapter of Dome '!!' " (Figure 9.8) and "The Gost Cat" (Figure 9.6) are both first-draft works, we can compare them for evidence of learning during the year, "The Rapter" coming early in the year and "The Gost Cat" in May. As noted earlier, Sadie was able to edit out all but six of her spelling errors without adult help in the May writing. However, she correctly spelled *would* and *could* in

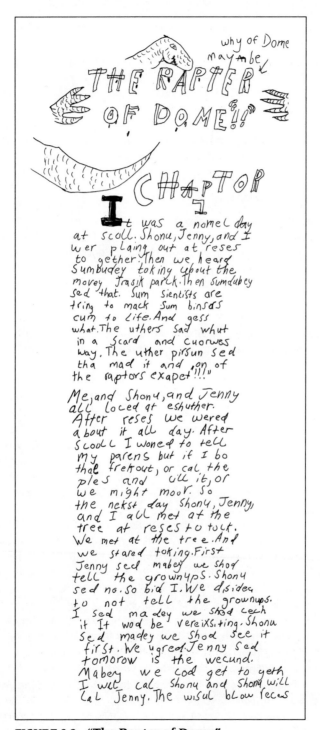

FIGURE 9.8 **"The Rapter of Dome"**

was over. We all started
to thenk on how we cod
cech a raptor. the nekst day
I cald evrebudey. We all
cam over to my house to all
Slep over and think udout
cech ing the raptor. We went
out sid. It was darck and
we hird a rusel in the
bishes. We all stod still. We
wer verey scord. It ternd out
to be just a racoon. Fuow.
We all Sed. Then we hird
the racoon screm! And a nuther
rusul in the bushis. We went
over. We saw a ded racoon
with blud driping from it. And
Somthing was iting it.

FIGURE 9.8 (*continued*)

her May first draft, having spelled *wod, cod,* and *shod* early in the year. She also correctly wrote *nobody* in the spring, having written *evrebudey* and *sumbudey* in the fall. She continues to reverse *b*s and *d*s, writing *bid/did* and *madey/maybe* in the fall and *dack/back* and *doat/boat* in May. *Sed* appears in both first drafts, as do *slep/sleep,* and Sadie continues to omit *e* in *-ed* endings (*scard, ternd, yeld*).

After intensive tutoring in spelling patterns and sight word spelling, Sadie has made modest gains in rough-draft spelling but demonstrates the ability to put the knowledge to use during editing. Her oral reading of her own writing (discussed later) also demonstrates that she recognizes errors on rereading, since she often paused for or corrected misspelled words.

Both "The Rapter" and "The Gost Cat" rely on subject-verb-object sentences, 21 of 38 in the former and 22 of 34 in the latter. Sadie also uses roughly the same small number of other structures in each. Four sentences begin with *and* or *but* in both stories; two in "The Rapter" start with *so,* and four begin that way in "The Gost Cat." She also begins with *It was* three times in the former, and she does so twice in the latter. Sadie's writing has grown in sentence structure, however. She begins four sentences in "The Rapter" with adverb phrases (*after recess,* and *after school*), and in "The Gost Cat" she uses adverbial clauses (*One night wen I was sleping* and *But when I looked to the door*). In the earlier story, she had limited herself to relative

clauses. Although she continued to use them in the second piece, Sadie spontaneously began using more forms of subordinated sentences.

"The Gost Cat" (Figure 9.6) rough draft also shows Sadie has learned more substantial writing content. Although "The Rapter of Dome" (Figure 9.8) is told mainly in conversation, Sadie uses quotation marks only around the exclamation points. In "The Gost Cat" she uses them around the spoken sentences to her mother and to the ghost. This use shows two developments. First, she has learned how to use quotation marks well enough to do so extemporaneously while composing. Second, she has limited conversation in her second story.

For young writers, Graves (1994) points out that writing is speech written down. Early on, this idea translates into *large* words for *loud* voices. Later, students tell all of a story with conversation but no exposition. In "The Rapter," students conversing on the playground deliver the expository information about the development and escape of the raptor. In "The Gost Cat," Sadie (as narrator) tells us about her research in the library and that people did not believe her story. The only spoken words come when she talks to other "characters." Sadie, then, has learned not only how to manipulate quotation marks (evidently an emphasis in the resource room, given the editing of "The Gost Cat" with the aide and the teacher) but also how to tell stories in forms other than "speech written down."

Current Assessment

Sadie correctly read 42 of the 70 first and last names on the Names Test (see Figure 9.9) in grade 5, as compared to 17 correct responses in grade 3 and 27 in grade 4. She correctly recognized the following percentages of phonic elements in the names in each of the three years:

Names Test

Phonics Category	Grade 3 (percent)	Grade 4 (percent)	Grade 5 (percent)
Initial consonants	92	87	84
Consonant blends	64	58	79
Consonant digraphs	73	53	80
Short vowels	50	75	83
Long Vowels/VC-*e*	43	52	78
Vowel digraphs	60	60	80
Controlled vowels	56	48	88
Schwa	20	73	80
Average	57%	63%	80%

Sadie has made consistent progress except in the area of consonants, blends, and digraphs. Even there, she has developed an 80 percent proficiency. I suspect

Name _____   Grade _____   Teacher _____   Date _____

✓ Crowny Jay Conway	✓ Cornul Tim Cornell	✓ ✓ Chuck Hoke	✓ Yorandie ✓ Yolanda Clark
✓ Blank ✓ Kimberly Blake	Robert Salde Roberta Slade	✓ ✓ Homer Preston	✓ Quinkly Gus Quincy
Kincy Spamshun Cindy Sampson	Christer ✓ Chester Wright	gynner/ginney ✓ Ginger Yale	✓ ✓ Patrick Tweed
Stacey ✓ Stanley Shaw	✓ Shane Wendy Swain	✓ ✓ Glen Spencer	✓ ✓ Fred Sherwood
✓ ✓ Flo Thornton	✓ Kidmore Dee Skidmore	✓ Brister Grace Brewster	✓ ✓ Ned Westmoreland
✓ Simmerman Ron Smitherman	✓ Whichlock Troy Whitlock	✓ ✓ Vance Middleton	✓ ✓ Zane Anderson
Brand Pintergraph Bernard Pendergraph	✓ Felter Shane Fletcher	✓ ✓ Floyd Sheldon	Dan Batman Dean Bateman ✓
✓ ✓ Austin Shepherd	Broth ✓ Bertha Dale	✓ ✓ Neal Wade	Jack ✓ Jake Murphy
John ✓ Joan Brooks	Jen ✓ Gene Loomis	Themeel Rinhart Thelma Rinehart	

Phonics Category	Errors		
Initial consonants	6/37	16%	84
Initial consonant blends	4/19	21%	79
Consonant digraphs	3/15	20%	80
Short vowels	6/36	17%	83
Long vowels/VC—final *e*	5/23	22%	78
Vowel digraphs	3/15	20%	80
Controlled vowels	3/25	12%	88
Schwa	3/15	20%	80

FIGURE 9.9   Sadie's Names Test: Grade 5

Source: Figure from Duffelmeyer, Frederick A., Kruse, Anne E., Merkley, Donna J., & Fyfe, Stephen A. (October, 1994). Further validation and enhancement of the Names Test. *The Reading Teacher, 38* (2), 118–129. Reprinted with permission of Frederick Duffelmeyer and the International Reading Association. All rights reserved.

her early reliance on solely initial consonant sounds and context inflated her scores on those sounds to the detriment of attention to medial vowel sounds. Her average score shows steady progress, especially in the second, and only full, year of tutoring. Overall, when she could reasonably substitute a known name for an unknown target name, she did (*Stacey/Stanley, John/Joan, Robert/Roberta, Jen/Gene, Dan/Dean,* and *Jack/Jake*). These miscues reflect her spelling difficulties with *c* sounds, vowel digraphs, and silent *e* words.

Oral Reading Passages

Easy Reading.   Sadie chose her "Rapter" story as an easy reading selection, and she read it with her invented spelling intact. Chapter 1 runs 298 words, which she read with 13 miscues and 5 self-corrections for an uncorrected accuracy rate of 96 percent and a corrected accuracy rate of 97 percent, clearly in the independent range. Her miscues are listed here:

Sadie	Text	Match Preceding Context	Match Following Context	Self-Corrects	Meaning Preserving	Meaning Preserving or Self-Corrected	Match Initial Sound	Match Middle Sound	Match Final Sound
then	when	yes	yes	no	yes	yes	no	yes	yes
then	when	yes	yes	no	yes	yes	no	yes	yes
the	we	yes	no	yes	no	yes	no	no	yes
thal (they'll)	tell	yes	no	yes	no	yes	no	no	yes
and	or	yes	yes	no	yes	yes	no	no	no
to	not	yes	yes	no	yes	yes	no	no	no
not	to	yes	yes	no	yes	yes	no	no	no
I will	I'll	yes	yes	no	yes	yes	yes	no	yes
thenk/ think	talk	yes	yes	yes	no	yes	no	no	yes
a	the	yes	yes	no	yes	yes	no	no	no
cald/ called	could	yes	no	yes	no	yes	yes	no	yes
went	heard	yes	no	yes	no	yes	no	no	no
we	and	yes	yes	no	yes	yes	no	no	no
		100%	69%	38%	62%	100%	15%	15%	54%

Sadie clearly read this text from memory, since only 15 percent of her miscues matched the first or middle sounds of words and only half matched the ending sounds. By contrast, 100 percent of the miscues followed the preceding context and 69 percent matched the following context. She self-corrected all 32 percent of the miscues that did not preserve meaning (68 percent did match), for a 100% comprehending or sentence-level comprehension score. Notice that she miscued on three of her invented spellings, clearly knowing what the correct spelling is when she reread her own writing.

Just-Right Reading.   Sadie decided to read jokes from several sections of *101 Silly Summertime Jokes* (Calmenson, 1989) as her just-right reading. She read some "knock-knock" jokes, some riddles, and some "hinky pinky" riddles, where the answer is two rhyming words. (We had to cover the answers so that I could do the running records without seeing the answers; the point was for her to *fool* me!) Altogether, she read 161 words with 16 miscues and 10 self-corrections, for an uncorrected accuracy rate of 90 percent and a corrected accuracy rate of 96 percent, putting her in the independent reading range with self-corrections. Her miscues are tabulated here:

Sadie	Text	Match Preceding Context	Match Following Context	Self-Corrects	Meaning Preserving	Meaning Preserving or Self-Corrected	Match Initial Sound	Match Middle Sound	Match Final Sound
call	do	yes	no	yes	no	yes	no	no	no
talkative	traffic	yes	no	yes	no	yes	yes	no	no
—	a	yes	yes	no	yes	yes	no	no	no
sunspots	sunspot	yes	yes	no	yes	yes	yes	yes	no
Debby	Dewey	yes	no	yes	no	yes	yes	no	yes
deli	Dewey	yes	no	yes	no	yes	yes	no	yes
Dehway	Dewey	no	no	yes	no	yes	yes	no	yes
Dew	Dewey	yes	no	yes	no	yes	yes	yes	no
none	no	yes	no	no	yes	yes	yes	no	no
visited	visit	yes	no	no	yes	yes	yes	yes	no
snorting	sorting	yes	yes	no	no	no	no	yes	yes
still	settle	no	no	no	no	no	no	no	yes
hundred	humid	yes	no	yes	no	yes	yes	no	yes
pounds	puds	no	no	yes	no	yes	yes	no	yes
hundred	humid	yes	no	yes	no	yes	yes	no	yes
pounds	puds	no	no	yes	no	yes	yes	no	yes
		75%	19%	63%	25%	81%	75%	25%	56%

Here, in unfamiliar reading, Sadie continued to predict from preceding context (75 percent) but much less frequently matched the following context (19 percent). She therefore corrected (63 percent) more often, yielding a sentence-level comprehension score of 81 percent. Sadie again relied heavily on initial consonants (75 percent) to the exclusion of middle sounds (25 percent) but used endings to help her decode (56 percent).

Considering the fact that Sadie received no prompting during her round-robin oral reading session to use the decoding strategies learned in Orton-Gillingham, she has admirably maintained her focus on sense when reading orally and self-corrected when necessary. (True Orton-Gillingham procedure does call for students to check their decodings against context in the controlled readings they have.)

Sadie laughed appropriately at the hinky pinky riddles but had more trouble understanding the plays on words in the knock-knock jokes. For instance, she read "Harriet all the watermelon, and there's none left for us," with no phrasing to indicate that she understood that *Harriet* is meant to sound the same as *Harry ate*. When I asked her if she got the joke, she said no. She had similar difficulty with "Dewey have to go into the water today?"

When Sadie becomes frustrated with oral reading, she relies on phonics elements without cross-checking with sense or looking for known words or phonograms. For instance, she read, "What is heavier: a hundred pounds of feathers or a hundred pounds of sand?" as "What is heavier: a humid puds of feathers or a humid puds of sand?" even with several repetitions of the preceding context to restart the sentence. When I asked her if that made sense, she said no. I covered all but *red* in *hundred* and asked her to read the word. She replied, "Red." I then uncovered the *d* and she read, "Dred," correctly. I then covered all but *hun* and she read it correctly, reading "hundred" when I uncovered the whole word. She was then able to rerun the entire passage and understand the joke.

I have suggested in the past that methods such as the Benchmark phonogram approach or Gunning's Word Building be used with Sadie. I know Orton-Gillingham tutoring has taught syllabication, but so far that concept does not appear to be useful for Sadie, whereas finding known words (Gunning) such as *red* or using phonograms such as /un/ in *hun* have helped her in each assessment I have done.

Challenging Reading. Sadie chose to continue reading *Where the Red Fern Grows* (Rawls, 1961), which she had started in school, as her challenge book. She wanted to read it silently, but I asked her to read at least some of it aloud, and she agreed when I told her I would not look over her shoulder but just tape her and check her reading later. "I can *read* it silently," she insisted, and I told her after a page or so aloud, I would ask her to read for a few minutes silently as well.

Sadie read 231 words on pages 7 through 9 with 20 miscues and 5 self-corrections, for an uncorrected accuracy rate of 91 percent and a corrected rate of 94 percent, which is borderline instructional. Bantam rates the book a grade-6 reading level, and the pages she read scanned as a grade-5 level by the Fry readability chart. Combined with her adequate retelling of the passage, these figures indicate Sadie can read grade-appropriate material, given time and some support. Her miscues are as follows:

Sadie	Text	Match Preceding Context	Match Following Context	Self-Corrects	Meaning Preserving	Meaning Preserving or Self-Corrected	Match Initial Sound	Match Middle Sound	Match Final Sound
particu-larly	practi-cally	yes	no	no	no	no	no	yes	yes
every-one	every	yes	no	yes	no	yes	yes	yes	no
dis-*	disease	no	no	no	no	no	yes	no	no
leaves	lives	yes	no	yes	no	yes	yes	no	yes
wiggy	wiggly	yes	no	yes	no	yes	yes	yes	yes
grind	gnaw	yes	yes	no	yes	yes	no	no	no
and	on	yes	no	no	no	no	no	yes	no
rope	romp	yes	yes	no	no	no	yes	no	yes
a	and	yes	no	no	no	no	yes	no	no
the	—	yes	no	yes	no	yes	—	—	—
trouble	terrible	yes	no	no	yes	yes	no	no	yes
di-*	disease	no	no	no	no	no	yes	no	no
no	not	yes	no	no	yes	yes	yes	no	no
any	a	yes	yes	no	yes	yes	yes	no	no

Sadie	Text	Match Preceding Context	Match Following Context	Self-Corrects	Meaning Preserving	Meaning Preserving or Self-Corrected	Match Initial Sound	Match Middle Sound	Match Final Sound
strange	starts	no	no	no	no	no	no	no	no
grow-ing	gnaw-ing	yes	yes	no	yes	yes	no	no	yes
to	on	yes	no	no	no	no	no	no	no
wanted	wanting	yes	no	no	no	no	yes	yes	no
a	—	yes	no	no	no	no	—	—	—
toll	boy	no	no	yes	no	yes	no	no	no
		85%	20%	25%	25%	50%	56%	28%	33%

*Waited for teacher assistance

Here, Sadie continued to predict heavily from preceding context (85 percent), but she self-corrected much less (25 percent) when the following context did not confirm her prediction (20 percent). I suspect fatigue had something to do with her lack of self-correction. In fact, she waited for me to give her the word *disease* twice, and if those are counted as self-corrections (she had isolated the first syllable each time), she corrected an adequate 35 percent of the time and her correction and meaning preservation (50 percent) would jump to 60 percent. Still, she only told me that the boy wanted another dog after he let the other one go. When I asked if he only wanted one, she said, "One or two."

I also notice that she paid less attention to print (last three columns) than she might have, particularly middle sounds (28 percent). Compared to the last two years, Sadie seemed to be attending more to ends of words, reading through words much less than last year:

Text and Grade	Matches Preceding Context	Matches Sound or Print	Matches Initial Sound	Matches Middle Sound	Matches Final Sound
Easy Grade 3	83%	100%	100%	0%	17%
Grade 4	60	100	90	70	60
Grade 5*	100	50	15	15	54
Just Right Grade 3	90	80	60	50	30
Grade 4	84	100	68	80	61
Grade 5	75	93	75	25	56
Hard Grade 3	83	100	58	58	50
Grade 4	100	82	64	55	45
Grade 5**	85	84	56	28	33

*This is reading of her own invented spelling story, unlike the earlier years.
**The hardest grade 5 passage was read with 94% corrected accuracy.

In fourth grade, Sadie dramatically changed the way she read easy and just-right text; she paid considerably more attention to the middles and ends of words than she had before Orton-Gillingham tutoring, exceeding at the automatic level even the attention she paid in consciously challenging text. In fifth grade, however, her easy text is her own "Rapter" story written in invented spelling, which she read with nearly total prediction from context (100 versus 50 percent matching of print). Interestingly, Sadie matched final sounds (54 percent) almost four times more frequently than initial or middle sounds (15 percent each). In the just-right and hard passages, as well, final sound matches exceeded middle sound matches. I suspect her most recent tutoring emphasis on inflectional endings may account for this new awareness.

More important, however, are Sadie's increased fluency and decreased frustration with oral reading. In grade 5, she never reached frustration-level reading, even with material rated by the publisher as grade-6 reading level. Further, she read the last section of the *Where the Red Fern Grows* selection more fluently than the earlier part (6 repetitions in the last 7 lines, versus 24 repetitions in the first 9 lines). In her just-right reading, she had only 16 repetitions in all, including 10 self-corrections. Overall, Sadie read more fluently in all her selections, compared to halting word-by-word reading in the easiest controlled vocabulary passages two years ago.

Three of Sadie's miscues in the challenging passage occurred on new vocabulary (*gnaw, romp,* and *gnawing*). Neither Sadie, Virginia, nor the Orton-Gillingham reports note any direct instruction in vocabulary, especially vocabulary selected and taught in the context of independent reading. As vocabulary grows more intensive in intermediate grade and secondary reading, Sadie will need instruction in this area. Her Woodcock scores and insensitivity to contextual word play in the joke book reinforce this concern.

Silent Reading

Sadie read the next 358 words silently in three minutes and 15 seconds for a speed of 110 words per minute. Gilmore and Gilmore (1968) list 116 words per minute as the average for third-grade readers, 177 for fifth-graders, and 206 for sixth-graders. This means Sadie's fifth-grade classmates have been reading assignments all year about 50 percent faster than she has, and that next year she will be reading about half as fast as her classmates. Therefore, Sadie will need extended time to complete reading assignments.

Sadie exhibited strong factual comprehension during silent reading in a number of ways. Before reading with me, she had read the first chapter of the book at school and was able to retell the plot up until the boy (whose name she could not remember) had released a dog he had saved from a fight:

> He saw this dog being beat up and his shoulder got ripped and people were watching the fight. And he went and shooed the dogs away and like he took his coat and wrapped it around him and took it home. And

the dog ate all the meat in the house and drank all the water and slept all that night and half the day. And he let him go and said good-bye to him because he had been traveling and didn't know where he'd been. Maybe he'd been stolen or something.

She could not tell me the boy's name. After reading the beginning of the second chapter orally, Sadie said, "The boy wants a dog after he let that one go and said good-bye. It's sad." When I asked her about how many dogs he wanted, she said one or two.

During her silent reading, Sadie paused and said, "His name's 'Billy.'" When she had finished the silent reading, she told me:

The boy like he asked his parents if he could have two bloodhounds and they're like, well, they say they're having puppies and it's the kind of dogs or puppies down the street. And they're having bloodhounds and it costs a lot of money and they don't have it.

When I asked what he was going to do about the problem, she said he was planning to ask his mother. Again, Sadie extracted the main plot elements (problem or initiating event, character's reaction, possible solution); however, she paid little attention to setting. I asked her where the story is taking place, and she said in a nice place. When I inquired if it was nice like the seaside area around her home, she replied that they had a lot of different types of trees. I asked her what it was a good place to do, and she said to have a dog. "Do you mean to have a dog to play with or something else? I asked. She said, "To hunt." I pointed out to her that the land must be good hunting land. Although that information was explicit in the text, the connection between the environment and the characters did not seem important to Sadie.

Current Abilities

At the end of her fifth-grade year, Sadie is able to read grade-appropriate text with adequate oral reading accuracy and silent reading comprehension at a rate considerably less than that of her average peers. She has mastered 80 percent of phonics generalizations tested through reading of naturally occurring English names. In connected reading, Sadie predicts words from context and acceptably self-corrects when her guesses do not make sense. She uses initial and final sounds more than medial sounds when decoding and continues to have difficulty with consonant clusters.

In writing, Sadie spells 80 percent of running text correctly on the first draft. She continues to have trouble with basic sight words (*through, said, when, what, father, come*), vowel digraphs (*sleeping*), and inflectional endings and doubled letters (*comming, disaperd/disappeared*), but she has shown that she can find and correct most of her errors when allowed to edit after composing.

Sadie chooses to write exciting stories dealing with animals, and has moved away from dialogue-only stories to ones with some narration. She writes in subject-object-verb simple sentences, but has begun using introductory adverbial clauses and has learned to use quotation marks to indicate actual speech. Sadie overuses periods, creating sentence fragments, but does not tend to write run-on sentences. Her writing, like her reading, tends to focus on actions and the main character's reactions.

Despite two years of code instruction divorced from regular classroom opportunities for practice, Sadie has developed a wider store of sight words for reading and writing, as evidenced by her more fluent reading and more conventional spelling. Moreover, without ever having been asked to write and present her work to an audience, Sadie has maintained a good sense of what writing and reading are for. She has consistently known how to choose books of interest to her (animals, marine life, dinosaurs, adventure) and to read with comprehension. She knows that writers have ideas that they cannot express any other way than in writing. Although Sadie has demonstrated considerable talent in both painting and drawing, she continues to write stories on her own that incorporate her friends, her interests, and intertextual links to her reading and viewing.

Suggested Instruction

Sadie has proven herself ready to return to the regular classroom for reading and writing instruction. Given enough time to finish assigned readings, she can read and comprehend grade-level material. Given the opportunity to edit separate from composing, Sadie can produce grade-appropriate texts. Although she has clearly learned a great deal about recognizing and producing print from two years of Orton-Gillingham training, she calls it "worse than boring," and there is little evidence that she has chances to practice learned routines in either her resource room or regular classroom. Therefore, rather than frustrate Sadie with further isolated instruction, we should give her the chance to practice what she knows by reading and writing to learn in extended, naturally occurring texts in the regular classroom. She may be provided with extra time to finish reading, to polish texts, or to elaborate on her stories or responses to literature in a resource room. In fact, I would hope that *all* students routinely have such opportunities in the regular classroom, making further pull-out time unnecessary.

I have evidence of only limited vocabulary development for Sadie: looking up words at the end of chapters and using them to fill in blanks in teacher-made worksheets. Her miscues indicate that she has begun reading sufficiently challenging texts so that she is often encountering new words. Sadie needs to be shown how to learn words from context and to begin self-collection of new words. Since she has responded well to learning common word endings for spelling and decoding, she can probably also benefit from more instruction in English morphology.

Perhaps because she has been out of class for code tutoring, Sadie shows little awareness of the literary elements of stories. On her own, she has noticed intertextual links in plot devices, but she needs to know more about character analysis, setting, and theme. Given her ability to write entertaining stories that incorporate her own experience and interests, as well as techniques from published writers, Sadie needs to be engaged in a meaningful writing process that goes beyond rough draft, type, edit, and publish. She needs to be given a chance to develop a sense of audience and voice by hearing reactions to her own writing as well as the writing of others. She also needs to be asked to develop her own innate sense that rewriting involves changing the meaning as well as the superficial form of the text, by engaging in sharing and discussion of both peer writing and that of published authors.

"Sixth Grade Is Soooo Good!"

At the beginning of Sadie's first year of independence following the Orton-Gillingham tutoring, her teacher says Sadie loves sixth grade. She got a B+ in reading for the first marking period and has finished *Tuck Everlasting, Pinballs,* and *The Red Pony.* Her mother can see the signs of growth outside of school, too. Sadie reads 30 to 45 minutes each day at school, and just as much at home. "I was reading over her shoulder, and it's much more sophisticated language, but she understands it," her mother comments. Sadie also has developed the ability to look ahead in the text as well as to look away from the page and back without losing her place. "It's a major accomplishment," her mother says, "for her to be able to jump into the sixth-grade reading program." Or, as Sadie would put it, "Sixth grade is soooo good!"

Descriptions of Tests Used in Case Reports

These descriptions are compiled from personal observation and from the following sources: McCabe (1978), Manzo and Manzo (1993), Salvia and Ysseldyke (1995), and Weaver (1984).

Bender Visual Motor Gestalt Test (BVMGT)

Koppitz, E. M. (1963). *Bender Gestalt Test for Young Children*. New York: Grune & Stratton.

The examiner presents nine geometric designs one at a time to the child, who must then copy the design exactly. The scorer uses a system designed by Koppitz (1963) for children ages 5 to 11 to record errors of distortion of shape, perseveration, integration, and rotation. The procedure samples perceptual-motor behavior, but results are routinely used to make decisions about the presence of emotional disorders, perceptual problems, or brain damage.

Boston Naming

In this test, the examiner presents a series of pictures one at a time, such as one of a protractor, and the child must name the object.

Bruininks Oseretsky Test of Motor Proficiency

Bruininks, R. H. (1978). *Bruininks Oseretsky Test of Motor Proficiency*. Circle Pines, MN: American Guidance Service.

This individually administered test includes eight subtests: Running Speech and Agility, Balance, Bilateral Coordination, Strength, Upper-Limb Coordination, Response Speed, Visual-Motor Control, and Upper-Limb Speed and Dexterity. It is designed for use with children ages 4.6 through 14.6 years.

Children's Apperception Test

Bellak, L., & Bellak, S. B. (1971). *The Children's Apperception Test*. Larchmont, NY: CPS, Inc.

This test is used to measure personality in children ages 3 to 10. Subjects are shown 10 pictures of animals in human situations (form A) one at a time and asked to tell a story about them. Form H uses pictures of human beings, and the Supplement uses pictures of animals in less frequent family situations.

Developmental Test of Visual-Motor Integration (VMI)

Beery, K. E. (1989). *Developmental Test of Visual-Motor Integration*. Cleveland: Modern Curriculum Press.

Students ages 2 to 19 are asked to copy 24 geometric designs using pencil and paper. The designs are arranged in order of increasing difficulty and take about 15 minutes to reproduce. The test administrator scores the drawings on a pass/fail basis.

Diagnostic Reading Scales (DRS)

Spache, G. D. (1981). *Diagnostic Reading Scales*. Monterey, CA: CTB/McGraw-Hill.

The DRS is essentially an informal reading inventory with norms originally derived in 1963. The student pronounces words at sight from up to three lists. Performance is used to indicate instructional reading level, word attack skills, and sight vocabulary development. The test also includes 12 passages for oral or silent reading comprehension or listening comprehension with literal and inferential questions. Miscues and reading speed are also recorded. The supplemental phonics and word analysis tests cover the spectrum of phonetic elements, using blending, substitution, and auditory discrimination tasks. The entire test can be administered orally in an hour.

Durrell Analysis of Reading Difficulty

Durrell, D., & Catterson, J. (1980). *Durrell Analysis of Reading Difficulty*. San Antonio, TX: Psychological Corp.

The Durrell Analysis is administered individually in 30 to 90 minutes with two sets of paragraphs, test cards, word lists, and a cardboard tachistoscope. Subtests include the following:

Oral Reading.   The student reads aloud a series of eight paragraphs that become more and more complex and then answers literal questions.

Silent Reading.   The student reads silently a similar series of paragraphs while the examiner notes eye movements. The student then retells the passage and answers questions.

Listening Comprehension.   The student listens to six graded paragraphs read aloud by the test giver and then answers questions.

Word Recognition and Analysis. Using the tachistoscope, the test giver flashes each word for a half second. If the student fails to recognize the word at sight, it is repeated without a time limit for the student to sound out the word.

Listening Vocabulary. The administrator reads aloud the words used in the previous subtest. The student must point to a picture that shows the meaning of the word.

Pronunciation of Word Elements. The student reads single letters, clusters, morphemes, and phonograms.

Spelling. The student writes words dictated by the examiner.

Visual Memory of Words. The student is shown words visually then writes them. Students reading orally at grade 3 or below circle words rather than write them.

Auditory Analysis of Words and Elements. The student spells words phonetically. Less able readers identify phonetic elements in words.

Prereading Phonics Abilities Inventories. The student is asked to identify phonemes, name letters, write letters, match syntactic units, and identify letters in spoken words.

Gardner Expressive One-Word Picture Vocabulary Test

Gardner, M. F. (1990). *Expressive One-Word Picture Vocabulary Test.* Novato, CA: Academic Therapy Publications.

This test is similar to the Boston Naming Test, in that students are asked to identify pictures with one-word oral responses. The pictures represent both objects and abstract ideas. If administered in small groups, students respond in writing.

Gray Oral Reading Test

Wiederholt, L., & Bryant, B. (1992). *Gray Oral Reading Tests–3.* Austin, TX: Pro-Ed.

Students are tested individually and asked to read from 13 paragraphs arranged in order of increasing difficulty. There are five comprehension questions for each paragraph.

Kaufman Assessment Battery for Children

Kaufman, A., & Kaufman, N. (1983). *Kaufman Assessment Battery for Children.* Circle Pines, MN: American Guidance Service.

Tasks are grouped into three required scales (Sequential Processing, Simultaneous Processing, and Achievement) and one optional scale (Nonverbal).

Sequential Processing

Hand Movements.   The student imitates a sequence of taps by the examiner.

Number Recall.   The examiner reads a series of digits and the student repeats them.

Word Order.   The tester names a series of objects and the student points to silhouettes of the objects in the order in which they were named.

Simultaneous Processing

Magic Window.   The examiner rotates a picture behind a slit and the student names the object.

Face Recognition.   The examiner presents one or two faces. Then the student finds the face(s) in a group photograph in which the pose is different.

Gestalt Closure.   The child is given an inkblot drawing, completes it, and names it.

Triangles.   The student must match a given design by arranging triangles that have different colors on each side.

Matrix Analogies.   The student is presented with a two-part by two-part visual analogy and chooses a picture or design to complete it.

Spatial Memory.   The student is shown an arrangement of pictures on a page, then must recall where they were.

Photo Series.   The child is given photographs to represent an event and must place them in the correct time order.

Achievement

Expressive Vocabulary.   The student is shown photographs and names them.

Faces and Places.   The student is shown pictures of famous places or people and must give the names.

Arithmetic.   The student names numbers, counts, and computes.

Riddles.   The student is given some of the characteristics of a concrete or abstract concept and must name the concept.

Reading/Decoding.   The child is presented with letters or words and must say them.

Reading/Understanding.   The student reads a sentence and then acts out the directions.

Nonverbal
The preceding subtests are presented with gestures and students respond without words (Age 4: Face Recognition, Hand Movements, Triangles; Age 5: Hand Movements, Triangles, Spatial Memory, Matrix Analogies; Age 6 or older: Hand Movements, Triangles, Matrix Analogies, Spatial Memory, Photo Series).

Lindamood Auditory Conceptualization Test

Lindamood, C. H., & Lindamood, P. C. (1971). *Lindamood Auditory Conceptualization Test*. Boston: Teaching Resources Corporation.

This test takes about 10 minutes to administer. Students are presented with either Isolated Sounds in Sequence or Sounds within Syllable Patterns. They use colored blocks to represent the sounds they hear.

Metropolitan Achievement Tests

Balow, I. H., Farr, R. C., & Hogan, T. P. (1992). *Metropolitan Achievement Tests* (7th ed.). San Antonio, TX: Psychological Corporation.

These are standardized group achievement tests for preprimer (K.0–K.5), Primer (K.5–1.5) and grades 1 through 12: Word Recognition, Reading Vocabulary, Reading Comprehension, Prereading, Prewriting/Composing/Editing, Language.

Peabody Picture Vocabulary Test–Revised

Dunn, L., & Dunn, L. (1981). *Peabody Picture Vocabulary Test–Revised*. Circle Pines, MN: American Guidance Service.

This individually administered test takes 10 to 15 minutes to give, and can be used with subjects from 2½ to 40 years of age. The test giver places an easel with plates of four pictures each in front of the student. The examiner says a word, and the student points to the picture that best represents the word.

Purdue Perceptual-Motor Survey

Roach, E., & Kephart, N. C. (1966). *The Purdue Perceptual-Motor Survey*. Columbus, OH: Merrill.

This individual test purports to measure laterality, directionality, and perceptual-motor matching skills. Students walk on a board, jump, name parts of the body, imitate movements, and go through an obstacle course. A chalkboard is used for rhythmic writing, ocular control, and form perception tasks.

Rorschach Psychodiagnostic Test

Rorschach, H. (1921). *Rorschach Psychodiagnostic Test*. New York: Grune & Stratton.

The student is shown 10 cards with inkblots on them and asked to describe what he or she sees.

Stanford Achievement Test

Psychological Corporation. (1992). *Stanford achievement test* (8th ed.). San Antonio, TX: Harcourt Brace Jovanovich.

This is a group-administered test. Subtests include the following:

Sounds and Letters. Students are asked to match beginning and ending sounds of words they hear, to recognize letters, and to match letters with the sounds they make.

Word Study Skills. In one of these skills, students are shown the same word divided into syllables in three different ways. They must select the correctly divided word.

Word Reading. Students match spoken words to pictures and printed words to pictures.

Reading Vocabulary. Students select from a list the word that best matches a definition read to them.

Sentence Reading. Students select a picture to match a sentence they read.

Reading Comprehension. Students read both functional and recreational selections and complete multiple-choice questions designed to be both literal and inferential.

Listening to Words and Stories. Students listen to words and stories and answer questions about details, word meaning, cause and effect, directions, main idea, and language structure.

Listening Comprehension. Similar to Reading Comprehension, but the selections are read to the students.

Language Arts. These multiple-choice items cover complete sentences, finding and organizing information, and spelling.

Language Mechanics. Students are asked to recognize on multiple-choice lists proper capitalization, punctuation, and grammar.

Language Expression. The items ask students to compare the use of words, phrases, and clauses, and to judge style and organization.

Spelling. Students select correct spellings from lists of words.

Stanford Diagnostic Reading Test (SDRT)

Karlsen, B., & Gardner, E. (1985). *Stanford Diagnostic Reading Test* (3rd ed.). San Antonio, TX: The Psychological Corporation.

This group-administered test is designed for use with low-achieving readers. It appears in red (grades 1–3), green (grades 3–5), brown (grades 5–8+), and blue (grades 8–14). Subtests include the following:

Auditory Vocabulary. Words from reading and literature, mathematics and science, or social studies and the arts are read aloud to students. They select the pictures that match the words.

Vocabulary. Words appear in context. Student select the proper meanings.

Auditory Discrimination. Word pairs are read. Students are asked if the words have the same beginning, middle, or ending sounds.

Phonetic Analysis. The task differs with the level of the test. Red identifies beginning and ending sounds; green and brown identify sounds and match to spellings; and blue identifies the sounds of unusual spellings.

Structural Analysis. (No red.) Green identifies the first syllable of two-syllable words and identifying word parts and blending them into words; brown and blue identify syllabicating three-syllable words.

Word Parts. (Blue only.) Students are asked the meanings of common affixes and roots.

Word Reading. Students match meanings to words read.

Reading Comprehension. Red requires students to match pictures with sentences read or to choose completion words from multiple choices for clozed sentences or paragraphs; green asks multiple-choice cloze questions; brown and blue give passages of varied types followed by multiple-choice questions.

Reading Rate. (Brown only.) Students mark how far through an easy passage they can read in a given time.

Skimming and Scanning. (Blue only.) Students scan passages for specific information, or skim a passage in a given time for both general and specific information.

Fast Reading. (Blue only.) Students read easy material in a given time and answer comprehension questions.

Test of Written Spelling–2

Larsen, S., & Hammill, D. (1986). *Test of Written Spelling–2*. Austin, TX: Pro-Ed.

This is a test given to individual students in grades 1 through 12. Subtests cover Predictable and Unpredictable words. Words are given in isolation, in a sentence, and repeated in isolation, as in a spelling bee.

Predictable Words. Students write 50 dictated words that have regular spellings.

Unpredictable Words. Students write 50 phonetically irregular words.

Wechsler Adult Intelligence Scale–Revised (WAIS–R)

Wechsler, D. (1981). *Wechsler Adult Intelligence Scale–Revised*. New York: The Psychological Corporation.

The subtests are the same as the WISC–R, except that Coding is called Digit Symbol, Mazes is not included, and Picture Completion is supplementary.

Weschler Individual Achievement Test (WIAT)

Psychological Corporation. (1992). *Weschler Individual Achievement Test*. San Antonio, TX: Harcourt Brace Jovanovich.

This norm-referenced, individually administered achievement test was based on the same norms as the Wechsler intelligence scales. It can be given in an hour. Language subtests include the following:

Basic Reading. The child points or responds orally to pictures and printed words as measures of decoding ability.

Spelling. The examiner dictates letters, sounds, and words and the student writes them down.

Reading Comprehension. The student reads brief passages and is asked and answers literal and inferential questions orally.

Listening Comprehension. The student identifies pictures that match words or passages read by the examiner.

Oral Expression. The student sees a picture and is given oral instructions. The child must respond with descriptions, instructions, or explanations of processes.

Written Expression. This is a timed, prompted writing sample. The student is given a topic or picture, and the piece is rated for development, organization, and mechanics.

Wechsler Intelligence Scales for Children–Revised (WISC–R)

Wechsler, D. (1974). *Wechsler Intelligence Scales for Children–Revised*. New York: The Psychological Corporation.

This test is given individually and contains 12 subtests, 6 of which are verbal and six of which are performance.

Verbal

Information. The child answers 30 questions about general information.

Similarities. Given 17 pair of words, the child must tell how the two things in each pair are similar.

Arithmetic. Without using paper and pencil, the student solves 18 word problems that are read aloud by the examiner.

Vocabulary. The examiner presents 32 words in order of increasing difficulty. The child must define each word.

Comprehension. The child answers 17 questions of common-sense reasoning ability, such as what he or she would do if someone else were in danger.

Digit Span. The child repeats backward or forward numbers in series pronounced one second apart.

Performance

Picture Completion. The child finds missing parts in 26 pictures presented.

Picture Arrangement. The student is given a group of pictures and asked to find a story behind them. Then the child puts the pictures in order.

Block Design. The student sees a design and then is given four, six, or nine blocks with which to re-create the design.

Object Assembly. The child is given four familiar objects that have been broken down into puzzles and is asked to reassemble them.

Coding. The child is shown a series of symbols and is asked to copy a symbol into a box when a matching number appears.

Mazes. This subtest is optional. Without lifting pencil from paper, the child completes nine mazes that become increasingly difficult.

Wechsler Intelligence Scale for Children–III (WISC–III)

Wechsler, D. (1991). *Wechsler Intelligence Scales for Children–III*. New York: The Psychological Corporation.

This is a 1991 revision of the WISC–R. Symbol Search can be substituted for Coding. The child is given two sets of symbols: a target and a search group. The child must tell whether the search group includes the target symbol.

Woodcock-Johnson Psychoeducational Battery–R (WJ–R)

Woodcock, R. W., & Johnson, M. B. (1989). *Woodcock-Johnson Psychoeducational Battery–Revised*. Allen, TX: DLM.

The Woodcock-Johnson is administered individually and contains 21 cognitive ability subtests and 14 achievement subtests, presented on easels or tapes.

Cognitive Ability

Memory for Names.   The student learns and uses names for nine space creatures pictured on the easel.

Memory for Sentences.   The student repeats sentences dictated from tapes.

Visual Matching.   The student matches sets of one- to three-digit numbers.

Incomplete Words.   The student identifies words with one or more phonemes deleted.

Visual Closure.   The student identifies objects that are distorted, incomplete, or obscured.

Picture Vocabulary.   The student sees a picture of an object and names it.

Analysis—Synthesis.   The student is presented with logical puzzles that are incomplete and must decide what elements are missing.

Visual-Auditory Learning.   The student learns visual symbols to stand for words and reads rebus sentences made from them.

Memory for Words.   The student repeats lists of random words read aloud by the examiner. Lists can be as long as eight words.

Cross Out.   In this timed test, the student is given a set of 20 drawings from which to find 5 that match the original stimulus drawing.

Sound Blending.   The student combines syllables into words.

Picture Recognition.   The student finds target pictures among sets of distracters.

Oral Vocabulary.   The administrator reads a word aloud and the student responds with a synonym or an antonym.

Concept Formation.   The student is given materials that represent both examples and nonexamples of concepts. The student must then identify the intended concept.

Delayed Recall—Memory for Names.   The student is asked to recall the names of the space creatures learned in the Memory for Names subtest after breaks of from one to eight days.

Delayed Recall—Visual-Auditory Learning.   The student is asked to recall one to eight days later the symbols that were memorized for the rebuses in the Visual-Auditory Learning subtest.

Numbers Reversed.   The examiner reads a series of digits, and the student repeats the list backward.

Sound Patterns.   The student hears two sound patterns at a time and says whether they are the same or different.

Spatial Relations.   The student is presented with shapes and must find the matches.

Listening Comprehension.   The administrator reads a passage aloud and the student supplies the missing last word.

Verbal Analogies.   The student completes analogies that are presented in ascending order of difficulty.

Achievement

Letter-Word Identification.   The student is asked to name letters presented in isolation and in words.

Passage Comprehension.   (Similar to the WRMT-R.) The student supplies the missing word in brief selections.

Calculation.   The student solves problems with whole numbers and mixed numbers. Difficulty ranges from basic operations to calculus.

Applied Problems.   The student solves math problems drawn from practical situations.

Dictation.   The student writes answers to questions in order to generate text from which mechanical correctness and usage can be assessed.

Writing Samples.   The student responds to questions that call for answers of one word or a sentence. He or she may be asked to describe a picture or to use designated words.

Science, Social Studies, and Humanities.   The student responds orally to questions about biology, physical science, geography, history, music, art, and literature.

Word Attack.   The student is asked to read nonsense words and low-frequency words.

Reading Vocabulary.   Given a list of words, the student reads them and responds with antonyms or synonyms.

Quantitative Concepts.   The student explains math vocabulary.

Proofing.   The student is given text contain mechanical errors and must correct them.

Writing Fluency.   Given a word or picture prompt, the student writes during a timed period. Samples are scored for mechanics and handwriting.

Woodcock Reading Mastery Tests–R (WRMT–R)

Woodcock, R. (1987). *Woodcock Reading Mastery Tests–Revised*. Circle Pines, MN: American Guidance Service.

This battery contains six tests to be administered individually. It was revised in 1987 to contain a readiness cluster by adding a Visual-Auditory learning subtest to the Letter Identification subtest present in the 1973 version. It also shares the Visual-Auditory Learning subtest with the Woodcock-Johnson Psychoeducational Battery–Revised (WJ–R). The newer version measures word comprehension with synonym and antonym tasks as well as the analogies that were present in the 1973 version. Vocabulary is broken down into general, science-math, social studies, and humanities categories in the newer edition. All responses are oral to stimuli presented on an easel.

In the Visual-Auditory learning subtest, the student must learn symbols and read rebuses containing them to make sentences. The Letter Identification subtest presents upper- and lower-case letters in several typefaces. The student pronounces words presented in isolation for the Word Identification subtest. Word attack skills are measured through the reading of nonsense words.

The administrator reads words and the student responds with an antonym for the antonym section of the Word Comprehension test, or a synonym for the synonym section. In the analogies section, the student reads the analogy aloud and completes it. For the Passage Comprehension subtest, the student reads a phrase or passage of no more than three sentences from which a word has been deleted and provides the missing word. Some synonyms are accepted. Pictures accompany the earliest examples.

APPENDIX B

Natural or Authentic Measures of Reading and Writing

Oral Reading

Running Records

Clay, M. (1993). *An Observational Survey of Early Literacy Achievement.* Portsmouth, NH: Heinemann.

Johnston, P. H. (1997). *Knowing Literacy: Constructive Literacy Assessment.* York, ME: Stenhouse Publishers.

Running records are a method of recording oral reading that does not require that the teacher have a copy of the student's text. You simply sit next to the reader and place a check mark on a piece of lined paper for each word the reader says correctly. Be sure to transcribe the marks in the same configuration that the words take on the page, and note page numbers and the book used. Following the reading, you can refer to the original text for help in interpreting exactly what the check marks mean.

Marie Clay, who developed this method, devised a notation system as well, which Johnston (1997) adopts. The recorder notes deviations from print, including substitutions, omissions, insertions, repetitions, attempts, requests for help, and teacher assistance. The running records not only provide an accuracy rate (in order to determine whether the text is easy, appropriate for learning, or too hard) but also a self-correction rate and the cueing systems used to decode words in connected reading. To determine the reading level of the text for the reader, I use the following percentages (combined with the comprehension percentages noted):

Easy/Independent	• 96–100 percent word recognition accuracy in context
	• Better than 80 percent comprehension (measured by questions or retelling of key ideas and information)
Learning/Just Right/Instructional	• 91–95 percent word recognition accuracy in context
	• 50 to 80 percent comprehension
Frustration/Too Hard/Challenge	• 90 percent or less
	• Less than 50 percent comprehension

Miscue Analysis

Weaver, C. (1988). *Reading Process and Practice: From Socio-Psycholinguistics to Whole Language*. Portsmouth, NH: Heinemann.

There are many forms of miscue analysis in use; all are intended to help the teacher reliably determine which cueing system (graphophonic, syntactic, semantic, pragmatic) the student is using to recognize words and construct meaning. I generally follow Weaver's method, although I have collapsed some columns of hers and added some of my own. Refer to Figure B.1, a sample grid adapted from Weaver (1988). In column 1, record the word printed in the text (below the line in the running record). In column 2, write what the student said (above the line in the running record). For the next five columns, decide whether the student has (Y) or has not (N) matched the part of the text indicated: the word's initial, middle, or final sound; the preceding context; or the following context. In the last three columns, write Y if the reader self-corrected the miscue, if the miscue preserved essential meaning, or if it was either self-corrected or meaning-preserving. At the bottom of the columns, calculate and fill in the percentage of Y answers.

Weaver calls this last column a comprehending score, or a measure of sentence-level comprehension. When the student gives an adequate retelling of the piece, Weaver suggests accepting 30 percent self-correction or 60 percent prediction from preceding context, correction from following context, or a 60 percent comprehending score. I use the match of initial, middle, and final sound columns to indicate whether the student is reading all the way through a word. In general, weaker readers will rely on the first sound and context, next attending to the final sound.

FIGURE B.1   Miscue Analysis Form

Text	Student	Initial Sound (Y/N)	Middle Sound (Y/N)	Final Sound (Y/N)	Precede Context (Y/N)	Follow Context (Y/N)	Self-Correct (Y/N)	Meaning Preserve (Y/N)	SC or Meaning Preserve (Y/N)
		%	%	%	%	%	%	%	%

Source: Adapted from Weaver (1998).

Phonics Knowledge

Yopp-Singer Test of Phonemic Awareness

Yopp, H. K. (1995). A test for assessing phonemic awareness in young children. *The Reading Teacher, 49,* 20–29.

This 20-item test is for use with young children just learning to read. Although it is not normed, it will allow the teacher to observe in a brief time whether the student can segment the phonemes in words. The teacher says a word, such as *dog,* and the student replies, with the phonemes /d/, /o/, /g/.

The Names Test

Duffelmeyer, F. A., Kruse, A. E., Merkley, D. J., & Fyfe, S. A. (1994). Further validation and enhancement of the Names Test. *The Reading Teacher, 48,* 118–128.

This test is designed for use with students in grades 2 through 5, but I have used it successfully with older students. It consists of 35 names (first and last) that the student is asked to read as if it were a class list for attendance or a team roster for practice. Therefore, the test is quick to give and provides a natural context familiar to most children. The names are English, not multicultural, since the test is one of English phonology. I print the names on individual 3″ × 5″ cards to prevent younger children or those overwhelmed by chunks of print from being intimidated. The authors include in the article a scoring chart that allows you to count the percentage of sounds in specific positions that the student has mastered.

Comprehension

Retelling

Rhodes, L. K., & Shanklin, N. L. (1993). *Windows into Literacy: Assessing Learners K–8.* Portsmouth, NH: Heinemann.

Retellings of passages just read are natural measures of comprehension, since nowhere other than school is a child likely to be quizzed by someone who has already read a piece the child is discussing. Such questions would be socially inappropriate. Frequently, however, people share books or articles with friends or suggest readings to them by retelling the piece, at least its main parts.

Retellings take two basic forms: free and elicited. In free retelling, simply tell the reader prior to beginning the passage that after reading, you would like him or her to retell the passage as if to a friend who has not read it (or some other socially appropriate reason, such as a recommendation). In elicited retelling, you can set a particular purpose; be prepared to retell the important idea, or the five most important things the author has to say, or something of a similar nature.

When the student finishes reading, have him or her put the book aside and ask for the retell. When she or he stops, ask if there is anything else to add. If not, you can then request more information. Depending on your purpose in reading the passage, you might ask about main ideas, sequence of events, the author's tone or purpose, important factors omitted from the initial retelling, or the reader's reaction. Remember that no retelling, even from a good reader, is likely to seem complete, since you are not apt to know the reader's purpose or preferences in reading. I would grade retellings based on information gained from both the free and elicited portions, but I would note the sections on which I gave help (questions).

For the purpose of generating a reading level or of interpreting word recognition adequacy in the miscue analysis, note whether the retell was adequate. Did the reader include most (80 percent, or 50 percent for inadequate) of the main ideas or key parts of the story grammar? Or did the reader set a purpose for the retelling and select details and conclusions appropriately? (See the next section for suggestions about how to make the retelling more dynamic in order to gain information for instructional strategies.)

I would avoid retelling grading schemes that simply rewrite the text in grammatical or story grammar units and ask you to check off the ones covered. As noted earlier, even good readers seldom repeat everything in a passage, and the purpose of the perceived relationship between you and the reader will likely dictate how the retell is constructed, not a verbatim list of the component sentences.

Intervention Assessment

Paratore, J., & Indrisano, R. (1987). Intervention assessment of reading comprehension. *The Reading Teacher, 40* (80), 778–782.

The authors have laid out procedures for dynamic assessment of comprehension, particularly in expository passages, but the principles can be used with narratives or fiction as well. Generally, you are attempting to couch the assessment in the setting of a lesson. Therefore, you ask the reader to do what he or she might in a Directed Reading-Thinking Activity (Stauffer, 1975) or the Survey Technique (Aukerman, 1972): Activate prior knowledge, set purposes for reading, and preview the sections and illustrations. At any stage, if the student does not know how to do the step, or if the response is inadequate, teach the procedure and try again.

After reading and retelling, if there are sections that are unclear or inaccurate, ask the student to reopen the text and find the answer or the details in question. If the student cannot do so, note this apparent insensitivity to text structure, and direct the reader to the appropriate page. Repeat as necessary, homing in on the paragraph or sentence, and finally pointing directly to the target information. Combined with Weaver's (1988) comprehending score, this technique will help you understand any difficulty the reader is having at the text or sentence level of comprehension.

Writing

Dictation

Clay, M. (1993). *An Observational Survey of Early Literacy Achievement.* Portsmouth, NH: Heinemann.

Johnston, P. H. (1997). *Knowing Literacy: Constructive Literacy Assessment.* York, ME: Stenhouse Publishers.

Clay has developed norm-referenced passages for dictation to beginning writers in order to assess how accurately they transcribe speech into print. Johnston suggests constructing our own sentences or brief passages that incorporate target spellings. In either case, you dictate the sentence(s) to the student, repeating phrases as necessary. Score, if you wish, by tabulating the number of sounds transcribed conventionally. Note the cueing systems used by the student (visual, phonetic, morphemic). Also compare spelling under this condition (no composing required) with spelling during composing. Composing drains away capacity that might be used for retrieval, formation of mental models, self-monitoring, and storage.

Write with Me

This is my own adaptation of Murray's (1985) procedures for the first day of writing class (see Figure 6.3). I use it to provide good writing conditions for students who have never had them in order to see how they react with good instruction. This procedure allows me to observe the writing processes of students I do not teach in class.

APPENDIX C

Instructional Approaches Mentioned

Elkonin Phonemic Segmentation Task

Elkonin, D. (1973). Reading in the USSR. In John Dowling (Ed.), *Comparative Reading*. New York: Macmillan.

In order to make concrete something as abstract as the association of a sound with a letter, which is part of a group of letters, which make another sound, which represents a thing, Elkonin used pictures, markers, and boxes. The child sees a picture, below which a series of boxes have been drawn to represent each sound in the word represented by the picture. The instructor demonstrates saying the word, then pushes a marker into each box in order for the sounds heard in the word. For a picture of a dog, for instance, the teacher would push a marker into the first box while saying /d/, one into the second box while saying /o/, and a third into its box while saying /g/. The child would repeat the task. Next, the child learns to use the markers to separate sounds heard in further words.

Language Experience Approach (LEA)

Van Allen, R., & Allen, C. (1966). *Language Experiences in Reading: Teachers' Resource Book*. Chicago: Encyclopedia Brittanica Press.

The LEA is used individually or in groups with beginning learners of written language. The point of the approach is to facilitate the association of print with speech. The instructor solicits from the student a story about a subject of study or from the student's personal life. The teacher transcribes the story *verbatim*, not changing the language to standard usage, but also not attempting to simulate dialectic pronunciation in spelling (e.g., "We be going to the store" is recorded, but not "We be goin' to dah sto'"). With groups, students can be asked to derive a "more usual way to say that" to prevent some students from practicing usage errors of others.

Once the language experience chart is recorded, the student reads it and the instructor underlines each word said immediately. The next day, a new chart is generated and the old chart is reread. When a word has been underlined three times, it is transferred to a 3" × 5" card to form a sight word bank. The word bank forms the basis for phonics instruction via analogy to other words. Words that are not instantly recognized from the word bank can be returned to a practice pile.

Orton-Gillingham Method

This individual tutoring program teaches letter-sound relationships and blending through visual, auditory, and kinesthetic means. This is a bottom-up approach based on rote drill of sequenced phonetic elements. Reading begins after sight words, major phonograms, and single-letter phonics are mastered.

Reading Recovery

Clay, M. (1993). *Reading Recovery: A Guidebook for Teachers in Training.* Portsmouth, NH: Heinemann.

Marie Clay devised this early intervention tutorial program of limited duration for underachieving first-graders. Schools who employ trained Reading Recovery teachers generally identify the lowest achieving 20 percent of first-graders for 30-minute daily sessions for 12 to 20 weeks. Although each session is based on the child's needs as assessed by the teacher, lessons usually contain four elements:

1. Reading a familiar book while the teacher observes
2. Reading the book introduced to the child the day before while the teacher takes a running record
3. Writing a daily message, usually a sentence with the help of the teacher, with this sentence forming the basis for word and/or syntactic study
4. Introducing a new book (by the teacher)

REFERENCES

Adams, M. J. (1990). *Beginning to read: Thinking and learning about print*. Cambridge, MA: The MIT Press.

American Psychological Association, American Research Association, National Council on Measurement in Education. (1985). *Standards for educational and psychological testing*. Washington, DC: American Psychological Association.

Anthony, R. J., Johnson, T. D., Mickelson, N. I., & Preece, A. (1991). *Evaluating literacy*. Portsmouth, NH: Heinemann.

Ascher, C. (1990, May). Assessing bilingual students for placement and instruction. *ERIC Clearinghouse on Urban Education Digest, 65,* 2–5.

Atwell, N. (1998). *In the middle: New understandings about writing, reading and learning* (2nd ed.). Portsmouth, NH: Heinemann Boynton/Cook.

Aukerman, R. C. (1972). *Reading in the secondary school classroom*. New York: McGraw Hill.

Bader, L. A., & Wiesendanger, K. (1994). *Bader Reading and Language Inventory* (2nd ed.). New York: Merrill.

Barr, R., Blachowicz, C., & Wogman-Sadow, M. (1995). *Reading diagnosis for teachers* (3rd ed.). White Plains, NY: Longman.

Betts, E. A. (1954). *Foundations of reading instruction*. New York: American Book Co.

Brazee, P., & Haynes, S. W. (1989). Special education and whole language: From an evaluator's viewpoint. In K. S. Goodman, Y. M. Goodman, & W. J. Hood (Eds.), *The whole language evaluation book*. Portsmouth, NH: Heinemann.

Brisk, M. E. (1998). *Bilingual education: From compensatory to quality schooling*. Mahwah, NJ: Lawrence Erlbaum.

Britton, J. N., et al. (1976). *The development of writing abilities, 11–18*. London: Macmillan.

Broadfoot, P. (1988). Profiles and records of achievement: A real alternative. *Educational Psychology, 8* (4), 291–297.

Brown, A. L. (1994). The advancement of learning. *Educational Researcher, 23* (8), 4–12.

Brown, R. G. (1993). *Schools of thought: How the politics of literacy shape thinking in the classroom*. San Francisco: Jossey-Bass.

California State Department of Education. (1992). *It's elementary! Elementary grades task force report*. Sacramento, CA: California State Department of Education.

Calkins, L. M., with Harwayne, S. (1991). *Living between the lines*. Portsmouth, NH: Heinemann.

Calmenson, S. (1989). *101 silly summertime jokes*. New York: Scholastic.

Carney, J., & Cioffi, G. (1990). Extending traditional diagnosis: The dynamic assessment of reading abilities. *Reading Psychology, 11,* 177–192.

Carver, R., & Leibert, R. (1995). The effect of reading library books at different levels of difficulty upon gain in reading ability. *Reading Research Quarterly, 30,* 26–48.

Cioffi, G., & Carney, J. (1983). Dynamic assessment of reading disabilities. *The Reading Teacher, 36,* 764–768.

Clarizio, H. F. (1982). Intellectual assessment of Hispanic children. *Psychology in the Schools, 19,* 61–71.

Clay, M. (1985). *The early detection of reading difficulties* (3rd ed.). Wellington: Heinemann.

Clay, M. (1993). *An observational survey of early literacy achievement*. Portsmouth, NH: Heinemann.

Cloud, N. (1994). Special education needs of second language learners. In F. Genesee (Ed.), *Educating second language children: The whole child, the whole curriculum, the whole community* (pp. 243–277). Cambridge: Cambridge University Press.

Coltheart, V., Laxon, V., Rickard, M., & Elton, C. (1988). Phonological recoding in reading for meaning by adults and children. *Journal of Experimental Psychology, 14,* 387–397.

Connor, U. (1984). Recall of texts: Differences between first and second language learners. *TEOSL Quarterly, 18,* 239–256.

Cook, L. K., & Mayer, R. E. (1988). Teaching readers about the structure of scientific text. *Journal of Educational Psychology, 80* (4), 448–456.

251

Cummins, J. (1984). *Bilingualism and special education: Issues in assessment and pedagogy.* San Diego: College Hill Press.

Cummins, J. (1986). Empowering minority students: A framework for intervention. *Harvard Educational Review, 56,* 18–36.

Cummins, J. (1991). Interdependence of first- and second-language proficiency in bilingual children. In E. Bialystok (Ed.), *Language processing in bilingual children* (pp. 70–89). New York: Cambridge University Press.

Cunningham, P. M., & Allington, R. L. (1994). *Classrooms that work: They can all read and write.* New York: HarperCollins.

Dahl, R. (1980). *The twits.* New York: Viking Penguin.

Damico, J. S. (1991). Descriptive assessment of communicative ability in limited English proficient students. In E. V. Hamayan & J. S. Damico (Eds.), *Limiting bias in the assessment of bilingual students* (pp. 157–217). Austin, TX: Pro-Ed.

Darling-Hammond, L., & Goodwin, L. (1993). Progress toward professionalism in teaching. In G. Kawelti (Ed.), *Challenges and achievements of American education* (pp. 19–52). Alexandria, VA: Association for Supervision and Curriculum Development.

Darling-Hammond, L. (1994). Performance-based assessment and educational equity. *Harvard Educational Review, 64,* 5–30.

Dixon-Krauss, L. (1996). *Vygotsky in the classroom: Mediated literacy instruction and assessment.* White Plains, NY: Longman.

Duffelmeyer, F. A., Kruse, A. E., Merkley, D. J., & Fyfe, S. A. (1994). Further validation and enhancement of the Names Test. *The Reading Teacher, 48,* 118–128.

Duran, R. P. (1983). *Hispanics' education and background: Predictors of college achievement.* New York: College Entrance Examination Board.

Duran, R. P. (1989). Testing of linguistic minorities. In R. L. Linn (Ed.), *Educational Measurement* (pp. 573–587). London: Collier Macmillan.

Edelsky, C., & Harman, S. (1988). One more critique or reading tests—With two differences. *English Education, 20* (3), 157–171.

Ehri, L. C. (1987). Learning to read and spell words. *Journal of Reading Behavior, 5,* 5–31.

Elkonin, D. (1973). Reading in the USSR. In John Dowling (Ed.), *Comparative reading.* New York: Macmillan.

Evans, M. A., & Carr, T. H. (1985). Cognitive abilities, conditions of learning and the early development of reading skill. *Reading Research Quarterly, 20,* 327–351.

Fink, R. (1995–1996). Successful dyslexics: A constructivist study of passionate interest reading. *Journal of Adolescent and Adult Literacy, 39,* 268–280.

Flower, L. (1990). Writer-based prose: A cognitive basis for problems in writing. In T. Newkirk (Ed.), *To compose: Teaching writing in high school and college* (2nd ed.). Wellington: Heinemann.

Freebody, P., & Byrne, B. (1988). Word-reading strategies in elementary school children: Relations to comprehension, reading time, and phonemic awareness. *Reading Research Quarterly,* Fall, 441–453.

Freire, P. (1985). *The politics of education.* South Hadley, MA: Bergin & Garvey.

Fry, E. (1977). Fry's readability graph: Clarifications, validity, and extension to level 17. *Journal of Reading, 21* (3), 242–252.

Garcia, G. E. (1988). *Factors influencing the English reading test performance of Spanish-English bilingual children.* Unpublished doctoral dissertation, University of Illinois at Urbana-Champaign.

Garcia, G. E. (1991). Factors influencing the English reading test performance of Spanish-speaking Hispanic children. *Reading Research Quarterly, 26* (1), 371–392.

Garcia, G. E. (1992). Ethnography and classroom communication: Taking an "emic" perspective. *Topics in Language Disorders, 12* (3), 123–141.

Garcia, G. E. (1994). Equity challenges in authentically assessing students from diverse backgrounds. *The Educational Forum, 59* (1), 64–73.

Garcia, G. E., & Pearson, P. D. (1991). The role of assessment in a diverse society. In E. H. Hiebert (Ed.), *Literacy in a diverse society: Perspectives, practices, and policies* (pp. 253–278). New York: Teachers College Press.

Garcia, G. E., & Pearson, P. D. (1994). Assessment and diversity. In L. Darling-Hammond (Ed.), *Review of research in education* (Vol. 20, pp. 337–391). Washington, DC: American Educational Research Association.

Gardner, H. (1982). *Art, mind, and brain.* New York: Basic Books.

Gaskins, I. W., Downer, M. A., Anderson, R. C., Cunningham, P. M., Gaskins, R. W., Schommer, M., & the Teachers of the Benchmark School. (1988). A metacognitive approach to phonics: Using what you know to decode what you don't know. *Remedial and Special Education, 9.*

Genesee, F., & Hamayan, E. V. (1994). Classroom-based assessment. In F. Genesee (Ed.), *Educating second language children: The whole child, the whole curriculum, the whole community* (pp. 212–239). Cambridge: Cambridge University Press.

Gentile, C. A., Martin-Rehrmann, J., & Kennedy, J. H. (1995). *Windows into the classroom: NAEP's 1992 writing portfolio study*. Washington, DC: U.S. Department of Education.

Gilmore, J. V., & Gilmore, E. C. (1968). *Gilmore Oral Reading Test*. New York: The Psychological Corporation.

Gonzalez, V., Brusca-Vega, R., & Yawkey, T. (1997). *Assessment and instruction of culturally and linguistically diverse students with or at-risk of learning problems*. Boston: Allyn and Bacon.

Goodman, Y. M., Watson, D., & Burke, C. L. (1987). *Reading miscue inventory: Alternate procedures*. Katonah, NY: Richard C. Owen.

Graves, D. (1983). *Writing: Teachers and children at work*. Portsmouth, NH: Heinemann.

Graves, D. (1994). *A fresh look at writing*. Portsmouth, NH: Heinemann.

Gunning, T. (1995). Word building: A strategic approach to the teaching of phonics. *The Reading Teacher, 48*, 484–488.

Gunning, T. G. (1996). *Creating reading instruction for all children* (2nd ed.). Boston: Allyn and Bacon.

Hansen, J. (1987). *When writers read*. Portsmouth, NH: Heinemann.

Harste, J., Woodward, V., & Burke, C. (1984). *Language stories and literacy lessons*. Portsmouth, NH: Heinemann.

Howe, D., & Howe, J. (1979). *Bunnicula*. New York: Avon.

Jenkins, C. B. (1996). *Inside the writing portfolio: What we need to know to assess children's writing*. Portsmouth, NH: Heinemann.

Johnson, T., & Louis, D. (1987). *Literacy through literature*. Portsmouth, NH: Heinemann.

Johnston, P. (1984a). Prior knowledge and reading comprehension test bias. *Reading Research Quarterly, 19* (2), 219–239.

Johnston, P. (1984b). *Reading comprehension assessment: A cognitive basis*. Newark, DE: International Reading Association.

Johnston, P. (1992). *Constructive evaluation of literate activity*. New York: Longman.

Johnston, P. (1997). *Knowing literacy: Constructive literacy assessment*. York, ME: Stenhouse Publishers.

Kibby, M. W. (1995). *Practical steps for informing literacy instruction: A diagnostic decision-making model*. Newark, DE: International Reading Association.

LaBerge, D., & Samuels, S. J. (1974). Toward a theory of automatic information processing in reading. *Cognitive Psychology, 6*, 293–323.

LaCelle-Peterson, M. W., & Rivera, C. (1994). Is it real for all kids? A framework for equitable assessment policies for English language learners. *Harvard Educational Review, 64* (1), 55–75.

Lahey, M., & Bloom, L. (1994). Variability and language learning disabilities. In G. P. Wallach & K. G. Butler (Eds.), *Language learning disabilities in school-age children and adolescents*. New York: Macmillan.

Lee, J. F. (1986). On the use of recall task to measure L2 reading comprehension. *Studies in Second Language Acquisition, 8* (2), 201–211.

Leslie, L., & Caldwell, J. (1995). *Qualitative reading inventory–II*. New York: HarperCollins.

Lyons, C. A. (1991). Helping a learning-disabled child enter the literate world. In D. E. DeFord, C. A. Lyons, & G. S. Pinnell (Eds.), *Bridges to literacy*. Portsmouth, NH: Heinemann.

Manzo, A., & Manzo, U. (1993). *Literacy disorders. Holistic diagnosis and remediation*. Fort Worth, TX: Harcourt Brace Jovanovich.

Marzollo, J. (1992). *I spy: A book of picture riddles*. New York: Scholastic.

Mason, J., & Au, K. (1990). *Reading instruction for today* (2nd ed.). Glenview, IL: Scott Foresman.

McCabe, R. (1978). *McCabe's test handbook: A guide to tests used by speech pathologists, learning disabilities specialists, and special educators*. Tigard, OR: C. C. Publications.

Mills, H., O'Keefe, T., & Stephens, D. (1992). *Looking closely: Phonics in the whole language classroom*. Newark, DE: International Reading Association.

Mills, I., Campbell, J., & Farstrup, A. (1993). *NAEP 1992 reading report card for the nation and the states*. Washington, DC: National Center for Education Statistics.

Murray, D. M. (1985). *A writer teaches writing* (2nd ed.). Boston: Houghton Mifflin.

National Council of Teachers of English & The International Reading Association. (1996). *Standards for the English Language Arts*. Urbana, IL: National Council of Teachers of English.

Newkirk, T. (1987). The non-narrative writing of young children. *Research in the Teaching of English, 21*, 121–145.

O'Brien, C. (1992). A large-scale assessment to support the process paradigm. *English Journal, 81*, 28–33.

O'Malley, J. M., & Valdez-Pierce, L. (1996). *Authentic assessment for English language learners: Practical approaches for teachers*. Reading, MA: Addison-Wesley.

Oxford, R., Poll, L., Lopez, D., Stupp, P., Gendell, M., & Peng, S. (1981). Projections of non-English background limited English proficient persons in the United States to the year 2000: Educational planning in the demographic context. *NABE Journal, 5* (3), 1–30.

Paratore, J. (1993). *Reading/language arts program evaluation.* Unpublished manuscript.

Paratore, J., Homza, A., Krol-Sinclair, B, Lewis-Barrow, T., Melzi, G., Stergis, R., & Haynes, H. (1995). Shifting boundaries in home and school responsibilities: The construction of home-based literacy portfolios by immigrant parents and their children. *Research in the Teaching of English, 29,* 367–389.

Paratore, J., & Indrisano, R. (1987). Intervention assessment of reading comprehension. *The Reading Teacher, 40* (80), 778–782.

Perfetti, C. A. (1984). Reading acquisition and beyond: Decoding includes cognition. *American Journal of Education, 93,* 40–60.

Pinnell, G. S., Fried, M. D., & Estice, R. M. (1991). Reading recovery: Learning how to make a difference. In D. E. DeFord, C. A. Lyons, & G. S. Pinnell (Eds.), *Bridges to literacy.* Portsmouth, NH: Heinemann.

Porter, C., & Cleland, J. (1995). *The portfolio as a learning strategy.* Portsmouth, NH: Heinemann.

Rhodes, L. K. (Ed.). (1993). *Literacy assessment: A handbook of instruments.* Portsmouth, NH: Heinemann.

Rhodes, L. K., & Dudley-Marling, C. (1996). *Readers and writers with a difference: A holistic approach to teaching learning disabled and remedial students* (2nd ed.). Portsmouth, NH: Heinemann.

Rhodes, L. K., & Shanklin, N. L. (1993). *Windows into literacy: Assessing learners K–8.* Portsmouth, NH: Heinemann.

Richard-Amato, P. A., & Snow, M. A. (1992). *The multicultural classroom: Readings for content-area teachers.* Reading, MA: Addison-Wesley.

Richek, M., Caldwell, J., Jennings, J., & Lerner, J. (1996). *Reading problems: Assessment and teaching strategies.* Boston: Allyn and Bacon.

Rief, L. (1992). *Seeking diversity.* Portsmouth, NH: Heinemann.

Rosenblatt, L. (1978). *The reader, the text, the poem: The transactional theory of the literary work.* Carbondale, IL: Southern Illinois University Press.

Rosinski, R. R., Golinkoff, R. M., & Kukish, K. S. (1975). Automatic semantic processing in a picture-word interference task. *Child Development, 46,* 247–253.

Rothman, R. (1988). Vermont plans to pioneer with "work portfolios": Assessment to include best pupil materials. *Education Week, 8* (8).

Rueda, R., & Garcia, E. (1994). Teachers' beliefs about reading assessment with Latino language minority students. In Office of Educational Research and Improvement (Ed.), *Research Report: 9.* Santa Cruz, CA: National Center for Research on Cultural Diversity and Second Language Learning.

Rueda, R., & Garcia, E. (1996). Teachers' perspectives on literacy assessment and instruction with language-minority students: A comparative study. *The Elementary School Journal, 96* (3), 311–332.

Sanchez, G. I. (1934). Implications of a basal vocabulary to the measurement of the abilities of bilingual children. *The Journal of Social Psychology, 5,* 395–402.

Salvia, J., & Ysseldyke, J. (1995). *Assessment* (6th ed.). Boston: Houghton Mifflin.

Savage, J. F. (1998). *Teaching reading and writing: Combing skills, strategies, and literature* (2nd ed.). Boston: McGraw Hill.

Shanker, J. L., & Ekwall, E. E. (1998). *Locating and correcting reading difficulties* (7th ed.). Upper Saddle River, NJ: Merrill.

Short, K. G., Harste, J., & Burke, C. (1996). *Creating classrooms for authors and inquirers* (2nd ed.). Portsmouth, NH: Heinemann.

Short, K. G., & Pierce, K. M. (Eds.). (1990). *Talking about books: Creating literate communities* (pp. 36–52). Portsmouth, NH: Heinemann.

Silliman, E. R., & Wilkinson, L. C. (1994). Observation is more than looking. In G. P. Wallach & K. G. Butler (Eds.), *Language learning disabilities in school-age children and adolescents.* New York: Macmillan.

Silvaroli, N. J. (1997). *Classroom Reading Inventory.* Madison, WI: Brown & Benchmark.

Simmons, J. (1977). *Report to the faculty.* Unpublished manuscript.

Simmons, J. (1990). Portfolios as large-scale assessment. *Language Arts, 67* (3), 262–267.

Simmons, J. (1992). Portfolios for large-scale assessment. In D. Graves & B. Sunstein (Eds.), *Portfolio portraits* (pp. 96–113). Portsmouth, NH: Heinemann.

Simmons, J. (1996). *Attack of the killer baby-faces: Gender similarities in third grade writing.* Paper presented at the Spring conference of the National Council of Teachers of English, Boston, March.

Spradley, J. (1979). *The ethnographic interview.* New York: Holt, Rinehart and Winston.

Stahl, S. A. (1988). Is there evidence to support matching reading styles and initial reading methods? A reply to Carbo. *Phi Delta Kappan, 70* (4), 317–327.

Stahl, S. A. (1992). Saying the "p" word: Nine guidelines for exemplary phonics instruction. *The Reading Teacher, 45,* 618–625.

Stanovich, K. (1980). Toward and interactive-compensatory model of individual differences in the development of reading fluency. *Reading Research Quarterly, 16,* 32–71.

Stanovich, K. (1986). Matthew effects in reading: Some consequences of individual differences in the acquisition of literacy. *Reading Research Quarterly, 20,* 360–407.

Stauffer, R. (1975). *Directing the reading-thinking process.* New York: Harper and Row.

Taylor, D. (1991). *Learning denied.* Portsmouth, NH: Heinemann.

Taylor, B., Harris, L. A., Pearson, P. D., & Garcia, G. (1995). *Reading difficulties: Instruction and assessment* (2nd ed.). New York: McGraw Hill.

Trachtenburg, P. (1990). Using children's literature to enhance phonics instruction. *The Reading Teacher, 43,* 648–652.

Ungerer, T. (1974). *Ningun beso para mama.* Barcelona, Spain: Editorial Lumen.

Vacca, R. T., & Vacca, J. L. (1996). *Content area reading* (5th ed.). New York: HarperCollins.

Valdes, G., & Figueroa, R. (1989). *The nature of bilingualism and the nature of testing: Towards the development of a coherent research agenda.* Prepared for the National Commission on Testing and Public Policy. Unpublished manuscript, University of California, Berkeley, & University of California, Davis.

Valencia, S. W., Hiebert, E. H., & Afflerbach, P. P. (1994). Realizing the possibilities of authentic assessment: Current trends and future issues. In S. W. Valencia, E. H. Hiebert, & P. P. Afflerbach (Eds.), *Authentic reading assessment: Practices and possibilities* (pp. 286–299). Newark, DE: International Reading Association.

Van Allen, R. & Allen, C. (1966). *Language experiences in reading: Teachers' resource book.* Chicago: Encyclopedia Brittanica Press.

Van Orden, G. C., Johnston, J. C., & Hale, B. L. (1988). Word identification in reading proceeds from spelling to sound to meaning. *Journal of Experimental Psychology, 14,* 371–386.

Vygotsky, L. S. (1978). *Mind in society: The development of higher psychological processes.* M. Cole, V. John-Steiner, S. Scribner, & E. Souberman (Eds.). Cambridge, MA: Harvard University Press.

Vygotsky, L. S. (1986). *Thought and language.* Cambridge, MA: MIT Press.

Weaver, C. (1988). *Reading process and practice: From socio-psycholinguistics to whole language.* Portsmouth, NH: Heinemann.

Weaver, S. J. (1984). *Testing children: A reference guide for effective clinical and psychoeducational assessments.* Kansas City, KS: Test Corporation of America.

Wixson, K. K., Peters, C. W., Weber, E. M., & Roeber, E. D. (1987). New directions in statewide reading assessment. *The Reading Teacher,* pp. 747–754.

Woods, M. L., & Moe, A. J. (1989). *Analytic reading inventory* (4th ed.). Columbus, OH: Merrill.

Yopp, H. K. (1995). A test for assessing phonemic awareness in young children. *The Reading Teacher, 49,* 20–29.

INDEX